A Week
on the
Concord
and Merrimack
Rivers

Henry David Thoreau

A Week on the Concord and Merrimack Rivers

Illustrated by
Clifton Johnson

BOOK-OF-THE-MONTH CLUB
NEW YORK

A Week on the Concord and Merrimack Rivers was first published in 1849.

Where'er thou sail'st who sailed with me
Though now thou climbest loftier mounts,
And fairer rivers dost ascend,
Be thou my Muse, my Brother—.

I am bound, I am bound, for a distant shore,
By a lonely isle, by a far Azore,
There it is, there it is, the treasure I seek,
On the barren sands of a desolate creek.

I sailed up a river with a pleasant wind,
New lands, new people, and new thoughts to find;
Many fair reaches and headlands appeared,
And many dangers were there to be feared;
But when I remember where I have been,
And the fair landscapes that I have seen,
THOU seemest the only permanent shore,
The cape never rounded, nor wandered o'er.

INTRODUCTION

IN my foreword to the several preceding volumes in this illustrated edition of Thoreau I have noted various phases of his life, but there is much else that is of interest, and the present preface, in further commenting on his characteristics, simply supplements, without repetition, what I have previously written.

Thoreau's racial ancestry included a mingling of the French, Scotch, and English. John Thoreau, the nature-lover's grandfather, emigrated to New England from the Isle of Jersey about 1773, and became a successful Boston merchant. It was only natural that Thoreau's father should be bred to a mercantile life; but his business career in the city ended in failure. When his son Henry was born he was "carrying on" a Concord farm. This farm belonged to his wife's mother, who had inherited it from her second husband, Jonas Minott, and thus it happened that the famous author's birthplace was the Minott house on the Virginia Road. The house was of a type common in New England at that period, with gray, unpainted boards, and a grassy, unfenced door-yard. It was somewhat isolated, for the Virginia Road was only

INTRODUCTION

a winding country by-way on the outskirts of the town; but round about were pleasant, sunny meadows, and in front ran a good-sized brook.

Thoreau's father removed to Chelmsford, ten miles north, in Henry's infancy, and three years later to Boston. He did not thrive in either place, and in 1823 was back in Concord where he engaged in pencil-making. Thenceforth he led a plodding, unambitious, and respectable life in Concord village. He became moderately prosperous, and at his death left at least a competency to his family.

Thoreau was fond of out-of-door life from his boyhood, and was always specially attracted by the streams and ponds and woods. At the age of sixteen he entered Harvard College, where he shunned making acquaintances and lived in rigid seclusion. He graduated in 1837, and with characteristic frugality saved five dollars by refusing his diploma. His opinion of the benefits conferred by his four years at Harvard seems not to have been very flattering. "Education," he says, "often makes a straight-cut ditch out of a free meandering brook." But it could scarcely be claimed that it had that effect on him.

While attending college he began to collect Indian relics, and was a diligent student of natural history. His expertness in finding Indian relics in later years became proverbial.

INTRODUCTION

Once, when out walking, a friend asked him where Indian arrow-heads could be found.

"Everywhere," he replied, and stooped down and picked up one.

As Thoreau and his brother and two sisters grew up they all took up school-teaching, and each displayed peculiar gifts in that profession. He himself, after his college course, began teaching in his home town. He gave notice that there would be no flogging in his school, and that instead he would talk morals as a substitute. At the end of a fortnight a deacon who was one of the school committee visited the school and told him that he must use the ferule or the pupils would be spoiled. So that day, after school, Thoreau flogged six pupils. But this was against his conscience, and he informed the committee that he should no longer serve them if they interfered with his methods of discipline.

After teaching for three years he turned to other employments, yet he only tied himself to these as much as his own simple needs required. His income from authorship was never more than a few hundred dollars a year, and the amount was not half enough in most years to supply even his few wants. He would not be dependent on others, and therefore eked out a subsistence by gardening, fence-building, white-washing, carpentering and kindred pursuits. In

INTRODUCTION

everything he undertook he showed a patient, conscientious industry, and took pride in the quality of his workmanship. He had a knack for raising the best melons, planting the orchard with the choicest trees, and for doing any odd jobs that needed mechanical ingenuity.

For general society, or for mixing with throngs Thoreau had no inclination. "I would rather," said he, "sit on a pumpkin and have the seat all to myself than be crowded on a velvet cushion."

He would sometimes dart through a hedge or over a neighbor's back fence to escape an encounter which meant boredom. Very few were acceptable companions to him on his walks. In response to a friend who invited him to spend a few weeks at the friend's "island lodge," Thoreau wrote: "Such are my engagements to myself that I dare not promise to wend your way."

The closest of his early companions was his brother John, a sunny and serene soul for whom he had a great affection. This brother's early death in 1842 was a loss which moved Thoreau deeply.

Of his later friendships, that with Emerson was perhaps the most intimate and important. A close acquaintance between the two began in 1837, and Thoreau was fully admitted into that inner circle of which Emerson, Alcott, and Mar-

INTRODUCTION

garet Fuller were the leaders. In the spring of
1841 he became an inmate of Mr. Emerson's
house, and Emerson wrote concerning this ar-
rangement: "He is to have his board, etc., for
what labor he chooses to do; and he is thus far
a great benefactor and physician to me, for he
is an indefatigable and skillful laborer."

From the year of his graduation down almost
to the time of his death he kept a journal which
recorded his thoughts and experiences. In it
he noted the temperature of springs and ponds,
the tints of the morning and evening skies, the
flowering and fruitage of plants, the habits of
birds and other animals, and indeed every aspect of nature both small and great. Much of
it is dry detail, but there are constantly recurring
strokes of beauty in what he says, and often a
delightful originality of thought and piquancy
of expression.

He never crossed the ocean, and saw only a
very limited portion of his homeland. Even
Boston, only twenty miles distant, was seldom
visited, except as he needed to pass through it
in going elsewhere. He says: "The only room
in Boston which I visit with alacrity, is the
Gentlemen's Room at the Fitchburg Depot,
where I wait for the cars, in order to get out of
town. It is a paradise to the Parker House, for
no smoking is allowed, and there is far more
retirement."

INTRODUCTION

Again he says: "When it was proposed to me to go abroad, rub off some of the rust, and better my condition in a worldly sense, I feared lest my life would lose some of its homeliness. If these fields, and streams and woods, and the simple occupations of the inhabitants should cease to interest and inspire me, no culture or wealth would atone for the loss."

Admiring friends offered to carry him at their own cost to the Yellowstone River, to the West Indies, to South America; but he always refused.

Yet however little he saw of distant places, he was a great traveller in the neighborhood of Concord. Every day he was afield, and no other writer of modern times has been so much awake and abroad at night, or has described better the phenomena of darkness and of moonlight. He could make his way unerringly through the gloomiest woods at night where most men would have been lost at mid-day. His keenness of scent was like a dog's. The time of day he could tell by the height of the sun; and he has said of the plants in a certain Concord swamp that he thought they would enable him to estimate the time of year within two days. He had a great fancy for huckleberries, wild strawberries, chestnuts, acorns, and wild apples; and sometimes he would cut a square of birch-bark, fashion it into a rustic

INTRODUCTION

basket, and fill it with the treasures he had discovered to carry home.

Unquestionably, he injured his naturally robust health by the way he pursued his out-door studies, and the hardships he imposed on himself. He was endowed with great strength of body and limb, and increased these physical advantages by a temperate youth and by manual labor, in which he took much pleasure; but he could not be moderate in those pursuits to which his taste inclined. He exposed himself in his journeys and night encampments to cold and hunger and changes of weather such as no one could brave with impunity.

A fellow townsman, writing in 1855, describes him as "a little under size, with a huge nose, bluish-gray eyes, brown hair, and a ruddy, weather-beaten face, which reminds me of some shrewd and honest animal's — some retired, philosophical woodchuck, or magnanimous fox. He dresses very plainly, wears his collar turned over, and often an old dress-coat, broad in the skirts, and by no means a fit. He walks about with a brisk, rustic air and never seems tired."

His hands and feet were rather large, and his shoulders were noticeably sloping. The weakest feature of his face was a receding chin. By choice he wore plain working clothes, and generally old ones. The fashion of his garments gave him no concern, and was often out-of-date and even grotesque.

He was an untiring worker and stooped from his devotion to desk and book. But his wild instincts were never so dulled by his booklore but that he knew how to coax the partridge to feed at his door, and the shy woodmice to scurry up his sleeve and share his bread.

He was fond of pets, and appreciated in particular his sister's kittens, with which he would play by the half-hour.

The companionship of children was enjoyable to him, and at the homes where he visited he would tell these little folks stories, or mystify them with juggler tricks, or pop corn for them in the winter evenings, using for a popper an old brass warming-pan brought from the garret. In the spring he used to make willow whistles, and in the summer he made trumpets out of the stems of squash leaves. Sometimes he took the children huckleberrying, or out on the river in his boat, and he added interest and value to such excursions by showing his youthful comrades many of nature's wonders.

After the public began to know something about his Walden life he had frequent lecture engagements. Until then, he had supported himself ever since he left college chiefly by the work of his hands. Yet in spite of this new source of income he continued to do some surveying, and occasionally devoted time to manual labor. It was, in fact, one of the serious doctrines of the Transcendentalists that each person should perform his quota of hand-work. Hence Alcott, Channing, Hawthorne, and the rest took their turn at wood-chopping, hay-making, plowing, etc. Even Emerson trimmed his own orchard, and sometimes assisted in raking hay and hoeing corn.

Thoreau first became the author of a printed book when his *Week on the Concord and Merrimack Rivers* was published. Alcott, to whom he read portions in manuscript at the hermitage beside Walden Pond, says: "The book is purely American, fragrant with the life of New England woods and streams, and could have been written nowhere else;" and he expressed great eagerness to see it in print. However, the manuscript went from publisher to publisher, and was only accepted at last on condition that the author should be responsible for the expense of issuing it. So Thoreau borrowed the necessary funds, and it appeared in 1849.

The book is a mixture of humor and wisdom, founded on broad reading, deep thought, and a very unusual love for Nature and insight into her ways. To take it for a steady diet and read it consecutively from cover to cover would be tedious to most persons, but for literary browsing the book is a gem. It abounds in suggestion and

INTRODUCTION

charm, and, like all of Thoreau's books, has come to be accepted as an open-air classic. Nevertheless, back in 1849, in spite of some complimentary notices, the first edition was not a success. Four years passed, and Thoreau was asked to remove the unsold copies from the cellar of the publishing house.

About this time he wrote to a friend: "I have been almost constantly in the fields surveying of late. It is long since I have spent so many days so profitably in a pecuniary sense; so unprofitably in a more important sense. I have earned a dollar a day for seventy-six days past. This is instead of lecturing, which has not offered of late, to pay for that book I printed."

Two hundred and fifteen had been sold, about a third as many more had been given away, and the rest were shipped to the author. When he received them he confided to his diary that he had a library of nearly nine hundred volumes, over seven hundred of which he had written himself.

Things have changed since then. Now all that he wrote is treasured as the legacy of a prophet and a poet.

The boat in which the trip on the Concord and Merrimack was made later became the property of Hawthorne, and is mentioned by him in his *Mosses from an Old Manse*. The day after Hawthorne bought the boat he took a lesson from Thoreau in paddling it. Apparently he was not a very apt pupil, for he says: "The boat seemed to be bewitched, and turned its head to every point of the compass except the right one. I suspect she has not yet transferred her affections from her old master to her new one."

The years passed on, until at length Thoreau's health began to fail, and in 1861 he went to Minnesota; but the climate there did not afford the hoped-for benefit, and he soon returned to Concord. After it became evident that he had not long to live he said the idea of death did not trouble him. His thoughts had entertained him all his life and did still. When he had wakeful nights he would ask his sister to arrange the furniture so as to make fantastic shadows on the wall.

He considered occupation not less necessary for the sick than for those in health, and he accomplished a vast amount of labor in his last months preparing papers for the press, working as long as he could hold a pencil in his trembling fingers. No murmur or complaint escaped him, and he was cheerful to the end. His room was made fragrant by the gifts of flowers from young and old. Fruit, too, of all kinds that the season afforded was sent to him, and the townspeople sought in every way to minister to his comfort. Only two hours before he passed away Judge

INTRODUCTION

Hoar called with a bouquet of hyacinths fresh from his garden, which Thoreau smelled and said he liked.

He died on the 6th of May, 1862, and a few days later he was given a public funeral from the parish church. His grave is in Concord's Sleepy Hollow Cemetery within a few rods of the graves of the rest of that wonderful Concord galaxy — Emerson, Hawthorne, Alcott, and Channing.

To quote the words of Emerson spoken at his funeral: "A truth-speaker he, a friend, knowing not only the secret of friendship, but almost worshipped by those few who resorted to him as their confessor and prophet, and knew the deep value of his mind and great heart."

The pictures for this edition were made at the very end of August to correspond with the time of year that Thoreau made his trip. Naturally the aspect of the river has changed in some ways since 1839. The embryo manufacturing towns of that day have expanded enormously, the dams are higher so that the backwater has obliterated certain of the lesser falls, and the picturesque canal-boat traffic is only a memory. The entire region is less primitive, yet the country as viewed from the stream, whether you are on the Concord or the Merrimack, presents for the most part the same appearance

INTRODUCTION

it did to Thoreau. You find that the varied trees, and flowers, and berries, the wild creatures, and the fishermen almost duplicate what he describes. Indeed, had he lived now instead of then I think he might go over the same route and produce a book that would not be essentially different from the one he did write. He remarked then how near the wild in nature was to be found to the long-settled towns and busy marts of men; and even yet in that populous New England manufacturing district hints of wildness abound and Thoreau would not lack inspiration.

CLIFTON JOHNSON.

HADLEY, MASS.

CONTENTS

LIST OF ILLUSTRATIONS

A WEEK ON THE CONCORD AND MERRIMACK RIVERS

CONCORD RIVER

"Beneath low hills, in the broad interval
Through which at will our Indian rivulet
Winds mindful still of sannup and of squaw,
Whose pipe and arrow oft the plough unburies,
Here, in pine houses, built of new-fallen trees,
Supplanters of the tribe, the farmers dwell."
— EMERSON.

THE Musketaquid, or Grass-ground River, though probably as old as the Nile or Euphrates, did not begin to have a place in civilized history, until the fame of its grassy meadows and its fish attracted settlers out of England in 1635, when it received the other but kindred name of CONCORD from the first plantation on its banks, which appears to have been commenced in a spirit of peace and harmony. It will be Grass-ground River as long as grass grows and water runs here; it will be Concord River only while men lead peaceable lives on its banks. To an extinct race it was grass-ground, where they hunted and fished, and it is still perennial grass-ground to Concord farmers, who own the Great Meadows, and get the hay from year to year. "One branch of it," according to

the Historian of Concord, for I love to quote so
good authority, "rises in the south part of Hopkinton, and another from a pond and a large
cedar swamp in Westborough," and flowing
between Hopkinton and Southborough, through
Framingham, and between Sudbury and Wayland, where it is sometimes called Sudbury
River, it enters Concord at the south part of
the town, and after receiving the North or Assa-
beth River, which has its source a little further
to the north and west, goes out at the north-
east angle, and flowing between Bedford, and
Carlisle, and through Billerica, empties into the
Merrimack at Lowell. In Concord it is, in
summer, from four to fifteen feet deep, and from
one hundred to three hundred feet wide, but in
the spring freshets, when it overflows its banks,
it is in some places nearly a mile wide. Between
Sudbury and Wayland the meadows acquire
their greatest breadth, and when covered with
water, they form a handsome chain of shallow
vernal lakes, resorted to by numerous gulls and
ducks. Just above Sherman's Bridge, between
these towns, is the largest expanse, and when
the wind blows freshly in a raw March day,
heaving up the surface into dark and sober
billows or regular swells, skirted as it is in the
distance with alder swamps and smoke-like
maples, it looks like a smaller Lake Huron, and
is very pleasant and exciting for a landsman to

row or sail over. The farm-houses along the Sudbury shore, which rises gently to a considerable height, command fine water prospects at this season. The shore is more flat on the Wayland side, and this town is the greatest loser by the flood. Its farmers tell me that thousands of acres are flooded now, since the dams have been erected, where they remember to have seen the white honeysuckle or clover growing once, and they could go dry with shoes only in summer. Now there is nothing but blue-joint and sedge and cut-grass there, standing in water all the year round. For a long time, they made the most of the driest season to get their hay, working sometimes till nine o'clock at night, sedulously paring with their scythes in the twilight round the hummocks left by the ice; but now it is not worth the getting, when they can come at it, and they look sadly round to their wood-lots and upland as a last resource.

It is worth the while to make a voyage up this stream, if you go no farther than Sudbury, only to see how much country there is in the rear of us; great hills, and a hundred brooks, and farm-houses, and barns, and hay-stacks, you never saw before, and men everywhere, Sudbury, that is *Southborough* men, and Wayland, and Nine-Acre-Corner men, and Bound Rock, where four towns bound on a rock in the river, Lincoln, Wayland, Sudbury, Concord.

Many waves are there agitated by the wind,
keeping nature fresh, the spray blowing in your
face, reeds and rushes waving; ducks by the
hundred, all uneasy in the surf, in the raw wind,
just ready to rise, and now going off with a
clatter and a whistling, like riggers straight for
Labrador, flying against the stiff gale with
reefed wings, or else circling round first, with all
their paddles briskly moving, just over the surf,
to reconnoitre you before they leave these parts;
gulls wheeling overhead, muskrats swimming
for dear life, wet and cold, with no fire to warm
them by that you know of; their labored homes
rising here and there like hay-stacks; and countless mice and moles and winged titmice along
the sunny, windy shore; cranberries tossed on
the waves and heaving up on the beach, their
little red skiffs beating about among the alders;
— such healthy natural tumult as proves the
last day is not yet at hand. And there stand all
around the alders, and birches, and oaks, and
maples full of glee and sap, holding in their buds
until the waters subside. You shall perhaps
run aground on Cranberry Island, only some
spires of last year's pipegrass above water, to
show where the danger is, and get as good a
freezing there as anywhere on the North-west
Coast. I never voyaged so far in all my life.
You shall see men you never heard of before,
whose names you don't know, going away down

through the meadows with long ducking guns, with water-tight boots, wading through the fowl-meadow grass, on bleak, wintry, distant shores, with guns at half cock, and they shall see teal, blue-winged, green-winged, shelldrakes, whistlers, black ducks, ospreys, and many other wild and noble sights before night, such as they who sit in parlors never dream of. You shall see rude and sturdy, experienced and wise men, keeping their castles, or teaming up their summer's wood, or chopping alone in the woods, men fuller of talk and rare adventure in the sun and wind and rain, than a chestnut is of meat; who were out not only in '75 and 1812, but have been out every day of their lives; greater men than Homer, or Chaucer, or Shakspeare, only they never got time to say so; they never took to the way of writing. Look at their fields, and imagine what they might write, if ever they should put pen to paper. Or what have they not written on the face of the earth already, clearing, and burning, and scratching, and harrowing, and plowing, and subsoiling, in and in, and out and out, and over and over, again and again, erasing what they had already written for want of parchment.

As yesterday and the historical ages are past, as the work of to-day is present, so some flitting perspectives, and demi-experiences of the life that is in nature are in time veritably future, or

rather outside to time, perennial, young, divine,
in the wind and rain which never die.

> The respectable folks, —
> Where dwell they?
> They whisper in the oaks,
> And they sigh in the hay;
> Summer and winter, night and day,
> Out on the meadow, there dwell they.
> They never die,
> Nor snivel, nor cry,
> Nor ask our pity
> With a wet eye.
> A sound estate they ever mend,
> To every asker readily lend;
> To the ocean wealth,
> To the meadow health,
> To Time his length,
> To the rocks strength,
> To the stars light,
> To the weary night,
> To the busy day,
> To the idle play;
> And so their good cheer never ends,
> For all are their debtors, and all their friends.

Concord River is remarkable for the gentleness of its current, which is scarcely perceptible, and some have referred to its influence the proverbial moderation of the inhabitants of Concord, as exhibited in the Revolution, and on later occasions. It has been proposed that the town should adopt for its coat of arms a field verdant, with the Concord circling nine times round. I have read that a descent of an

Concord meadows

eighth of an inch in a mile is sufficient to produce a flow. Our river has, probably, very near the smallest allowance. The story is current, at any rate, though I believe that strict history will not bear it out, that the only bridge ever carried away on the main branch, within the limits of the town, was driven up stream by the wind. But wherever it makes a sudden bend it is shallower and swifter, and asserts its title to be called a river. Compared with the other tributaries of the Merrimack, it appears to have been properly named Musketaquid, or Meadow River, by the Indians. For the most part, it creeps through broad meadows, adorned with scattered oaks, where the cranberry is found in abundance, covering the ground like a moss-bed. A row of sunken dwarf willows borders the stream on one or both sides, while at a greater distance the meadow is skirted with maples, alders, and other fluviatile trees, over-run with the grape vine, which bears fruit in its season, purple, red, white, and other grapes. Still further from the stream, on the edge of the firm land, are seen the gray and white dwellings of the inhabitants. According to the valuation of 1831, there were in Concord two thousand one hundred and eleven acres, or about one-seventh of the whole territory, in meadow; this standing next in the list after pasturage and unimproved lands, and, judging from the returns of previous

years, the meadow is not reclaimed so fast as
the woods are cleared.

The sluggish artery of the Concord meadows
steals thus unobserved through the town, without a murmur or a pulse-beat, its general course
from south-west to north-east, and its length
about fifty miles; a huge volume of matter,
ceaselessly rolling through the plains and valleys
of the substantial earth, with the moccasined
tread of an Indian warrior, making haste from
the high places of the earth to its ancient reser-
voir. The murmurs of many a famous river on
the other side of the globe reach even to us here,
as to more distant dwellers on its banks; many
a poet's stream floating the helms and shields of
heroes on its bosom. The Xanthus or Sca-
mander is not a mere dry channel and bed of
a mountain torrent, but fed by the ever-flowing
springs of fame; —

> "And thou Simois, that as an arrowe, clere
> Through Troy rennest, aie downward to the sea;" —

and I trust that I may be allowed to associate
our muddy but much abused Concord River
with the most famous in history.

> "Sure there are poets which did never dream
> Upon Parnassus, nor did taste the stream
> Of Helicon; we therefore may suppose
> Those made not poets, but the poets those."

The Mississippi, the Ganges, and the Nile, those journeying atoms from the Rocky Mountains, the Himmaleh, and Mountains of the Moon, have a kind of personal importance in the annals of the world. The heavens are not yet drained over their sources, but the Mountains of the Moon still send their annual tribute to the Pasha without fail, as they did to the Pharaohs, though he must collect the rest of his revenue at the point of the sword. Rivers must have been the guides which conducted the footsteps of the first travellers. They are the constant lure, when they flow by our doors, to distant enterprise and adventure, and, by a natural impulse, the dwellers on their banks will at length accompany their currents to the lowlands of the globe, or explore at their invitation the interior of continents. They are the natural highways of all nations, not only levelling the ground, and removing obstacles from the path of the traveller, quenching his thirst, and bearing him on their bosoms, but conducting him through the most interesting scenery, the most populous portions of the globe, and where the animal and vegetable kingdoms attain their greatest perfection.

I had often stood on the banks of the Concord, watching the lapse of the current, an emblem of all progress, following the same law with the system, with time, and all that is made; the

weeds at the bottom gently bending down the
stream, shaken by the watery wind, still planted
where their seeds had sunk, but ere long to die
and go down likewise; the shining pebbles, not
yet anxious to better their condition, the chips
and weeds, and occasional logs and stems of
trees, that floated past, fulfilling their fate, were
objects of singular interest to me, and at last
I resolved to launch myself on its bosom, and
float whither it would bear me.

SATURDAY

"Come, come, my lovely fair, and let us try
These rural delicates."
                            — *Invitation to the Soul.* QUARLES.

A T length, on Saturday, the last day of
August, 1839, we two, brothers, and natives of Concord, weighed anchor in this
river port; for Concord, too, lies under the sun,
a port of entry and departure for the bodies as
well as the souls of men; one shore at least
exempted from all duties but such as an honest
man will gladly discharge. A warm drizzling
rain had obscured the morning, and threatened
to delay our voyage, but at length the leaves and
grass were dried, and it came out a mild afternoon, as serene and fresh as if nature were maturing some greater scheme of her own. After
this long dripping and oozing from every pore,
she began to respire again more healthily than
ever. So with a vigorous shove we launched
our boat from the bank, while the flags and bulrushes curtseyed a God-speed, and dropped
silently down the stream.

Our boat, which had cost us a week's labor in
the spring, was in form like a fisherman's dory,
fifteen feet long by three and a half in breadth

at the widest part, painted green below, with a border of blue, with reference to the two elements in which it was to spend its existence. It had been loaded the evening before at our door, half a mile from the river, with potatoes and melons from a patch which we had cultivated, and a few utensils, and was provided with wheels in order to be rolled around falls, as well as with two sets of oars, and several slender poles for shoving in shallow places, and also two masts, one of which served for a tent-pole at night; for a buffalo skin was to be our bed, and a tent of cotton cloth our roof. It was strongly built but heavy, and hardly of better model than usual. If rightly made, a boat would be a sort of amphibious animal, a creature of two elements, related by one half its structure to some swift and shapely fish, and by the other to some strong-winged and graceful bird. The fish shows where there should be the greatest breadth of beam and depth in the hold; its fins direct where to set the oars, and the tail gives some hint for the form and position of the rudder. The bird shows how to rig and trim the sails, and what form to give to the prow that it may balance the boat and divide the air and water best. These hints we had but partially obeyed. But the eyes, though they are no sailors, will never be satisfied with any model, however fashionable, which does not answer all the

requisitions of art. However, as art is all of a
ship but the wood, and yet the wood alone will
rudely serve the purpose of a ship, so our boat
being of wood gladly availed itself of the old
law that the heavier shall float the lighter, and
though a dull water fowl, proved a sufficient
buoy for our purpose.

"Were it the will of Heaven, an osier bough
Were vessel safe enough the seas to plow."

Some village friends stood upon a promontory
lower down the stream to wave us a last farewell; but we, having already performed these
shore rites with excusable reserve, as befits
those who are embarked on unusual enterprises,
who behold but speak not, silently glided past
the firm lands of Concord, both peopled cape
and lonely summer meadow, with steady sweeps.
And yet we did unbend so far as to let our guns
speak for us, when at length we had swept out
of sight, and thus left the woods to ring again
with their echoes; and it may be many russet-
clad children lurking in those broad meadows,
with the bittern and the woodcock and the rail,
though wholly concealed by brakes and hard-
hack and meadow-sweet, heard our salute that
afternoon.

We were soon floating past the first regular
battle ground of the Revolution, resting on our
oars between the still visible abutments of that

"North Bridge," over which in April, 1775, rolled the first faint tide of that war, which ceased not, till, as we read on the stone on our right, it "gave peace to these United States." As a Concord poet has sung, —

"By the rude bridge that arched the flood,
    Their flag to April's breeze unfurled,
Here once the embattled farmers stood,
    And fired the shot heard round the world.

"The foe long since in silence slept;
    Alike the conqueror silent sleeps;
And Time the ruined bridge has swept
    Down the dark stream which seaward creeps."

Our reflections had already acquired a historical remoteness from the scenes we had left, and we ourselves essayed to sing.

Ah, 't is in vain the peaceful din
    That wakes the ignoble town,
Not thus did braver spirits win
    A patriot's renown.

There is one field beside this stream,
    Wherein no foot does fall,
But yet it beareth in my dream
    A richer crop than all.

Let me believe a dream so dear,
    Some heart beat high that day,
Above the petty Province here,
    And Britain far away;

The bridge at the Battleground

Some hero of the ancient mould,
  Some arm of knightly worth,
Of strength unbought, and faith unsold,
  Honored this spot of earth;

Who sought the prize his heart described,
  And did not ask release,
Whose free born valor was not bribed
  By prospect of a peace.

The men who stood on yonder height
  That day are long since gone;
Not the same hand directs the fight
  And monumental stone.

Ye were the Grecian cities then,
  The Romes of modern birth,
Where the New England husbandmen
  Have shown a Roman worth.

In vain I search a foreign land,
  To find our Bunker Hill,
And Lexington and Concord stand
  By no Laconian rill.

With such thoughts we swept gently by this now peaceful pasture ground, on waves of Concord, in which was long since drowned the din of war.

But since we sailed
Some things have failed,
And many a dream
Gone down the stream.

Here then an aged shepherd dwelt,
Who to his flock his substance dealt,
And ruled them with a vigorous crook,
By precept of the sacred Book;
But he the pierless bridge passed o'er,
And solitary left the shore.

Anon a youthful pastor came,
Whose crook was not unknown to fame,
His lambs he viewed with gentle glance,
Spread o'er the country's wide expanse,
And fed with "Mosses from the Manse."
Here was our Hawthorne in the dale,
And here the shepherd told his tale.

That slight shaft had now sunk behind the
hills, and we had floated round the neighboring
bend, and under the new North Bridge between
Ponkawtasset and the Poplar Hill, into the
Great Meadows, which, like a broad moccasin
print, have levelled a fertile and juicy place in
nature.

On Ponkawtasset, since, with such delay,
Down this still stream we took our meadowy way,
A poet wise has settled, whose fine ray
Doth faintly shine on Concord's twilight day.

Like those first stars, whose silver beams on high,
Shining more brightly as the day goes by,
Most travellers cannot at first descry,
But eyes that wont to range the evening sky,

And know celestial lights, do plainly see,
And gladly hail them, numbering two or three;
For lore that's deep must deeply studied be,
As from deep wells men read star-poetry.

These stars are never pal'd, though out of sight,
But like the sun they shine forever bright;
Aye, *they* are suns, though earth must in its flight
Put out its eyes that it may see their light.

Who would neglect the least celestial sound,
Or faintest light that falls on earthly ground,
If he could know it one day would be found
That star in Cygnus whither we are bound,
And pale our sun with heavenly radiance round?

Gradually the village murmur subsided, and
we seemed to be embarked on the placid current
of our dreams, floating from past to future as
silently as one awakes to fresh morning or evening thoughts. We glided noiselessly down the
stream, occasionally driving a pickerel from the
covert of the pads, or a bream from her nest,
and the smaller bittern now and then sailed
away on sluggish wings from some recess in the
shore, or the larger lifted itself out of the long
grass at our approach, and carried its precious
legs away to deposit them in a place of safety.
The tortoises also rapidly dropped into the
water, as our boat ruffled the surface amid the
willows, breaking the reflections of the trees.
The banks had passed the height of their beauty,
and some of the brighter flowers showed by
their faded tints that the season was verging
towards the afternoon of the year; but this
sombre tinge enhanced their sincerity, and in
the still unabated heats they seemed like a

mossy brink of some cool well. The narrow-
leaved willow lay along the surface of the water
in masses of light green foliage, interspersed
with the large white balls of the button-bush.
The rose-colored polygonum raised its head
proudly above the water on either hand, and,
flowering at this season, and in these localities,
in the midst of dense fields of the white species
which skirted the sides of the stream, its little
streak of red looked very rare and precious.
The pure white blossoms of the arrow-head
stood in the shallower parts, and a few cardinals
on the margin still proudly surveyed themselves
reflected in the water, though the latter, as
well as the pickerel-weed, was now nearly out
of blossom. The snake-head, *chelone glabra*,
grew close to the shore, while a kind of coreop-
sis, turning its brazen face to the sun, full and
rank, and a tall dull red flower, *eupatorium
purpureum*, or trumpet weed, formed the rear
rank of the fluvial array. The bright blue flowers of the soap-wort gentian were sprinkled here
and there in the adjacent meadows, like flowers
which Proserpine had dropped, and still further
in the fields, or higher on the bank, were seen
the Virginian rhexia, and drooping neottia or
ladies'-tresses; while from the more distant
waysides, which we occasionally passed, and
banks where the sun had lodged, was reflected
a dull yellow beam from the ranks of tansy, now

in its prime. In short, nature seemed to have
adorned herself for our departure with a pro-
fusion of fringes and curls, mingled with the
bright tints of flowers, reflected in the water.
But we missed the white water-lily, which is
the queen of river flowers, its reign being over
for this season. He makes his voyage too late,
perhaps, by a true water clock who delays so
long. Many of this species inhabit our Concord
water. I have passed down the river before
sunrise on a summer morning between fields of
lilies still shut in sleep; and when at length the
flakes of sunlight from over the bank fell on the
surface of the water, whole fields of white blossoms seemed to flash open before me, as I floated
along, like the unfolding of a banner, so sensible
is this flower to the influence of the sun's rays.

As we were floating through the last of these
familiar meadows, we observed the large and
conspicuous flowers of the hibiscus, covering the
dwarf willows, and mingled with the leaves of
the grape, and wished that we could inform one
of our friends behind of the locality of this somewhat rare and inaccessible flower before it was
too late to pluck it; but we were just gliding out
of sight of the village spire before it occurred to
us that the farmer in the adjacent meadow
would go to church on the morrow, and would
carry this news for us; and so by the Monday,
while we should be floating on the Merrimack,

our friend would be reaching to pluck this blossom on the bank of the Concord.

After a pause at Ball's Hill, the St. Ann's of Concord voyageurs, not to say any prayer for the success of our voyage, but to gather the few berries which were still left on the hills, hanging by very slender threads, we weighed anchor again, and were soon out of sight of our native village. The land seemed to grow fairer as we withdrew from it. Far away to the south-west lay the quiet village, left alone under its elms and button-woods in mid afternoon; and the hills, notwithstanding their blue, ethereal faces, seemed to cast a saddened eye on their old playfellows; but, turning short to the north, we bade adieu to their familiar outlines, and addressed ourselves to new scenes and adventures. Nought was familiar but the heavens, from under whose roof the voyageur never passes; but with their countenance, and the acquaintance we had with river and wood, we trusted to fare well under any circumstances.

From this point, the river runs perfectly straight for a mile or more to Carlisle Bridge, which consists of twenty wooden piers, and when we looked back over it, its surface was reduced to a line's breadth, and appeared like a cobweb gleaming in the sun. Here and there might be seen a pole sticking up, to mark the place where some fisherman had enjoyed un-

Ball's Hill, in the middle distance on the left

usual luck, and in return had consecrated
his rod to the deities who preside over these
shallows. It was full twice as broad as before,
deep and tranquil, with a muddy bottom, and
bordered with willows, beyond which spread
broad lagoons covered with pads, bulrushes,
and flags.

Late in the afternoon we passed a man on
the shore fishing with a long birch pole, its
silvery bark left on, and a dog at his side, rowing so near as to agitate his cork with our oars,
and drive away luck for a season; and when we
had rowed a mile as straight as an arrow, with
our faces turned towards him, and the bubbles
in our wake still visible on the tranquil surface,
there stood the fisher still with his dog, like
statues under the other side of the heavens,
the only objects to relieve the eye in the extended meadow; and there would he stand abiding his luck, till he took his way home through
the fields at evening with his fish. Thus, by
one bait or another, Nature allures inhabitants
into all her recesses. This man was the last of
our townsmen whom we saw, and we silently
through him bade adieu to our friends.

The characteristics and pursuits of various
ages and races of men are always existing in
epitome in every neighborhood. The pleasures
of my earliest youth have become the inherit-

ance of other men. This man is still a fisher, and belongs to an era in which I myself have lived. Perchance he is not confounded by many knowledges, and has not sought out many inventions, but how to take many fishes before the sun sets, with his slender birchen pole and flaxen line, that is invention enough for him. It is good even to be a fisherman in summer and in winter. Some men are judges these August days, sitting on benches, even till the court rises; they sit judging there honorably, between the seasons and between meals, leading a civil politic life, arbitrating in the case of Spaulding *versus* Cummings, it may be, from highest noon till the red vesper sinks into the west. The fisherman, meanwhile, stands in three feet of water, under the same summer's sun, arbitrating in other cases between muckworm and shiner, amid the fragrance of water-lilies, mint, and pontederia, leading his life many rods from the dry land, within a pole's length of where the larger fishes swim. Human life is to him very much like a river,

— "renning aie downward to the sea."

This was his observation. His honor made a great discovery in bailments.

I can just remember an old brown-coated man who was the Walton of this stream, who had come over from Newcastle, England, with

his son, the latter a stout and hearty man who
had lifted an anchor in his day. A straight old
man he was who took his way in silence through
the meadows, having passed the period of communication with his fellows; his old experienced
coat hanging long and straight and brown as
the yellow pine bark, glittering with so much
smothered sunlight, if you stood near enough,
no work of art but naturalized at length.   I
often discovered him unexpectedly amid the
pads and the gray willows when he moved,
fishing in some old country method, — for
youth and age then went a-fishing together, —
full of incommunicable thoughts, perchance
about his own Tyne and Northumberland. He
was always to be seen in serene afternoons
haunting the river, and almost rustling with
the sedge; so many sunny hours in an old man's
life, entrapping silly fish, almost grown to be
the sun's familiar; what need had he of hat or
raiment any, having served out his time, and
seen through such thin disguises? I have seen
how his coeval fates rewarded him with the
yellow perch, and yet I thought his luck was
not in proportion to his years; and I have seen
when, with slow steps and weighed down with
aged thoughts, he disappeared with his fish
under his low-roofed house on the skirts of the
village. I think nobody else saw him; nobody
else remembers him now, for he soon after died,

and migrated to new Tyne streams. His fishing was not a sport, nor solely a means of subsistence, but a sort of solemn sacrament and
withdrawal from the world, just as the aged
read their bibles.

Whether we live by the sea-side, or by the
lakes and rivers, or on the prairie, it concerns
us to attend to the nature of fishes, since they
are not phenomena confined to certain localities only, but forms and phases of the life
in nature universally dispersed. The countless
shoals which annually coast the shores of
Europe and America are not so interesting to
the student of nature as the more fertile law
itself, which deposits their spawn on the tops
of mountains, and on the interior plains; the
fish principle in nature, from which it results
that they may be found in water in so many
places, in greater or less numbers. The natural
historian is not a fisherman, who prays for
cloudy days and good luck merely, but as fishing has been styled "a contemplative man's
recreation," introducing him profitably to woods
and water, so the fruit of the naturalist's ob-
servations is not in new genera or species, but
in new contemplations still, and science is only
a more contemplative man's recreation. The
seeds of the life of fishes are everywhere dis-
seminated, whether the winds waft them, or
the waters float them, or the deep earth holds

them; wherever a pond is dug, straightway it is stocked with this vivacious race. They have a lease of nature, and it is not yet out. The Chinese are bribed to carry their ova from province to province in jars or in hollow reeds, or the water-birds to transport them to the mountain tarns and interior lakes. There are fishes wherever there is a fluid medium, and even in clouds and in melted metals we detect their semblance. Think how in winter you can sink a line down straight in a pasture through snow and through ice, and pull up a bright, slippery, dumb, subterranean silver or golden fish! It is curious, also, to reflect how they make one family, from the largest to the smallest. The least minnow, that lies on the ice as bait for pickerel, looks like a huge sea-fish cast up on the shore. In the waters of this town there are about a dozen distinct species, though the inexperienced would expect many more.

It enhances our sense of the grand security and serenity of nature to observe the still undisturbed economy and content of the fishes of this century, their happiness a regular fruit of the summer. The fresh-water Sun Fish, Bream, or Ruff, *Pomotis vulgaris*, as it were, without ancestry, without posterity, still represents the Fresh Water Sun Fish in nature. It is the most

common of all, and seen on every urchin's
string; a simple and inoffensive fish, whose
nests are visible all along the shore, hollowed
in the sand, over which it is steadily poised
through the summer hours on waving fin.
Sometimes there are twenty or thirty nests in
the space of a few rods, two feet wide by half
a foot in depth, and made with no little labor,
the weeds being removed, and the sand shoved
up on the sides, like a bowl. Here it may be
seen early in summer assiduously brooding, and
driving away minnows and larger fishes, even
its own species, which would disturb its ova,
pursuing them a few feet, and circling round
swiftly to its nest again: the minnows, like
young sharks, instantly entering the empty
nests meanwhile, and swallowing the spawn,
which is attached to the weeds and to the
bottom, on the sunny side. The spawn is exposed to so many dangers that a very small
proportion can ever become fishes, for beside
being the constant prey of birds and fishes, a
great many nests are made so near the shore,
in shallow water, that they are left dry in a
few days, as the river goes down. These and
the lamprey's are the only fishes' nests that I
have observed, though the ova of some species
may be seen floating on the surface. The
breams are so careful of their charge that you
may stand close by in the water and examine

them at your leisure. I have thus stood over them half an hour at a time, and stroked them familiarly without frightening them, suffering them to nibble my fingers harmlessly, and seen them erect their dorsal fins in anger when my hand approached their ova, and have even taken them gently out of the water with my hand; though this cannot be accomplished by a sudden movement, however dexterous, for instant warning is conveyed to them through their denser element, but only by letting the fingers gradually close about them as they are poised over the palm, and with the utmost gentleness raising them slowly to the surface. Though stationary, they keep up a constant sculling or waving motion with their fins, which is exceedingly graceful, and expressive of their humble happiness; for unlike ours, the element in which they live is a stream which must be constantly resisted. From time to time they nibble the weeds at the bottom or overhanging their nests, or dart after a fly or a worm. The dorsal fin, besides answering the purpose of a keel, with the anal, serves to keep the fish upright, for in shallow water, where this is not covered, they fall on their sides. As you stand thus stooping over the bream in its nest, the edges of the dorsal and caudal fins have a singular dusty golden reflection, and its eyes, which stand out from the head, are transparent

and colorless. Seen in its native element, it is
a very beautiful and compact fish, perfect in all
its parts, and looks like a brilliant coin fresh
from the mint. It is a perfect jewel of the river,
the green, red, coppery, and golden reflections
of its mottled sides being the concentration of
such rays as struggle through the floating pads
and flowers to the sandy bottom, and in harmony with the sunlit brown and yellow pebbles.
Behind its watery shield it dwells far from many
accidents inevitable to human life.

There is also another species of bream found
in our river, without the red spot on the oper-
culum, which, according to M. Agassiz, is
undescribed.

The Common Perch, *Perca flavescens*, which
name describes well the gleaming, golden reflections of its scales as it is drawn out of the
water, its red gills standing out in vain in the
thin element, is one of the handsomest and
most regularly formed of our fishes, and at such
a moment as this reminds us of the fish in the
picture, which wished to be restored to its
native element until it had grown larger; and
indeed most of this species that are caught are
not half grown. In the ponds there is a light-
colored and slender kind, which swim in shoals
of many hundreds in the sunny water, in company with the shiner, averaging not more than
six or seven inches in length, while only a few

larger specimens are found in the deepest water,
which prey upon their weaker brethren. I have
often attracted these small perch to the shore
at evening, by rippling the water with my
fingers, and they may sometimes be caught
while attempting to pass inside your hands. It
is a tough and heedless fish, biting from impulse, without nibbling, and from impulse re-
fraining to bite, and sculling indifferently past.
It rather prefers the clear water and sandy
bottoms, though here it has not much choice.
It is a true fish, such as the angler loves to put
into his basket or hang at the top of his willow
twig, in shady afternoons along the banks of
the stream. So many unquestionable fishes he
counts, and so many shiners, which he counts
and then throws away.

The Chivin, Dace, Roach, Cousin Trout, or
whatever else it is called, *Leuciscus pulchellus*,
white and red, always an unexpected prize,
which, however, any angler is glad to hook for
its rarity. A name that reminds us of many an
unsuccessful ramble by swift streams, when the
wind rose to disappoint the fisher. It is commonly a silvery soft-scaled fish, of graceful,
scholarlike, and classical look, like many a
picture in an English book. It loves a swift
current and a sandy bottom, and bites inad-
vertently, yet not without appetite for the bait.
The minnows are used as bait for pickerel in

the winter. The red chivin, according to some,
is still the same fish, only older, or with its tints
deepened as they think by the darker water it
inhabits, as the red clouds swim in the twilight
atmosphere. He who has not hooked the red
chivin is not yet a complete angler. Other
fishes, methinks, are slightly amphibious, but
this is a denizen of the water wholly. The cork
goes dancing down the swift-rushing stream,
amid the weeds and sands, when suddenly, by
a coincidence never to be remembered, emerges
this fabulous inhabitant of another element,
a thing heard of but not seen, as if it were the
instant creation of an eddy, a true product of
the running stream. And this bright cupreous
dolphin was spawned and has passed its life
beneath the level of your feet in your native
field. Fishes, too, as well as birds and clouds,
derive their armor from the mine. I have heard
of mackerel visiting the copper banks at a particular season; this fish, perchance, has its habi-
tat in the Coppermine River. I have caught
white chivin of great size in the Aboljack-
nagesic, where it empties into the Penobscot,
at the base of Mount Ktaadn, but no red ones
there. The latter variety seems not to have
been sufficiently observed.

The Dace, *Leuciscus argenteus*, is a slight
silvery minnow, found generally in the middle
of the stream, where the current is most

rapid, and frequently confounded with the last
named.

The Shiner, *Leuciscus crysoleucas*, is a soft-
scaled and tender fish, the victim of its stronger
neighbors, found in all places, deep and shallow,
clear and turbid; generally the first nibbler at
the bait, but, with its small mouth and nibbling
propensities, not easily caught. It is a gold or
silver bit that passes current in the river, its
limber tail dimpling the surface in sport or
flight. I have seen the fry when frightened by
something thrown into the water, leap out by
dozens, together with the dace, and wreck
themselves upon a floating plank. It is the
little light-infant of the river, with body armor
of gold or silver spangles, slipping, gliding its
life through with a quirk of the tail, half in the
water, half in the air, upward and ever upward
with flitting fin to more crystalline tides, yet
still abreast of us dwellers on the bank. It is
almost dissolved by the summer heats. A
slighter and lighter colored shiner is found in
one of our ponds.

The Pickerel, *Esox reticulatus*, the swiftest,
wariest, and most ravenous of fishes, is very
common in the shallow and weedy lagoons along
the sides of the stream. It is a solemn, stately,
ruminant fish, lurking under the shadow of a
pad at noon, with still, circumspect, voracious
eye, motionless as a jewel set in water, or mov-

ing slowly along to take up its position, darting
from time to time at such unlucky fish or frog
or insect as comes within its range, and swallowing it at a gulp.   I have caught one which
had swallowed a brother pickerel half as large
as itself, with the tail still visible in its mouth,
while the head was already digested in its
stomach.   Sometimes a striped snake, bound to
greener meadows across the stream, ends its
undulatory progress in the same receptacle.
They are so greedy and impetuous that they are
frequently caught by being entangled in the
line the moment it is cast.   Fishermen also distinguish the brook pickerel, a shorter and
thicker fish than the former.

The Horned Pout, *Pimelodus nebulosus*, sometimes called Minister, from the peculiar squeak-
ing noise it makes when drawn out of the water,
is a dull and blundering fellow, and like the eel
vespertinal in his habits, and fond of the mud.
It bites deliberately as if about its business.
They are taken at night with a mass of worms
strung on a thread, which catches in their teeth,
sometimes three or four, with an eel, at one
pull.   They are extremely tenacious of life,
opening and shutting their mouths for half an
hour after their heads have been cut off.   A
bloodthirsty and bullying race of rangers, in-
habiting the fertile river bottoms, with ever a
lance in rest, and ready to do battle with their

nearest neighbor. I have observed them in summer, when every other one had a long and bloody scar upon his back, where the skin was gone, the mark, perhaps, of some fierce encounter. Sometimes the fry, not an inch long, are seen darkening the shore with their myriads.

The Suckers, *Catostomi Bostonienses* and *tuberculati*, Common and Horned, perhaps on an average the largest of our fishes, may be seen in shoals of a hundred or more, stemming the current in the sun, on their mysterious migrations, and sometimes sucking in the bait which the fisherman suffers to float toward them. The former, which sometimes grow to a large size, are frequently caught by the hand in the brooks, or, like the red chivins, are jerked out by a hook fastened firmly to the end of a stick and placed under their jaws. They are hardly known to the mere angler, however, not often biting at his baits, though the spearer carries home many a mess in the spring. To our village eyes, these shoals have a foreign and imposing aspect, realizing the fertility of the seas.

The Common Eel, too, *Muræna Bostoniensis*, the only species known in the State, a slimy, squirming creature, informed of mud, still squirming in the pan, is speared and hooked up with various success. Methinks it too occurs in picture, left after the deluge, in many a meadow high and dry.

In the shallow parts of the river, where the
current is rapid, and the bottom pebbly, you
may sometimes see the curious circular nests of
the Lamprey Eel, *Petromyzon Americanus*, the
American Stone-Sucker, as large as a cart wheel,
a foot or two in height, and sometimes rising
half a foot above the surface of the water. They
collect these stones, of the size of a hen's egg,
with their mouths, as their name implies, and
are said to fashion them into circles with their
tails. They ascend falls by clinging to the
stones, which may sometimes be raised by lifting the fish by the tail. As they are not seen
on their way down the streams, it is thought
by fishermen that they never return, but waste
away and die, clinging to rocks and stumps of
trees for an indefinite period; a tragic feature
in the scenery of the river bottoms, worthy to
be remembered with Shakspeare's description
of the sea-floor. They are rarely seen in our
waters at present, on account of the dams,
though they are taken in great quantities at
the mouth of the river in Lowell. Their nests,
which are very conspicuous, look more like art
than anything in the river.

If we had leisure this afternoon, we might
turn our prow up the brooks in quest of the
classical trout and the minnows. Of the last
alone, according to M. Agassiz, several of the
species found in this town are yet undescribed.

These would, perhaps, complete the list of our finny contemporaries in the Concord waters.

Salmon, Shad, and Alewives were formerly abundant here, and taken in weirs by the Indians, who taught this method to the whites, by whom they were used as food and as manure, until the dam, and afterward the canal at Billerica, and the factories at Lowell, put an end to their migrations hitherward; though it is thought that a few more enterprising shad may still occasionally be seen in this part of the river. It is said, to account for the destruction of the fishery, that those who at that time represented the interests of the fishermen and the fishes, remembering between what dates they were accustomed to take the grown shad, stipulated that the dams should be left open for that season only, and the fry, which go down a month later, were consequently stopped and destroyed by myriads. Others say that the fish-ways were not properly constructed. Perchance, after a few thousands of years, if the fishes will be patient, and pass their summers elsewhere, meanwhile, nature will have levelled the Billerica dam, and the Lowell factories, and the Grass-ground River run clear again, to be explored by new migratory shoals, even as far as the Hopkinton pond and Westborough swamp.

One would like to know more of that race,

now extinct, whose seines lie rotting in the
garrets of their children, who openly professed
the trade of fishermen, and even fed their
townsmen creditably, not skulking through the
meadows to a rainy afternoon sport. Dim
visions we still get of miraculous draughts of
fishes, and heaps uncountable by the river-
side, from the tales of our seniors sent on horse-
back in their childhood from the neighboring
towns, perched on saddle-bags, with instructions to get the one bag filled with shad, the
other with alewives. At least one memento of
those days may still exist in the memory of this
generation, in the familiar appellation of a
celebrated train-band of this town, whose un-
trained ancestors stood creditably at Concord
North Bridge. Their captain, a man of pisca-
tory tastes, having duly warned his company
to turn out on a certain day, they, like obedient
soldiers, appeared promptly on parade at the
appointed time, but, unfortunately, they went
undrilled, except in the manœuvres of a soldier's wit and unlicensed jesting, that May
day; for their captain, forgetting his own ap-
pointment, and warned only by the favorable
aspect of the heavens, as he had often done
before, went a fishing that afternoon, and his
company thenceforth was known to old and
young, grave and gay, as "The Shad," and by
the youths of this vicinity this was long re-

garded as the proper name of all the irregular
militia in Christendom.   But, alas, no record
of these fishers' lives remains, that we know
of, unless it be one brief page of hard but unquestionable history, which occurs in Day
Book No. 4, of an old trader of this town, long
since dead, which shows pretty plainly what
constituted a fisherman's stock in trade in
those days.   It purports to be a Fisherman's
Account Current, probably for the fishing season of the year 1805, during which months he
purchased daily rum and sugar, sugar and
rum, N. E. and W. I., "one cod line," "one
brown mug," and "a line for the seine;" rum
and sugar, sugar and rum, "good loaf sugar,"
and "good brown," W. I. and N. E., in short
and uniform entries to the bottom of the page,
all carried out in pounds, shillings, and pence,
from March 25th to June 5th, and promptly
settled by receiving "cash in full" at the last
date.   But perhaps not so settled altogether.
These were the necessaries of life in those days;
with salmon, shad, and alewives, fresh and
pickled, he was thereafter independent on the
groceries.   Rather a preponderance of the fluid
elements; but such was this fisherman's nature.
I can faintly remember to have seen the same
fisher in my earliest youth, still as near the
river as he could get, with uncertain undulatory step, after so many things had gone down

stream, swinging a scythe in the meadow, his bottle like a serpent hid in the grass; himself as yet not cut down by the Great Mower.

Surely the fates are forever kind, though Nature's laws are more immutable than any despot's, yet to man's daily life they rarely seem rigid, but permit him to relax with license in summer weather. He is not harshly reminded of the things he may not do. She is very kind and liberal to all men of vicious habits, and certainly does not deny them quarter; they do not die without priest. Still they maintain life along the way, keeping this side the Styx, still hearty, still resolute, "never better in their lives;" and again, after a dozen years have elapsed, they start up from behind a hedge, asking for work and wages for able-bodied men. Who has not met such

—— "a beggar on the way,
Who sturdily could gang?" . . .
"Who cared neither for wind nor wet,
In lands where'er he past?"

"That bold adopts each house he views, his own;
Makes every pulse his checquer, and, at pleasure,
Walks forth, and taxes all the world, like Cæsar;" —

As if consistency were the secret of health, while the poor inconsistent aspirant man, seeking to live a pure life, feeding on air, divided against himself, cannot stand, but pines and dies after a life of sickness, on beds of down.

The unwise are accustomed to speak as if some were not sick; but methinks the difference between men in respect to health is not great enough to lay much stress upon. Some are reputed sick and some are not. It often happens that the sicker man is the nurse to the sounder.

Shad are still taken in the basin of Concord River at Lowell, where they are said to be a month earlier than the Merrimack shad, on account of the warmth of the water. Still patiently, almost pathetically, with instinct not to be discouraged, not to be *reasoned* with, revisiting their old haunts, as if their stern fates would relent, and still met by the Corporation with its dam. Poor shad! where is thy redress? When Nature gave thee instinct, gave she thee the heart to bear thy fate? Still wandering the sea in thy scaly armor to inquire humbly at the mouths of rivers if man has perchance left them free for thee to enter. By countless shoals loitering uncertain meanwhile, merely stemming the tide there, in danger from sea foes in spite of thy bright armor, awaiting new instructions, until the sands, until the water itself, tell thee if it be so or not. Thus by whole migrating nations, full of instinct, which is thy faith, in this backward spring, turned adrift, and perchance knowest not where men do *not* dwell, where there are *not* factories, in these

days. Armed with no sword, no electric shock,
but mere Shad, armed only with innocence and
a just cause, with tender dumb mouth only
forward, and scales easy to be detached. I for
one am with thee, and who knows what may
avail a crow-bar against that Billerica dam? —
Not despairing when whole myriads have gone
to feed those sea monsters during thy suspense,
but still brave, indifferent, on easy fin there,
like shad reserved for higher destinies. Willing
to be decimated for man's behoof after the
spawning season. Away with the superficial
and selfish phil-*anthropy* of men, — who knows
what admirable virtue of fishes may be below
low-water mark, bearing up against a hard
destiny, not admired by that fellow creature
who alone can appreciate it! Who hears the
fishes when they cry? It will not be forgotten
by some memory that we were contemporaries.
Thou shalt ere long have thy way up the rivers,
up all the rivers of the globe, if I am not mistaken. Yea, even thy dull watery dream shall
be more than realized. If it were not so, but
thou wert to be overlooked at first and at last,
then would not I take their heaven. Yes, I say
so, who think I know better than thou canst.
Keep a stiff fin then, and stem all the tides thou
mayest meet.

    At length it would seem that the interests,
not of the fishes only, but of the men of Way-

land, of Sudbury, of Concord, demand the levelling of that dam. Innumerable acres of meadow are waiting to be made dry land, wild native grass to give place to English. The farmers stand with scythes whet, waiting the subsiding of the waters, by gravitation, by evaporation or otherwise, but sometimes their eyes do not rest, their wheels do not roll, on the quaking meadow ground during the haying season at all. So many sources of wealth inaccessible. They rate the loss hereby incurred in the single town of Wayland alone as equal to the expense of keeping a hundred yoke of oxen the year round. One year, as I learn, not long ago, the farmers standing ready to drive their teams afield as usual, the water gave no signs of falling; without new attraction in the heavens, without freshet or visible cause, still standing stagnant at an unprecedented height. All hydrometers were at fault; some trembled for their English even. But speedy emissaries revealed the unnatural secret, in the new float-board, wholly a foot in width, added to their already too high privileges by the dam proprietors. The hundred yoke of oxen, meanwhile, standing patient, gazing wishfully meadowward, at that inaccessible waving native grass, uncut but by the great mower Time, who cuts so broad a swathe, without so much as a wisp to wind about their horns.

That was a long pull from Ball's Hill to Carlisle Bridge, sitting with our faces to the south, a slight breeze rising from the north, but nevertheless water still runs and grass grows, for now, having passed the bridge between Carlisle and Bedford, we see men haying far off in the meadow, their heads waving like the grass which they cut.   In the distance the wind seemed to bend all alike.   As the night stole over, such a freshness was wafted across the meadow that every blade of cut-grass seemed to teem with life.   Faint purple clouds began to be reflected in the water, and the cow-bells tinkled louder along the banks, while, like sly water rats, we stole along nearer the shore, looking for a place to pitch our camp.

At length, when we had made about seven miles, as far as Billerica, we moored our boat on the west side of a little rising ground which in the spring forms an island in the river.   Here we found huckleberries still hanging upon the bushes, where they seemed to have slowly ripened for our especial use.   Bread and sugar, and cocoa boiled in river water, made our repast, and as we had drank in the fluvial prospect all day, so now we took a draught of the water with our evening meal to propitiate the river gods, and whet our vision for the sights it was to behold.   The sun was setting on the one hand, while our eminence was contributing its

A Billerica bridge

shadow to the night, on the other. It seemed insensibly to grow lighter as the night shut in, and a distant and solitary farm-house was revealed, which before lurked in the shadows of the noon. There was no other house in sight, nor any cultivated field. To the right and left, as far as the horizon, were straggling pine woods with their plumes against the sky, and across the river were rugged hills, covered with shrub oaks, tangled with grape vines and ivy, with here and there a gray rock jutting out from the maze. The sides of these cliffs, though a quarter of a mile distant, were almost heard to rustle while we looked at them, it was such a leafy wilderness; a place for fauns and satyrs, and where bats hung all day to the rocks, and at evening flitted over the water, and fireflies husbanded their light under the grass and leaves against the night. When we had pitched our tents on the hill-side, a few rods from the shore, we sat looking through its triangular door in the twilight at our lonely mast on the shore, just seen above the alders, and hardly yet come to a stand-still from the swaying of the stream; the first encroachment of commerce on this land. There was our port, our Ostia. That straight geometrical line against the water and the sky stood for the last refinements of civilized life, and what of sublimity there is in history was there symbolized.

For the most part, there was no recognition of human life in the night, no human breathing was heard, only the breathing of the wind. As we sat up, kept awake by the novelty of our situation, we heard at intervals foxes stepping about over the dead leaves, and brushing the dewey grass close to our tent, and once a musquash fumbling among the potatoes and melons in our boat, but when we hastened to the shore we could detect only a ripple in the water ruffling the disk of a star. At intervals we were serenaded by the song of a dreaming sparrow or the throttled cry of an owl, but after each sound which near at hand broke the stillness of the night, each crackling of the twigs, or rustling among the leaves, there was a sudden pause, and deeper and more conscious silence, as if the intruder were aware that no life was rightfully abroad at that hour. There was a fire in Lowell, as we judged, this night, and we saw the horizon blazing, and heard the distant alarm bells, as it were a faint tinkling music borne to these woods. But the most constant and memorable sound of a summer's night, which we did not fail to hear every night afterward, though at no time so incessantly and so favorably as now, was the barking of the house dogs, from the loudest and hoarsest bark to the faintest aerial palpitation under the eaves of heaven, from the patient but anxious mastiff

to the timid and wakeful terrier, at first loud
and rapid, then faint and slow, to be imitated
only in a whisper; wow-wow-wow-wow — wo —
wo — w — w.   Even in a retired and uninhabited district like this, it was a sufficiency of
sound for the ear of night, and more impressive
than any music.   I have heard the voice of a
hound, just before daylight, while the stars
were shining, from over the woods and river,
far in the horizon, when it sounded as sweet
and melodious as an instrument.   The hound-
ing of a dog pursuing a fox or other animal in
the horizon, may have first suggested the notes
of the hunting horn to alternate with and relieve the lungs of the dog.   This natural bugle
long resounded in the woods of the ancient
world before the horn was invented.   The very
dogs that sullenly bay the moon from farm-
yards in these nights, excite more heroism in
our breasts than all the civil exhortations or
war sermons of the age.   "I had rather be a
dog, and bay the moon," than many a Roman
that I know.   The night is equally indebted to
the clarion of the cock, with wakeful hope,
from the very setting of the sun, prematurely
ushering in the dawn.   All these sounds, the
crowing of cocks, the baying of dogs, and the
hum of insects at noon, are the evidence of
nature's health or *sound* state.   Such is the
never failing beauty and accuracy of language,

the most perfect art in the world; the chisel of a thousand years retouches it.

At length the antepenultimate and drowsy hours drew on, and all sounds were denied entrance to our ears.

> Who sleeps by day and walks by night,
> Will meet no spirit but some sprite.

SUNDAY

"The river calmly flows,
  Through shining banks, through lonely glen,
Where the owl shrieks, though ne'er the cheer of men
    Has stirred its mute repose,
Still if you should walk there, you would go there again."
                                    — CHANNING.

"The Indians tell us of a beautiful River lying far to the south,
which they call Merrimac."
          SIEUR DE MONTS.   *Relations of the Jesuits*, 1604.

IN the morning the river and adjacent country were covered with a dense fog, through
which the smoke of our fire curled up like a
still subtiler mist; but before we had rowed
many rods, the sun arose and the fog rapidly
dispersed, leaving a slight steam only to curl
along the surface of the water. It was a quiet
Sunday morning, with more of the auroral rosy
and white than of the yellow light in it, as if it
dated from earlier than the fall of man, and
still preserved a heathenish integrity; —

    An early unconverted Saint,
    Free from noontide or evening taint,
    Heathen without reproach,
    That did upon the civil day encroach,
    And ever since its birth
    Had trod the outskirts of the earth.

But the impressions which the morning makes
vanish with its dews, and not even the most
"persevering mortal" can preserve the memory
of its freshness to mid-day. As we passed the
various islands, or what were islands in the
spring, rowing with our backs down stream, we
gave names to them. The one on which we
had camped we called Fox Island, and one fine
densely wooded island surrounded by deep
water and overrun by grape vines, which looked
like a mass of verdure and of flowers cast upon
the waves, we named Grape Island. From
Ball's Hill to Billerica meeting-house, the river
was still twice as broad as in Concord, a deep,
dark, and dead stream, flowing between gentle
hills and sometimes cliffs, and well wooded all
the way. It was a long woodland lake bordered
with willows. For long reaches we could see
neither house nor cultivated field, nor any sign
of the vicinity of man. Now we coasted along
some shallow shore by the edge of a dense pali-
sade of bulrushes, which straightly bounded
the water as if clipt by art, reminding us of the
reed forts of the East Indians, of which we had
read; and now the bank slightly raised was
overhung with graceful grasses and various
species of brake, whose downy stems stood
closely grouped and naked as in a vase, while
their heads spread several feet on either side.
The dead limbs of the willow were rounded and

Billerica Meeting-house

adorned by the climbing mikania, *mikania scandens*, which filled every crevice in the leafy bank, contrasting agreeably with the gray bark of its supporter and the balls of the button-bush. The water willow, *salix Purshiana*, when it is of large size and entire, is the most graceful and ethereal of our trees. Its masses of light green foliage, piled one upon another to the height of twenty or thirty feet, seemed to float on the surface of the water, while the slight gray stems and the shore were hardly visible between them. No tree is so wedded to the water, and harmonizes so well with still streams. It is even more graceful than the weeping willow, or any pendulous trees, which dip their branches in the stream instead of being buoyed up by it. Its limbs curved outward over the surface as if attracted by it. It had not a New England but an oriental character, reminding us of trim Persian gardens, of Haroun Alraschid, and the artificial lakes of the east.

As we thus dipped our way along between fresh masses of foliage overrun with the grape and smaller flowering vines, the surface was so calm, and both air and water so transparent, that the flight of a kingfisher or robin over the river was as distinctly seen reflected in the water below as in the air above. The birds seemed to flit through submerged groves, alighting on the yielding sprays, and their clear notes to come up

from below.   We were uncertain whether the
water floated the land, or the land held the water
in its bosom.   It was such a season, in short, as
that in which one of our Concord poets sailed on
its stream, and sung its quiet glories.

> "There is an inward voice, that in the stream
> Sends forth its spirit to the listening ear,
> And in a calm content it floweth on.
> Like wisdom, welcome with its own respect.
> Clear in its breast lie all these beauteous thoughts,
> It doth receive the green and graceful trees,
> And the gray rocks smile in its peaceful arms, — "

And more he sung, but too serious for our page.
For every oak and birch too growing on the hill-
top, as well as for these elms and willows, we
knew that there was a graceful, ethereal and ideal
tree making down from the roots, and sometimes
Nature in high tides brings her mirror to its foot
and makes it visible.   The stillness was intense
and almost conscious, as if it were a natural
Sabbath.   The air was so elastic and crystalline
that it had the same effect on the landscape that
a glass has on a picture, to give it an ideal remoteness and perfection.   The landscape was
clothed in a mild and quiet light, in which the
woods and fences checkered and partitioned it
with new regularity, and rough and uneven
fields stretched away with lawn-like smoothness
to the horizon, and the clouds, finely distinct
and picturesque, seemed a fit drapery to hang
over fairy-land.   The world seemed decked for

some holyday or prouder pageantry, with silken streamers flying, and the course of our lives to wind on before us like a green lane into a country maze, at the season when fruit trees are in blossom.

Why should not our whole life and its scenery be actually thus fair and distinct? All our lives want a suitable background. They should at least, like the life of the anchorite, be as impressive to behold as objects in the desert, a broken shaft or crumbling mound against a limitless horizon. Character always secures for itself this advantage, and is thus distinct and unrelated to near or trivial objects, whether things or persons. On this same stream a maiden once sailed in my boat, thus unattended but by invisible guardians, and as she sat in the prow there was nothing but herself between the steersman and the sky. I could then say with the poet: —

"Sweet falls the summer air
Over her frame who sails with me;
Her way like that is beautifully free,
Her nature far more rare,
And is her constant heart of virgin purity."

At evening still the very stars seem but this maiden's emissaries and reporters of her progress.

Low in the eastern sky
Is set thy glancing eye;
And though its gracious light
Ne'er riseth to my sight,

Yet every star that climbs
Above the gnarled limbs
    Of yonder hill,
Conveys thy gentle will.

Believe I knew thy thought,
And that the zephyrs brought
Thy kindest wishes through,
As mine they bear to you,
That some attentive cloud
Did pause amid the crowd
    Over my head,
While gentle things were said.

Believe the thrushes sung,
And that the flower bells rung,
That herbs exhaled their scent,
And beasts knew what was meant,
The trees a welcome waved,
And lakes their margins laved,
    When thy free mind
To my retreat did wind.

It was a summer eve,
The air did gently heave,
While yet a low hung cloud
Thy eastern skies did shroud;
The lightning's silent gleam,
Startling my drowsy dream,
    Seemed like the flash
Under thy dark eyelash.

Still will I strive to be
As if thou wert with me;
Whatever path I take,
It shall be for thy sake,
Of gentle slope and wide,
As thou wert by my side,
    Without a root
To trip thy gentle foot.

I'll walk with gentle pace,
And choose the smoothest place,
And careful dip the oar,
And shun the winding shore,
And gently steer my boat
Where water lilies float,
    And cardinal flowers
Stand in their sylvan bowers.

It required some rudeness to disturb with our boat the mirror-like surface of the water, in which every twig and blade of grass was so faithfully reflected; too faithfully indeed for art to imitate, for only Nature may exaggerate herself. The shallowest still water is unfathomable. Wherever the trees and skies are reflected there is more than Atlantic depth, and no danger of fancy running aground. We noticed that it required a separate intention of the eye, a more free and abstracted vision, to see the reflected trees and the sky, than to see the river bottom merely; and so are there manifold visions in the direction of every object, and even the most opaque reflect the heavens from their surface. Some men have their eyes naturally intended to the one, and some to the other object.

"A man that looks on glass,
    On it may stay his eye,
Or, if he pleaseth, through it pass,
    And the heavens espy."

Two men in a skiff, whom we passed hereabouts, floating buoyantly amid the reflections

of the trees, like a feather in mid air, or a leaf
which is wafted gently from its twig to the water
without turning over, seemed still in their element, and to have very delicately availed themselves of the natural laws. Their floating there
was a beautiful and successful experiment in
natural philosophy, and it served to ennoble in
our eyes the art of navigation, for as birds fly
and fishes swim, so these men sailed. It reminded
us how much fairer and nobler all the actions of
man might be, and that our life in its whole
economy might be as beautiful as the fairest
works of art or nature.

The sun lodged on the old gray cliffs, and
glanced from every pad; the bulrushes and flags
seemed to rejoice in the delicious light and air;
the meadows were a-drinking at their leisure;
the frogs sat meditating, all Sabbath thoughts,
summing up their week, with one eye out on the
golden sun, and one toe upon a reed, eyeing the
wondrous universe in which they act their part;
the fishes swam more staid and soberly, as
maidens go to church; shoals of golden and silver
minnows rose to the surface to behold the heavens, and then sheered off into more sombre aisles;
they swept by as if moved by one mind, continually gliding past each other, and yet preserving the form of their battalion unchanged,
as if they were still embraced by the transparent
membrane which held the spawn; a young band

of brethren and sisters, trying their new fins; now they wheeled, now shot ahead, and when we drove them to the shore and cut them off, they dexterously tacked and passed underneath the boat. Over the old wooden bridges no traveller crossed, and neither the river nor the fishes avoided to glide between the abutments.

Here was a village not far off behind the woods, Billerica, settled not long ago, and the children still bear the names of the first settlers in this late "howling wilderness;" yet to all intents and purposes it is as old as Fernay or as Mantua, an old gray town, where men grow old and sleep already under moss-grown monuments, — outgrow their usefulness. This is ancient Billerica (Villarica?), now in its dotage. I never heard that it was young. See, is not Nature here gone to decay, farms all run out, meeting-house grown gray and racked with age? If you would know of its early youth, ask those old gray rocks in the pasture. It has a bell that sounds sometimes as far as Concord woods; I have heard that, aye, — hear it now. No wonder that such a sound startled the dreaming Indian, and frightened his game, when the first bells were swung on trees, and sounded through the forest beyond the plantations of the white man. But to-day I like best the echo amid these cliffs and woods. It is no feeble imitation, but rather its original, or as if some rural Orpheus played over the strain again to show how it should sound.

Dong, sounds the brass in the east,
As if to a funeral feast,
But I like that sound the best
Out of the fluttering west.

The steeple ringeth a knell,
But the fairies' silvery bell
Is the voice of that gentle folk,
Or else the horizon that spoke.

Its metal is not of brass,
But air, and water, and glass,
And under a cloud it is swung,
And by the wind it is rung.

When the steeple tolleth the noon,
It soundeth not so soon,
Yet it rings a far earlier hour,
And the sun has not reached its tower.

On the other hand, the road runs up to Carlisle, city of the woods, which, if it is less civil, is the more natural. It does well hold the earth together. It gets laughed at because it is a small town, I know, but nevertheless it is a place where great men may be born any day, for fair winds and foul blow right on over it without distinction. It has a meeting-house and horse-sheds, a tavern and a blacksmith's shop for centre, and a good deal of wood to cut and cord yet. And

"Bedford, most noble Bedford,
I shall not thee forget."

History has remembered thee; especially that meek and humble petition of thy old planters,

The road to Carlisle

like the wailing of the Lord's own people, "To
the gentlemen, the selectmen" of Concord, praying to be erected into a separate parish. We
can hardly credit that so plaintive a psalm resounded but little more than a century ago along
these Babylonish waters. "In the extreme difficult seasons of heat and cold," said they, "we
were ready to say of the Sabbath, Behold what
a weariness is it." — "Gentlemen, if our seeking
to draw off proceed from any disaffection to our
present reverend pastor, or the Christian society
with whom we have taken such sweet counsel
together, and walked unto the house of God in
company, then hear us not this day, but we
greatly desire, if God please, to be eased of our
burden on the Sabbath, the travel and fatigue
thereof, that the word of God may be nigh to us,
near to our houses, and in our hearts, that we
and our little ones may serve the Lord. We
hope that God, who stirred up the spirit of
Cyrus to set forward temple work, has stirred
us up to ask, and will stir you up to grant, the
prayer of our petition; so shall your humble
petitioners ever pray, as in duty bound, —."
And so the temple work went forward here to a
happy conclusion. Yonder in Carlisle the building of the temple was many wearisome years delayed, not that there was wanting of Shittim
wood, or the gold of Ophir, but a site therefor
convenient to all the worshippers; whether on

"Buttrick's Plain," or rather on "Poplar Hill:" it was a tedious question.

In this Billerica solid men must have lived, select from year to year, a series of town clerks, at least, and there are old records that you may search. Some spring the white man came, built him a house, and made a clearing here, letting in the sun, dried up a farm, piled up the old gray stones in fences, cut down the pines around his dwelling, planted orchard seeds brought from the old country, and persuaded the civil apple tree to blossom next to the wild pine and the juniper, shedding its perfume in the wilderness. Their old stocks still remain. He culled the graceful elm from out the woods and from the river-side, and so refined and smoothed his village plot. And thus he plants a town. He rudely bridged the stream, and drove his team afield into the river meadows, cut the wild grass, and laid bare the homes of beaver, otter, muskrat, and with the whetting of his scythe scared off the deer and bear. He set up a mill, and fields of English grain sprang in the virgin soil. And with his grain he scattered the seeds of the dandelion and the wild trefoil over the meadows, mingling his English flowers with the wild native ones. The bristling burdock, the sweet scented catnip, and the humble yarrow, planted themselves along his woodland road, they too seeking "freedom to worship God" in their way. The white man's mullein soon reigned in Indian corn-fields, and sweet scented English grasses clothed the new soil.   Where, then, could the red man set his foot?   The honey bee hummed through the Massachusetts woods, and sipped the wild flowers round the Indian's wigwam, perchance unnoticed, when, with prophetic warning, it stung the red child's hand, forerunner of that industrious tribe that was to come and pluck the wild flower of his race up by the root.

The white man comes, pale as the dawn, with a load of thought, with a slumbering intelligence as a fire raked up, knowing well what he knows, not guessing but calculating; strong in community, yielding obedience to authority; of experienced race; of wonderful, wonderful common sense; dull but capable, slow but persevering, severe but just, of little humor but genuine; a laboring man, despising game and sport; building a house that endures, a framed house.   He buys the Indian's moccasins and baskets, then buys his hunting grounds, and at length forgets where he is buried, and plows up his bones.   And here town records, old, tattered, time-worn, weather-stained chronicles, contain the Indian sachem's mark, perchance an arrow or a beaver, and the few fatal words by which he deeded his hunting grounds away.   He comes with a list of ancient Saxon, Norman, and Celtic names, and strews them up and down this river, — Framingham, Sudbury, Bedford, Carlisle, Billerica, Chelmsford, — and this is New Angle-land, and these are the new West Saxons, whom the red men call, not Angle-ish or English, but Yengeese, and so at last they are known for Yankees.

When we were opposite to the middle of Billerica, the fields on either hand had a soft and cultivated English aspect, the village spire being seen over the copses which skirt the river, and sometimes an orchard straggled down to the water side, though, generally, our course this forenoon was the wildest part of our voyage. It seemed that men led a quiet and very civil life there. The inhabitants were plainly cultivators of the earth, and lived under an organized political government. The school-house stood with a meek aspect, entreating a long truce to war and savage life. Every one finds by his own experience, as well as in history, that the era in which men cultivate the apple, and the amenities of the garden, is essentially different from that of the hunter and forest life, and neither can displace the other without loss. We have all had our day dreams, as well as more prophetic nocturnal visions, but as for farming, I am convinced that my genius dates from an older era than the agricultural. I would at least strike my spade into the earth with such careless freedom but accuracy as the woodpecker his bill into a tree. There is in my nature, methinks, a singular yearning toward all wildness. I know of no redeeming qualities in myself but a sincere love for some things, and when I am reproved I fall back on to this ground. What have I to do with plows? I cut another furrow than you see. Where the off ox treads, there is it not, it is further off; where the nigh ox walks, it will not be, it is nigher still. If corn fails, my crop fails not, and what are drought and rain to me? The rude Saxon pioneer will sometimes pine for that refinement and artificial beauty which are English, and love to hear the sound of such sweet and classical names as the Pentland and Malvern Hills, the Cliffs of Dover and the Trossacks, Richmond, Derwent, and Winandermere, which are to him now instead of the Acropolis and Parthenon, of Baiæ, and Athens with its sea walls, and Arcadia and Tempe.

> Greece, who am I that should remember thee,
> Thy Marathon and thy Thermopylæ?
> Is my life vulgar, my fate mean,
> Which on these golden memories can lean?

We are apt enough to be pleased with such books as Evelyn's Sylva, Acetarium, and Kalendarium Hortense, but they imply a relaxed nerve in the reader. Gardening is civil and social, but it wants the vigor and freedom of the forest and the outlaw. There may be an excess of cultivation as well as of anything else, until civilization becomes pathetic. A highly cultivated man, — all whose bones can be bent! whose heaven-born virtues are but good manners! The young pines springing up in the corn-fields from year to year are to me a refreshing fact. We talk of civilizing the Indian, but that is not the name for his improvement. By the wary independence and aloofness of his dim forest life he preserves his intercourse with his native gods, and is admitted from time to time to a rare and peculiar society with Nature. He has glances of starry recognition to which our saloons are strangers. The steady illumination of his genius, dim only because distant, is like the faint but satisfying light of the stars compared with the dazzling but ineffectual and short-lived blaze of candles. The Society Islanders had their day-born gods, but they were not supposed to be "of equal antiquity with the *atua fauau po*, or night-born gods." It is true, there are the innocent pleasures of country life, and it is sometimes pleasant to make the earth yield her increase, and gather the fruits in their season, but the heroic spirit will not fail to dream of remoter retirements and more rugged paths. It will have its garden plots and its parterres elsewhere than on the earth, and gather nuts and berries by the way for its subsistence, or orchard fruits with such heedlessness as berries. We would not always be soothing and taming Nature, breaking the horse and the ox, but sometimes ride the horse wild and chase the buffalo. The Indian's intercourse with Nature is at least such as admits of the greatest independence of each. If he is somewhat of a stranger in her midst, the gardener is too much of a familiar. There is something vulgar and foul in the latter's closeness to his mistress, something noble and cleanly in the former's distance. In civilization, as in a southern latitude, man degenerates at length, and yields to the incursion of more northern tribes,

> "Some nation yet shut in
> With hills of ice."

There are other, savager, and more primeval aspects of Nature than our poets have sung. It is only white man's poetry. Homer and Ossian even can never revive in London or Boston. And yet behold how these cities are refreshed by the mere tradition, or the imperfectly transmitted fragrance and flavor of these wild fruits. If we could listen but for an instant to the chaunt of the Indian muse, we should understand why he will not exchange his savageness for civilization. Nations are not whimsical. Steel and blankets are strong temptations; but the Indian does well to continue Indian.

After sitting in my chamber many days, reading the poets, I have been out early on a foggy morning, and heard the cry of an owl in a neighboring wood as from a nature behind the common, unexplored by science or by literature. None of the feathered race has yet realized my youthful conceptions of the woodland depths. I had seen the red Election-bird brought from their recesses on my comrades' string, and fancied that their plumage would assume stranger and more dazzling colors, like the tints of evening, in proportion as I advanced further into the darkness and solitude of the forest. Still less have I seen such strong and wild tints on any poet's string.

These modern ingenious sciences and arts do not affect me as those more venerable arts of hunting and fishing, and even of husbandry in its primitive and simple form; as ancient and honorable trades as the sun and moon and winds pursue, coeval with the faculties of man, and invented when these were invented. We do not know their John Gutenberg, or Richard Arkwright, though the poets would fain make them to have been gradually learned and taught. According to Gower,

"And Iadahel, as saith the boke,
Firste made nette, and fishes toke.
Of huntyng eke he fond the chace,
Whiche nowe is knowe in many place;
A tent of clothe, with corde and stake,
He sette up first, and did it make."

Also, Lydgate says:

> "Jason first sayled, in story it is tolde,
> Toward Colchos, to wynne the flees of golde.
> Ceres the Goddess fond first the tilthe of londe;
>
> *   *   *   *   *
>
> Also, Aristeus fonde first the usage
> Of mylke, and cruddis, and of honey swote;
> Peryodes, for grete avauntage,
> From flyntes smote fuyre, daryng in the roote."

We read that Aristeus "obtained of Jupiter and Neptune, that the pestilential heat of the dog days, wherein was great mortality, should be mitigated with wind." This is one of those dateless benefits conferred on man, which have no record in our vulgar day, though we still find some similitude to them in our dreams, in which we have a more liberal and juster apprehension of things, unconstrained by habit, which is then in some measure put off, and divested of memory, which we call history.

According to fable, when the island of Ægina was depopulated by sickness, at the instance of Æacus, Jupiter turned the ants into men, that is, as some think, he made men of the inhabitants who lived meanly like ants. This is perhaps the fullest history of those early days extant.

The fable which is naturally and truly composed, so as to satisfy the imagination, ere it addresses the understanding, beautiful though strange as a wild flower, is to the wise man an apothegm, and admits of his most generous interpretation. When we read that Bacchus made the Tyrrhenian mariners mad, so that they leapt into the sea, mistaking it for a meadow full of flowers, and so became dolphins, we are not concerned about the historical truth of this, but rather a higher poetical truth. We seem to hear the music of a thought, and care not if the understanding be not gratified. For their beauty, consider the fables of Narcissus, of Endymion, of Memnon son of Morning, the representative of all promising youths who have died a premature death, and whose memory is melodiously prolonged to the latest morning; the beautiful stories of Phaeton, and of the Sirens whose isle shone afar off white with the bones of unburied men; and the pregnant ones of Pan, Prometheus, and the Sphynx; and that long list of names which have already become part of the universal language of civilized men, and from proper are becoming common names or nouns, — the Sibyls, the Eumenides, the Parcæ, the Graces, the Muses, Nemesis, &c.

It is interesting to observe with what singular unanimity the furthest sundered nations and generations consent to give completeness and roundness to an ancient fable, of which they indistinctly appreciate the beauty or the truth.

By a faint and dream-like effort, though it be only by the vote of a scientific body, the dullest posterity slowly add some trait to the mythus. As when astronomers call the lately discovered planet Neptune; or the asteroid Astræa, that the Virgin who was driven from earth to heaven at the end of the golden age, may have her local habitation in the heavens more distinctly assigned her, — for the slightest recognition of poetic worth is significant. By such slow aggregation has mythology grown from the first. The very nursery tales of this generation, were the nursery tales of primeval races. They migrate from east to west, and again from west to east; now expanded into the "tale divine" of bards, now shrunk into a popular rhyme. This is an approach to that universal language which men have sought in vain. This fond reiteration of the oldest expressions of truth by the latest posterity, content with slightly and religiously re-touching the old material, is the most impressive proof of a common humanity.

All nations love the same jests and tales, Jews, Christians, and Mahometans, and the same translated suffice for all. All men are children, and of one family. The same tale sends them all to bed, and wakes them in the morning. Joseph Wolff, the missionary, distributed copies of Robinson Crusoe, translated into Arabic, among the Arabs, and they made a great sensation. "Robinson Crusoe's adventures and wisdom," says he, "were read by Mahometans in the market-places of Sanaa, Hodyeda, and Loheya, and admired and believed!" On reading the book, the Arabians exclaimed, "Oh, that Robinson Crusoe must have been a great prophet!"

To some extent, mythology is only the most ancient history and biography. So far from being false or fabulous in the common sense, it contains only enduring and essential truth, the I and you, the here and there, the now and then, being omitted. Either time or rare wisdom writes it. Before printing was discovered, a century was equal to a thousand years. The poet is he who can write some pure mythology to-day without the aid of posterity. In how few words, for instance, the Greeks would have told the story of Abelard and Heloise, making but a sentence for our classical dictionary, — and then, perchance have stuck up their names to shine in some corner of the firmament. We moderns, on the other hand, collect only the raw materials of biography and history, "memoirs to serve for a history," which itself is but materials to serve for a mythology. How many volumes folio would the Life and Labors of Prometheus have filled, if perchance it had fallen, as perchance it did

first, in days of cheap printing! Who knows
what shape the fable of Columbus will at length
assume, to be confounded with that of Jason
and the expedition of the Argonauts? And
Franklin, — there may be a line for him in the
future classical dictionary, recording what that
demigod did, and referring him to some new
genealogy. "Son of —— and ——. He aided
the Americans to gain their independence, instructed mankind in economy, and drew down
lightning from the clouds."

The hidden significance of these fables which
is sometimes thought to have been detected,
the ethics running parallel to the poetry and
history, are not so remarkable as the readiness
with which they may be made to express a
variety of truths. As if they were the skeletons
of still older and more universal truths than
any whose flesh and blood they are for the
time made to wear. It is like striving to make
the sun, or the wind, or the sea, symbols to
signify exclusively the particular thoughts of
our day. But what signifies it? In the mythus
a superhuman intelligence uses the unconscious thoughts and dreams of men as its
hieroglyphics to address men unborn. In the
history of the human mind, these glowing and
ruddy fables precede the noon-day thoughts of
men, as Aurora the sun's rays. The matutine
intellect of the poet, keeping in advance of the

glare of philosophy, always dwells in this auroral atmosphere.

As we said before, the Concord is a dead stream, but its scenery is the more suggestive to the contemplative voyager, and this day its water was fuller of reflections than our pages even. Just before it reaches the falls in Billerica it is contracted, and becomes swifter and shallower, with a yellow pebbly bottom, hardly passable for a canal boat, leaving the broader and more stagnant portion above like a lake among the hills. All through the Concord, Bedford, and Billerica meadows, we had heard no murmur from its stream, except where some tributary runnel tumbled in, —

> Some tumultuous little rill,
>   Purling round its storied pebble,
> Tinkling to the self-same tune,
> From September until June,
>   Which no drought doth e'er enfeeble.
>
> Silent flows the parent stream,
>   And if rocks do lie below,
> Smothers with her waves the din,
> As it were a youthful sin,
>   Just as still, and just as slow.

But now at length we heard this staid and primitive river rushing to her fall, like any rill. We here left its channel, just above the Billerica Falls, and entered the canal, which

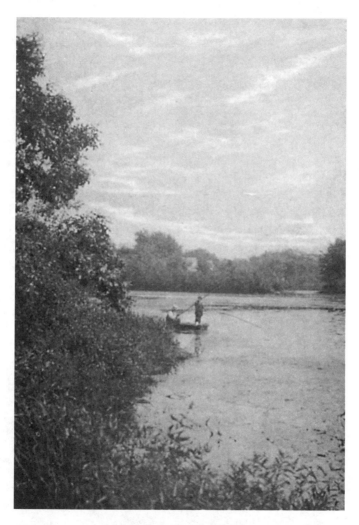

Above Billerica Falls

runs, or rather is conducted, six miles through
the woods to the Merrimack at Middlesex, and
as we did not care to loiter in this part of our
voyage, while one ran along the tow-path drawing the boat by a cord, the other kept it off the
shore with a pole, so that we accomplished the
whole distance in little more than an hour.
This canal, which is the oldest in the country,
and has even an antique look beside the more
modern railroads, is fed by the Concord, so
that we were still floating on its familiar waters.
It is so much water which the river *lets* for the
advantage of commerce.   There appeared some
want of harmony in its scenery, since it was not
of equal date with the woods and meadows
through which it is led, and we missed the con-
ciliatory influence of time on land and water;
but in the lapse of ages, Nature will recover and
indemnify herself, and gradually plant fit shrubs
and flowers along its borders.   Already the
kingfisher sat upon a pine over the water,
and the bream and pickerel swam below.   Thus
all works pass directly out of the hands of the
architect into the hands of Nature, to be
perfected.

It was a retired and pleasant route, without
houses or travellers, except some young men
who were lounging upon a bridge in Chelmsford, who leaned impudently over the rails to
pry into our concerns, but we caught the eye

of the most forward, and looked at him till he was visibly discomfited. Not that there was any peculiar efficacy in our look, but rather a sense of shame left in him which disarmed him.

It is a very true and expressive phrase, "He looked daggers at me," for the first pattern and prototype of all daggers must have been a glance of the eye. First, there was the glance of Jove's eye, then his fiery bolt, then, the material gradually hardening, tridents, spears, javelins, and finally, for the convenience of private men, daggers, krisses, and so forth, were invented. It is wonderful how we get about the streets without being wounded by these delicate and glancing weapons, a man can so nimbly whip out his rapier, or without being noticed carry it unsheathed. Yet after all, it is rare that one gets seriously looked at.

As we passed under the last bridge over the canal, just before reaching the Merrimack, the people coming out of church paused to look at us from above, and apparently, so strong is custom, indulged in some heathenish comparisons; but we were the truest observers of this sunny day. According to Hesiod,

> "The seventh is a holy day,
> For then Latona brought forth golden-rayed Apollo,"

and by our reckoning this was the seventh day of the week, and not the first. I find among the papers of an old Justice of the Peace and Deacon of the town of Concord, this singular memorandum, which is worth preserving as a relic of an ancient custom. After reforming the spelling and grammar, it runs as follows: — "Men that travelled with teams on the Sabbath, Dec. 18th, 1803, were Jeremiah Richardson and Jonas Parker, both of Shirley. They had teams with rigging such as is used to carry barrels, and they were travelling westward. Richardson was questioned by the Hon. Ephraim Wood, Esq., and he said that Jonas Parker was his fellow traveller, and he further said that a Mr. Longley was his employer, who promised to bear him out." We were the men that were gliding northward, this Sept. 1st, 1839, with still team, and rigging not the most convenient to carry barrels, unquestioned by any Squire or Church Deacon, and ready to bear ourselves out, if need were. In the latter part of the seventeenth century, according to the historian of Dunstable, "Towns were directed to erect '*a cage*' near the meeting-house, and in this all offenders against the sanctity of the Sabbath were confined." Society has relaxed a little from its strictness, one would say, but I presume that there is not less *religion* than formerly. If the *ligature* is found to be loosened in one part, it is only drawn the tighter in another.

You can hardly convince a man of an error

in a life-time, but must content yourself with
the reflection that the progress of science is
slow. If he is not convinced, his grand-children
may be. The geologists tell us that it took one
hundred years to prove that fossils are organic,
and one hundred and fifty more, to prove that
they are not to be referred to the Noachian
deluge. I am not sure but I should betake myself in extremities to the liberal divinities of
Greece, rather than to my country's God.
Jehovah, though with us he has acquired new
attributes, is more absolute and unapproach-
able, but hardly more divine, than Jove. He is
not so much of a gentleman, among gods, not so
gracious and catholic, he does not exert so intimate and genial an influence on nature, as many
a god of the Greeks. I should fear the infinite
power and inflexible justice of the almighty
mortal, hardly as yet apotheosized, so wholly
masculine, with no sister Juno, no Apollo,
no Venus, nor Minerva, to intercede for me,
θυμῷ φιλέουσά τε, κηδομένη τε. The Grecian are
youthful and erring and fallen gods, with the
vices of men, but in many important respects
essentially of the divine race. In my Pantheon,
Pan still reigns in his pristine glory, with his
ruddy face, his flowing beard, and his shaggy
body, his pipe and his crook, his nymph Echo,
and his chosen daughter Iambe; for the great
God Pan is not dead, as was rumored. Perhaps

of all the gods of New England and of ancient
Greece, I am most constant at his shrine.

It seems to me that the god that is commonly
worshipped in civilized countries is not at all
divine, though he bears a divine name, but is
the overwhelming authority and respectability
of mankind combined. Men reverence one another, not yet God. If I thought that I could
speak with discrimination and impartiality of
the nations of Christendom, I should praise
them, but it tasks me too much. They seem to
be the most civil and humane, but I may be
mistaken. Every people have gods to suit
their circumstances; the Society Islanders had
a god called Toahitu, "in shape like a dog; he
saved such as were in danger of falling from
rocks and trees." I think that we can do without him, as we have not much climbing to do.
Among them a man could make himself a god
out of a piece of wood in a few minutes, which
would frighten him out of his wits.

I fancy that some indefatigable spinster of
the old school, who had the supreme felicity to
be born in "days that tried men's souls," hearing this, may say with Nestor, another of the
old school, "But you are younger than I. For
time was when I conversed with greater men
than you. For not at any time have I seen
such men nor shall see them, as Perithous, and
Dryas, and ποιμένα λαῶν," that is probably

Washington, sole "Shepherd of the People."
And when Apollo has now six times rolled westward, or seemed to roll, and now for the sixth
time shows his face in the east, eyes well nigh
glazed, long glassed, which have fluctuated only
between lamb's wool and worsted, explore ceaselessly some good sermon book. For six days
shalt thou labor and do all thy knitting, but on
the seventh, forsooth thy reading. Happy we
who can bask in this warm September sun,
which illumines all creatures, as well when they
rest as when they toil, not without a feeling of
gratitude; whose life is as blameless, how blame-
worthy soever it may be, on the Lord's Mona-
day as on his Suna-day.

There are various, nay incredible faiths; why
should we be alarmed at any of them? What
man believes, God believes. Long as I have
lived, and many blasphemers as I have heard and
seen, I have never yet heard or witnessed any
direct and conscious blasphemy or irreverence;
but of indirect and habitual enough. Where is
the man who is guilty of direct and personal in-
solence to Him that made him? — Yet there are
certain current expressions of blasphemous modes
of viewing things, — as, frequently, when we
say, "He is doing a good business," — more
profane than cursing and swearing. There is sin
and death in such words. Let not the children
hear them. — My neighbor says that his hill

farm is "poor stuff," "only fit to hold the world together," — and much more to that effect. He deserves that God should give him a better for so free a treating of his gifts, more than if he patiently put up therewith. But perhaps my farmer forgets that his lean soil has sharpened his wits. This is a crop it was good for.

One memorable addition to the old mythology is due to this era, — the Christian fable. With what pains, and tears, and blood, these centuries have woven this and added it to the mythology of mankind. The new Prometheus. With what miraculous consent, and patience, and persistency, has this mythus been stamped upon the memory of the race? It would seem as if it were in the progress of our mythology to dethrone Jehovah, and crown Christ in his stead.

If it is not a tragical life we live, then I know not what to call it. Such a story as that of Jesus Christ, — the history of Jerusalem, say, being a part of the Universal History. The naked, the embalmed, unburied death of Jerusalem amid its desolate hills, — think of it. In Tasso's poem I trust some things are sweetly buried. Consider the snappish tenacity with which they preach Christianity still. What are time and space to Christianity, eighteen hundred years, and a new world? — that the humble life of a Jewish peasant should have force to make a New York bishop so bigoted. Forty-four lamps, the gift of kings, now burning in a place called the Holy Sepulchre; — a church bell ringing; — some unaffected tears shed by a pilgrim on Mount Calvary within the week. —

"Jerusalem, Jerusalem, when I forget thee, may my right hand forget her cunning."

"By the waters of Babylon there we sat down, and we wept when we remembered Zion."

I trust that some may be as near and dear to Buddha or Christ, or Swedenborg, who are without the pale of their churches. It is necessary not to be Christian, to appreciate the beauty and significance of the life of Christ. I know that some will have hard thoughts of me, when they hear their Christ named beside my Buddha, yet I am sure that I am willing they should love their Christ more than my Buddha, for the love is the main thing, and I like him too. Why need Christians be still intolerant and superstitious? The simple-minded sailors were unwilling to cast overboard Jonah at his own request. —

> "Where is this love become in later age?
> Alas! 't is gone in endless pilgrimage
> From hence, and never to return, I doubt,
> Till revolution wheel those times about."

One man says, —

> "The world's a popular disease, that reigns
> Within the froward heart and frantic brains
> Of poor distempered mortals."

Another that

> — "all the world's a stage,
> And all the men and women merely players."

The world is a strange place for a play-house to stand within it. Old Drayton thought that a man that lived here, and would be a poet, for instance, should have in him certain "brave translunary things," and a "fine madness" should possess his brain. Certainly it were as well that he might be up to the occasion. That is a superfluous wonder, which Dr. Johnson expresses at the assertion of Sir Thomas Browne, that "his life has been a miracle of thirty years, which to relate, were not history, but a piece of poetry, and would sound like a fable." The wonder is rather that all men do not assert as much.

Think what a mean and wretched place this world is; that half the time we have to light a lamp that we may see to live in it. This is half our life. Who would undertake the enterprise if it were all? And, pray, what more has day to offer? A lamp that burns more clear, a purer oil, say winter-strained, that so we may pursue our idleness with less obstruction. Bribed with a little sunlight and a few prismatic tints, we bless our Maker, and stave off his wrath with hymns.

> I make ye an offer,
> Ye gods, hear the scoffer,

The scheme will not hurt you,
If ye will find goodness, I will find virtue.
Though I am your creature,
And child of your nature,
I have pride still unbended,
And blood undescended,
Some free independence,
And my own descendants.
I cannot toil blindly,
Though ye behave kindly,
And I swear by the rood,
I'll be slave to no God.
If ye will deal plainly,
I will strive mainly,
If ye will discover,
Great plans to your lover,
And give him a sphere
Somewhat larger than here.

"Verily, my angels! I was abashed on account of my servant, who had no Providence but me; therefore did I pardon him." — *The Gulistan of Sadi.*

Most people with whom I talk, men and women even of some originality and genius, have their scheme of the universe all cut and dried, — very *dry*, I assure you, to hear, dry enough to burn, dry-rotted and powder-post, methinks, — which they set up between you and them in the shortest intercourse; an ancient and tottering frame with all its boards blown off. They do not walk without their bed. Some to me seemingly very unimportant and unsubstantial things and relations, are for them everlastingly settled, — as Father, Son, and Holy Ghost, and the like. These are like the everlasting hills to them. But in all my wanderings, I never came across the least vestige of authority for these things. They have not left so distinct a trace as the delicate flower of a remote geological period on the coal in my grate. The wisest man preaches no doctrines; he has no scheme; he sees no rafter, not even a cobweb, against the heavens. It is clear sky. If I ever see more clearly at one time than at another, the medium through which I see is clearer. To see from earth to heaven, and see there standing, still a fixture, that old Jewish scheme! What right have you to hold up this obstacle to my understanding you, to your understanding me! You did not invent it; it was imposed on you. Examine your authority. Even Christ, we fear, had his scheme, his conformity to tradition, which slightly vitiates his teaching. He had not swallowed all formulas. He preached some mere doctrines. As for me, Abraham, Isaac, and Jacob are now only the subtilest imaginable essences, which would not stain the morning sky. Your scheme must be the framework of the universe; all other schemes will soon be ruins. The perfect God in his revelations of himself has never got to the length of one such proposition as you, his prophets, state. Have

you learned the alphabet of heaven, and can
count three? Do you know the number of
God's family? Can you put mysteries into
words? Do you presume to fable of the ineffable?
Pray, what geographer are you, that speak of
heaven's topography? Whose friend are you
that speak of God's personality? Do you,
Miles Howard, think that he has made you his
confidant? Tell me of the height of the mountains of the moon, or of the diameter of space,
and I may believe you, but of the secret history
of the Almighty, and I shall pronounce thee
mad. Yet we have a sort of family history of
our God, — so have the Tahitians of theirs, —
and some old poet's grand imagination is imposed
on us as adamantine everlasting truth, and God's
own word!

The New Testament is an invaluable book,
though I confess to having been slightly prejudiced against it in my very early days by the
church and the Sabbath school, so that it seemed,
before I read it, to be the yellowest book in the
catalogue. Yet I early escaped from their
meshes. It was hard to get the commentaries
out of one's head, and taste its true flavor. — I
think that Pilgrim's Progress is the best sermon
which has been preached from this text; almost
all other sermons that I have heard or heard of,
have been but poor imitations of this. — It

would be a poor story to be prejudiced against
the Life of Christ, because the book has been
edited by Christians.   In fact, I love this book
rarely, though it is a sort of castle in the air to
me, which I am permitted to dream.   Having
come to it so recently and freshly, it has the
greater charm, so that I cannot find any to
talk with about it.   I never read a novel, they
have so little real life and thought in them.
The reading which I love best is the scriptures
of the several nations, though it happens that
I am better acquainted with those of the Hindoos, the Chinese, and the Persians, than of
the Hebrews, which I have come to last.   Give
me one of these Bibles, and you have silenced
me for a while.   When I recover the use of my
tongue, I am wont to worry my neighbors with
the new sentences, but commonly they cannot
see that there is any wit in them.   Such has been
my experience with the New Testament.   I have
not yet got to the crucifixion, I have read it over
so many times.   I should love dearly to read it
aloud to my friends, some of whom are seriously
inclined; it is so good, and I am sure that they
have never heard it, it fits their case exactly,
and we should enjoy it so much together, —
but I instinctively despair of getting their ears.
They soon show, by signs not to be mistaken,
that it is inexpressibly wearisome to them.   I do
not mean to imply that I am any better than my

neighbors; for, alas! I know that I am only as
good, though I love better books than they. It
is remarkable, that notwithstanding the universal favor with which the New Testament is
outwardly received, and even the bigotry with
which it is defended, there is no hospitality
shown to, there is no appreciation of, the order
of truth with which it deals. I know of no book
that has so few readers. There is none so truly
strange, and heretical, and unpopular. To
Christians, no less than Greeks and Jews, it is
foolishness and a stumbling block. There are,
indeed, severe things in it which no man should
read aloud but once. — "Seek first the kingdom
of heaven." — "Lay not up for yourselves treasures on earth." — "If thou wilt be perfect, go
and sell that thou hast, and give to the poor,
and thou shalt have treasure in heaven." —
"For what is a man profited, if he shall gain the
whole world, and lose his own soul? or what
shall a man give in exchange for his soul?" —
Think of this, Yankees! — "Verily I say unto
you, if ye have faith as a grain of mustard seed,
ye shall say unto this mountain, Remove hence
to yonder place; and it shall remove; and nothing
shall be impossible unto you." — Think of repeating these things to a New England audience!
thirdly, fourthly, fifteenthly, till there are three
barrels of sermons! Who, without cant, can read
them aloud? Who, without cant, can hear them,

and not go out of the meeting-house? They never *were* read, they never *were* heard. Let but one of these sentences be rightly read from any pulpit in the land, and there would not be left one stone of that meeting-house upon another.

Yet the New Testament treats of man and man's so-called spiritual affairs too exclusively, and is too constantly moral and personal, to alone content me, who am not interested solely in man's religious or moral nature, or in man even. I have not the most definite designs on the future. Absolutely speaking, Do unto others as you would that they should do unto you, is by no means a golden rule, but the best of current silver. An honest man would have but little occasion for it. It is golden not to have any rule at all in such a case. The book has never been written which is to be accepted without any allowance. Christ was a sublime actor on the stage of the world. He knew what he was thinking of when he said, "Heaven and earth shall pass away, but my words shall not pass away." I draw near to him at such a time. Yet he taught mankind but imperfectly how to live; his thoughts were all directed toward another world. There is another kind of success than his. Even here we have a sort of living to get, and must buffet it somewhat longer. There are various tough problems yet to solve, and we must make shift to live, betwixt spirit and matter, such a human life as we can.

A healthy man, with steady employment, as wood chopping at fifty cents a cord, and a camp in the woods, will not be a good subject for Christianity. The New Testament may be a choice book to him on some, but not on all or most of his days. He will rather go a-fishing in his leisure hours. The apostles, though they were fishers too, were of the solemn race of sea-fishers, and never trolled for pickerel on inland streams.

Men have a singular desire to be good without being good for anything, because, perchance, they think vaguely that so it will be good for them in the end. The sort of morality which the priest inculcates is a very subtle policy, far finer than the politicians, and the world is very successfully ruled by them as the policemen. It is not worth the while to let our imperfections disturb us always. The conscience really does not, and ought not to, monopolize the whole of our lives, any more than the heart or the head. It is as liable to disease as any other part. I have seen some whose consciences, owing undoubtedly to former indulgence, had grown to be as irritable as spoilt children, and at length gave them no peace. They did not know when to swallow their cud, and their lives of course yielded no milk.

Conscience is instinct bred in the house,
Feeling and Thinking propagate the sin
By an unnatural breeding in and in.
I say, Turn it out doors,
Into the moors.
I love a life whose plot is simple,
And does not thicken with every pimple;
A soul so sound no sickly conscience binds it,
That makes the universe no worse than 't finds it.
I love an earnest soul,
Whose mighty joy and sorrow
Are not drowned in a bowl,
And brought to life to-morrow;
That lives one tragedy,
And not seventy;
A conscience worth keeping,
Laughing not weeping;
A conscience wise and steady,
And forever ready;
Not changing with events,
Dealing in compliments;
A conscience exercised about
Large things, where one *may* doubt,
I love a soul not all of wood,
Predestinated to be good,
But true to the backbone
Unto itself alone,
And false to none;
Born to its own affairs,
Its own joys and own cares;
By whom the work which God begun
Is finished, and not undone;
Taken up where he left off,
Whether to worship or to scoff;
If not good, why then evil,
If not good god, good devil.
Goodness! — you hypocrite, come out of that,
Live your life, do your work, then take your hat.

I have no patience towards
Such conscientious cowards.
Give me simple laboring folk,
Who love their work,
Whose virtue is a song
To cheer God along.

I was once reproved by a minister who was driving a poor beast to some meeting-house horse-sheds among the hills of New Hampshire, because I was bending my steps to a mountain-top on the Sabbath, instead of a church, when I would have gone further than he to hear a true word spoken on that or any day. He declared that I was "breaking the Lord's fourth commandment," and proceeded to enumerate, in a sepulchral tone, the disasters which had befallen him whenever he had done any ordinary work on the Sabbath. He really thought that a god was at work to trip up those men who followed any secular work on this day, and did not see that it was the evil conscience of the workers that did it. The country is full of this superstition, so that when one enters a village, the church, not only really but from association, is the ugliest looking building in it, because it is the one in which human nature stoops the lowest and is most disgraced. Certainly, such temples as these shall ere long cease to deform the landscape.

If I should ask the minister of Middlesex to let me speak in his pulpit on a Sunday, he would object, because I do not pray as he does, or because I am not ordained. What under the sun are these things?

Really, there is no infidelity, now-a-days, so great as that which prays, and keeps the Sabbath, and rebuilds the churches. The sealer of the South Pacific preaches a truer doctrine. The church is a sort of hospital for men's souls, and as full of quackery as the hospital for their bodies. Those who are taken into it live like pensioners in their Retreat or Sailor's Snug Harbor, where you may see a row of religious cripples sitting outside in sunny weather. Let not the apprehension that he may one day have to occupy a ward therein discourage the cheerful labors of the able-souled man. While he remembers the sick in their extremities, let him not look thither as to his goal. One is sick at heart of this pagoda worship. It is like the beating of gongs in a Hindoo subterranean temple. In dark places and dungeons the preacher's words might perhaps strike root and grow, but not in broad daylight in any part of the world that I know. The sound of the Sabbath bell far away, now breaking on these shores, does not awaken pleasing associations, but melancholy and sombre ones rather. One involuntarily rests on his oar, to humor his unusually meditative mood. It is as the sound of many catechisms and religious books twanging a cant-

ing peal round the earth, seeming to issue from
some Egyptian temple and echo along the shore
of the Nile, right opposite to Pharaoh's palace
and Moses in the bulrushes, startling a multi-
tude of storks and alligators basking in the sun.

Everywhere "good men" sound a retreat, and
the word has gone forth to fall back on innocence. Fall forward rather on to whatever there
is there. Christianity only hopes. It has hung
its harp on the willows, and cannot sing a song
in a strange land. It has dreamed a sad dream,
and does not yet welcome the morning with joy.
The mother tells her falsehoods to her child, but
thank Heaven, the child does not grow up in
its parent's shadow. Our mother's faith has
not grown with her experience. Her experience
has been too much for her. The lesson of life
was too hard for her to learn.

It is remarkable, that almost all speakers and
writers feel it to be incumbent on them, sooner
or later, to prove or to acknowledge the personality of God. Some Earl of Bridgewater, thinking
it better late than never, has provided for it in
his will. It is a sad mistake. In reading a work
on agriculture, we have to skip the author's
moral reflections, and the words "Providence"
and "He" scattered along the page, to come at
the profitable level of what he has to say. What
he calls his religion is for the most part offensive
to the nostrils. He should know better than ex-

pose himself, and keep his foul sores covered till they are quite healed. There is more religion in men's science than there is science in their religion. Let us make haste to the report of the committee on swine.

A man's real faith is never contained in his creed, nor is his creed an article of his faith. The last is never adopted. This it is that permits him to smile ever, and to live even as bravely as he does. And yet he clings anxiously to his creed, as to a straw, thinking that that does him good service because his sheet anchor does not drag.

In most men's religion, the ligature, which should be its umbilical cord connecting them with divinity, is rather like that thread which the accomplices of Cylon held in their hands when they went abroad from the temple of Minerva, the other end being attached to the statue of the goddess. But frequently, as in their case, the thread breaks, being stretched, and they are left without an asylum.

"A good and pious man reclined his head on the bosom of contemplation, and was absorbed in the ocean of a revery. At the instant when he awaked from his vision, one of his friends, by way of pleasantry, said: What rare gift have you brought us from that garden, where you have been recreating? He replied; I fancied to

myself and said, when I can reach the rose-
bower, I will fill my lap with the flowers, and
bring them as a present to my friends; but
when I got there, the fragrance of the roses so
intoxicated me, that the skirt dropped from my
hands. — 'O bird of dawn! learn the warmth
of affection from the moth; for that scorched
creature gave up the ghost, and uttered not a
groan: These vain pretenders are ignorant of
him they seek after; for of him that knew him
we never heard again: — O thou! who towerest
above the flights of conjecture, opinion, and
comprehension; whatever has been reported of
thee we have heard and read; the congregation
is dismissed, and life drawn to a close; and we
still rest at our first encomium of thee!'" —
Sadi.

By noon we were let down into the Merrimack through the locks at Middlesex, just
above Pawtucket Falls, by a serene and liberal-
minded man, who came quietly from his book,
though his duties, we supposed, did not require
him to open the locks on Sundays. With him
we had a just and equal encounter of the eyes,
as between two honest men.

The movements of the eyes express the perpetual and unconscious courtesy of the parties.
It is said that a rogue does not look you in the
face, neither does an honest man look at you

Above Pawtucket Falls

as if he had his reputation to establish. I have
seen some who did not know when to turn aside
their eyes in meeting yours. A truly confident
and magnanimous spirit is wiser than to contend for the mastery in such encounters. Ser-
pents alone conquer by the steadiness of their
gaze. My friend looks me in the face and sees
me, that is all.

The best relations were at once established
between us and this man, and though few words
were spoken, he could not conceal a visible interest in us and our excursion. He was a lover
of the higher mathematics, as we found, and in
the midst of some vast sunny problem, when
we overtook him and whispered our conjectures.
By this man we were presented with the freedom
of the Merrimack. We now felt as if we were
fairly launched on the ocean-stream of our
voyage, and were pleased to find that our boat
would float on Merrimack water. We began
again busily to put in practice those old arts of
rowing, steering, and paddling. It seemed a
strange phenomenon to us that the two rivers
should mingle their waters so readily, since we
had never associated them in our thoughts.

As we glided over the broad bosom of the
Merrimack, between Chelmsford and Dracut,
at noon, here a quarter of a mile wide, the rat-
tling of our oars was echoed over the water to
those villages, and their slight sounds to us.

Their harbors lay as smooth and fairy-like as the Lido, or Syracuse, or Rhodes, in our imagination, while, like some strange roving craft, we flitted past what seemed the dwellings of noble home-staying men, seemingly as conspicuous as if on an eminence, or floating upon a tide which came up to those villagers' breasts. At a third of a mile over the water we heard distinctly some children repeating their catechism in a cottage near the shore, while in the broad shallows between, a herd of cows stood lashing their sides, and waging war with the flies.

Two hundred years ago other catechising than this was going on here; for here came the sachem Wannalancet, and his people, and sometimes Tahatawan, our Concord Sachem, who afterwards had a church at home, to catch fish at the falls; and here also came John Elliot, with the Bible and Catechism, and Baxter's Call to the Unconverted, and other tracts, done into the Massachusetts tongue, and taught them Christianity meanwhile. "This place," says Gookin, referring to Wamesit,

"being an ancient and capital seat of Indians, they come to fish; and this good man takes this opportunity to spread the net of the gospel, to fish for their souls." — "May 5th, 1674," he continues, "according to our usual custom, Mr. Eliot and myself took our journey to Wamesit, or Pawtuckett; and arriving there that evening, Mr. Eliot preached to as many of them as could be got together, out of Matt. xxii. 1–14, the parable of the marriage of the king's son. We met at the wigwam of one called Wannalancet, about two miles from the town, near Pawtuckett falls, and bordering upon Merrimak river. This person, Wannalancet, is the eldest son of old Pasaconaway, the chiefest sachem of Pawtuckett. He is a sober and grave person, and of years, between fifty and sixty. He hath been always loving and friendly to the English." As yet, however, they had not prevailed on him to embrace the Christian religion. "But at this time," says Gookin, "May 6, 1674," — "after some deliberation and serious pause, he stood up, and made a speech to this effect: — 'I must acknowledge I have, all my days, used to pass in an old canoe, (alluding to his frequent custom to pass in a canoe upon the river) and now you exhort me to change and leave my old canoe, and embark in a new canoe, to which I have hitherto been unwilling; but now I yield up myself to your advice, and enter into a new canoe, and do engage to pray to God hereafter.'" One "Mr. Richard Daniel, a gentleman that lived in Billerica," who with other "persons of quality" was present, "desired brother Eliot to tell the sachem from him, that it may be, while he went in his old canoe, he passed in a quiet stream; but the end thereof was death and destruction to soul and body. But now he went into a new canoe, perhaps he would meet with storms and trials, but yet he should be encouraged to persevere, for the end of his voyage would be everlasting rest." — "Since that time, I hear this sachem doth persevere, and is a constant and diligent hearer of God's word, and sanctifieth the Sabbath, though he doth travel to Wamesit meeting every Sabbath, which is above two miles; and though sundry of his people have deserted him, since he subjected to the gospel, yet he continues and persists." — *Gookin's Hist. Coll. of the Indians in New England*, 1674.

Already, as appears from the records, "At a General Court held at Boston in New England, the 7th of the first month, 1643–4." — "Wassamequin, Nashoonon, Kutchamaquin, Massaconomet, and Squaw Sachem, did voluntarily submit themselves" to the English; and among other things did "promise to be willing from time to time to be instructed in the knowledge of God." Being asked "Not to do any unnecessary work on the Sabbath day, especially within the gates of Christian towns," they answered, "It is easy to them; they have not much to do on any day, and they can well take their rest on that day." — "So," says Winthrop, in his Journal, "we causing them to understand the articles, and all the ten commandments of God, and they freely assenting to all, they were solemnly received, and then presented the Court with twenty-six fathom more of wampom; and the Court gave each of them a coat of two yards of cloth, and their dinner; and to them and their men, every of them, a cup of sack at their departure; and so they took leave and went away."

What journeying on foot and on horseback through the wilderness, to preach the gospel to these minks and muskrats! who first, no doubt, listened with their red ears out of a natural hospitality and courtesy, and afterward from curiosity or even interest, till at length there were "praying Indians," and, as the General Court wrote to Cromwell, the "work is brought to this perfection, that some of the Indians themselves can pray and prophesy in a comfortable manner."

It was in fact an old battle and hunting ground through which we had been floating, the ancient dwelling-place of a race of hunters and warriors. Their weirs of stone, their arrowheads and hatchets, their pestles, and the mortars in which they pounded Indian corn before the white man had tasted it, lay concealed in the mud of the river bottom. Tradition still points out the spots where they took fish in the greatest numbers, by such arts as they possessed. It is a rapid story the historian will have to put to-

gether. Miantonimo, — Winthrop, — Webster.
Soon he comes from Mount Hope to Bunker
Hill, from bear-skins, parched corn, bows and
arrows, to tiled roofs, wheat fields, guns and
swords. Pawtucket and Wamesit, where the
Indians resorted in the fishing season, are now
Lowell, the city of spindles, and Manchester of
America, which sends its cotton cloth round the
globe. Even we youthful voyagers had spent a
part of our lives in the village of Chelmsford,
when the present city, whose bells we heard, was
its obscure north district only, and the giant
weaver was not yet fairly born. So old are we;
so young is it.

We were thus entering the State of New
Hampshire on the bosom of the flood formed by
the tribute of its innumerable valleys. The river
was the only key which could unlock its maze,
presenting its hills and valleys, its lakes and
streams, in their natural order and position.
The MERRIMACK, or Sturgeon River, is formed
by the confluence of the Pemigewasset, which
rises near the Notch of the White Mountains,
and the Winnepisiogee, which drains the lake of
the same name, signifying "The Smile of the
Great Spirit." From their junction it runs south
seventy-eight miles to Massachusetts, and thence
east thirty-five miles to the sea. I have traced
its stream from where it bubbles out of the rocks
of the White Mountains above the clouds, to

where it is lost amid the salt billows of the ocean on Plum Island beach. At first it comes on murmuring to itself by the base of stately and retired mountains, through moist primitive woods whose juices it receives, where the bear still drinks it, and the cabins of settlers are far between, and there are few to cross its stream; enjoying in solitude its cascades still unknown to fame; by long ranges of mountains of Sandwich and of Squam, slumbering like tumuli of Titans, with the peaks of Moosehillock, the Haystack, and Kearsarge reflected in its waters; where the maple and the raspberry, those lovers of the hills, flourish amid temperate dews; — flowing long and full of meaning, but untranslatable as its name Pemigewasset, by many a pastured Pelion and Ossa, where unnamed muses haunt, tended by Oreads, Dryads, Naiads, and receiving the tribute of many an untasted Hippocrene. There are earth, air, fire, and water, — very well, this is water, and down it comes.

> Such water do the gods distil,
> And pour down every hill
>   For their New England men;
> A draught of this wild nectar bring,
> And I'll not taste the spring
>   Of Helicon again.

Falling all the way, and yet not discouraged by the lowest fall. By the law of its birth never to become stagnant, for it has come out of the clouds, and down the sides of precipices worn in the flood, through beaver dams broke loose, not splitting but splicing and mending itself, until it found a breathing place in this low land. There is no danger now that the sun will steal it back to heaven again before it reach the sea, for it has a warrant even to recover its own dews into its bosom again with interest at every eve.

It was already the water of Squam and New-found Lake and Winnepisiogee, and White Mountain snow dissolved, on which we were floating, and Smith's and Baker's and Mad rivers, and Nashua and Souhegan and Piscata-quoag, and Suncook and Soucook and Contoo-cook, mingled in incalculable proportions, still fluid, yellowish, restless all, with an ancient, ineradicable inclination to the sea.

So it flows on down by Lowell and Haverhill, at which last place it first suffers a sea change, and a few masts betray the vicinity of the ocean. Between the towns of Amesbury and Newbury it is a broad commercial river, from a third to half a mile in width, no longer skirted with yellow and crumbling banks, but backed by high green hills and pastures, with frequent white beaches on which the fishermen draw up their nets. I have passed down this portion of the river in a steam-boat, and it was a pleasant sight to watch from its deck the fishermen drag-ging their seines on the distant shore, as in pictures of a foreign strand. At intervals you may meet with a schooner laden with lumber, standing up to Haverhill, or else lying at anchor or aground, waiting for wind or tide; until, at last, you glide under the famous Chain Bridge, and are landed at Newburyport. Thus she who at first was "poore of waters, naked of renowne," having received so many fair tributaries, as was said of the Forth,

"Doth grow the greater still, the further downe;
    Till that abounding both in power and fame,
    She long doth strive to give the sea her name;"

or if not her name, in this case, at least the impulse of her stream. From the steeples of Newburyport, you may review this river stretching far up into the country, with many a white sail glancing over it like an inland sea, and behold, as one wrote who was born on its head-waters, "Down out at its mouth, the dark inky main blending with the blue above. Plum Island, its sand ridges scolloping along the horizon like the sea serpent, and the distant outline broken by many a tall ship, leaning, *still*, against the sky."

Rising at an equal height with the Connecticut, the Merrimack reaches the sea by a course only half as long, and hence has no leisure to form broad and fertile meadows like the former, but is hurried along rapids, and down numerous falls without long delay. The banks are generally steep and high, with a narrow interval reaching back to the hills, which is only occasionally and partially overflown at present, and is much valued by the farmers. Between Chelmsford and Concord in New Hampshire, it varies from twenty to seventy-five rods in width. It is probably wider than it was formerly, in many places, owing to the trees having been cut down, and the consequent wasting away of its banks. The influence of the Pawtucket dam is felt as far up as Cromwell's Falls, and many think that the banks are being abraded and the river filled up again by this cause. Like all our rivers, it is liable to freshets, and the Pemigewasset has been known to rise twenty-five feet in a few hours. It is navigable for vessels of burden about twenty miles, for canal boats by means of locks as far as Concord in New Hampshire, about seventy-five miles from its mouth, and for smaller boats to Plymouth, one hundred and thirteen miles. A small steam-boat once plied between Lowell and Nashua, before the railroad was built, and one now runs from Newburyport to Haverhill.

Unfitted to some extent for the purposes of commerce by the sand-bar at its mouth, see how this river was devoted from the first to the service of manufactures. Issuing from the iron region of Franconia, and flowing through still uncut forests, by inexhaustible ledges of granite,

The Newburyport "Chain Bridge"

with Squam, and Winnepisiogee, and Newfound, and Massabesic lakes for its millponds, it falls over a succession of natural dams, where it has been offering its *privileges* in vain for ages, until at last the Yankee race came to *improve* them. Standing here at its mouth, look up its sparkling stream to its source, — a silver cascade which falls all the way from the White Mountains to the sea, — and behold a city on each successive plateau, a busy colony of human beaver around every fall. Not to mention Newburyport and Haverhill, see Lawrence, and Lowell, and Nashua, and Manchester, and Concord, gleaming one above the other. When at length it has escaped from under the last of the factories it has a level and unmolested passage to the sea, a mere *waste water*, as it were, bearing little with it but its fame; its pleasant course revealed by the morning fog which hangs over it, and the sails of the few small vessels which transact the commerce of Haverhill and Newburyport. But its real vessels are railroad cars, and its true and main stream, flowing by an iron channel further south, may be traced by a long line of vapor amid the hills, which no morning wind ever disperses, to where it empties into the sea at Boston. This side is the louder murmur now. Instead of the scream of a fish-hawk scaring the fishes, is heard the whistle of the steam-engine, arousing a country to its progress.

This river too was at length discovered by the white man, "trending up into the land," he knew not how far, possibly an inlet to the South Sea. Its valley, as far as the Winnepisiogee, was first surveyed in 1652. The first settlers of Massachusetts supposed that the Connecticut, in one part of its course, ran north-west, "so near the great lake as the Indians do pass their canoes into it over land." From which lake and the "hideous swamps" about it, as they supposed, came all the beaver that was traded between Virginia and Canada, — and the Potomac was thought to come out of or from very near it. Afterward the Connecticut came so near the course of the Merrimack, that with a little pains they expected to divert the current of the trade into the latter river, and its profits from their Dutch neighbors into their own pockets.

Unlike the Concord, the Merrimack is not a dead but a living stream, though it has less life within its waters and on its banks. It has a swift current, and, in this part of its course, a clayey bottom, almost no weeds, and comparatively few fishes. We looked down into its yellow water with the more curiosity, who were accustomed to the Nile-like blackness of the former river. Shad and alewives are taken here in their season, but salmon, though at one time more numerous than shad, are now more rare. Bass, also, are taken occasionally; but locks and dams have proved more or less destructive to the fisheries. The shad make their appearance early in May, at the same time with the blossoms of the pyrus, one of the most conspicuous early flowers, which is for this reason called the shad-blossom. An insect, called the shad-fly, also appears at the same time, covering the houses and fences. We are told that "their greatest run is when the apple trees are in full blossom. The old shad return in August; the young, three or four inches long, in September. These are very fond of flies." A rather picturesque and luxurious mode of fishing was formerly practised on the Connecticut, at Bellows Falls, where a large rock divides the stream. "On the steep sides of the island rock," says Belknap, "hang several arm chairs, fastened to ladders, and secured by a counterpoise, in which fishermen sit to catch salmon and shad with dipping nets." The remains of Indian weirs, made of large stones, are still to be seen in the Winnepisiogee, one of the head-waters of this river.

It cannot but affect our philosophy favorably to be reminded of these shoals of migratory fishes, of salmon, shad, alewives, marsh-bankers, and others, which penetrate up the innumerable rivers of our coast in the spring, even to the interior lakes, their scales gleaming in the sun; and again, of the fry, which in still greater num-

bers wend their way downward to the sea. "And
is it not pretty sport," wrote Capt. John Smith,
who was on this coast as early as 1614, "to pull
up twopence, sixpence, and twelvepence, as fast
as you can haul and veer a line?" — "And
what sport doth yield a more pleasing content,
and less hurt or charge, than angling with a
hook, and crossing the sweet air from isle to isle,
over the silent streams of a calm sea."

On the sandy shore, opposite the Glass-house
village in Chelmsford, at the Great Bend, where
we landed to rest us and gather a few wild
plums, we discovered the *campanula rotundi-
folia*, a new flower to us, the harebell of the
poets, which is common to both hemispheres,
growing close to the water. Here, in the shady
branches of an apple tree on the sand, we took
our nooning, where there was not a zephyr to
disturb the repose of this glorious Sabbath day,
and we reflected serenely on the long past and
successful labors of Latona.

> "So silent is the cessile air,
>   That every cry and call,
> The hills and dales, and forest fair,
>   Again repeats them all.
>
> "The herds beneath some leafy trees,
>   Amidst the flowers they lie,
> The stable ships upon the seas
>   Tend up their sails to dry."

As we thus rested in the shade, or rowed leisurely along, we had recourse, from time to time, to the Gazetteer, which was our Navigator, and from its bald natural facts extracted the pleasure of poetry. Beaver river comes in a little lower down, draining the meadows of Pelham, Windham, and Londonderry. The Scotch-Irish settlers of the latter town, according to this authority, were the first to introduce the potato into New England, as well as the manufacture of linen cloth.

Everything that is printed and bound in a book contains some echo at least of the best that is in literature. Indeed, the best books have a use like sticks and stones, which is above or beside their design, not anticipated in the preface, nor concluded in the appendix. Even Virgil's poetry serves a very different use to me to-day from what it did to his contemporaries. It has often an acquired and accidental value merely, proving that man is still man in the world. It is pleasant to meet with such still lines as,

"Jam læto turgent in palmite gemmæ;"
Now the buds swell on the joyful stem;

or

"Strata jacent passim sua quæque sub arbore poma."
The apples lie scattered everywhere, each under its tree.

In an ancient and dead language, any recognition of living nature attracts us. These are such sentences as were written while grass grew and water ran. It is no small recommendation when a book will stand the test of mere unobstructed sunshine and daylight.

What would we not give for some great poem to read now, which would be in harmony with the scenery, — for if men read aright, methinks they would never read anything but poems. No history nor philosophy can supply their place.

The wisest definition of poetry the poet will instantly prove false by setting aside its requisitions. We can, therefore, publish only our advertisement of it.

There is no doubt that the loftiest written wisdom is either rhymed, or in some way musically measured, — is, in form as well as substance, poetry; and a volume which should contain the condensed wisdom of mankind, need not have one rhythmless line.

Yet poetry, though the last and finest result, is a natural fruit. As naturally as the oak bears an acorn, and the vine a gourd, man bears a poem, either spoken or done. It is the chief and most memorable success, for history is but a prose narrative of poetic deeds. What else have the Hindoos, the Persians, the Babylonians, the Egyptians done, that can be told? It is the simplest relation of phenomena, and describes the commonest sensations with more truth than science does, and the latter at a distance slowly mimics its style and methods. The poet sings how the blood flows in his veins. He performs his functions, and is so well that he needs such stimulus to sing only as plants to put forth leaves and blossoms. He would strive in vain to modulate the remote and transient music which he sometimes hears, since his song is a vital function like breathing, and an integral result like weight. It is not the overflowing of life but of its subsidence rather, and is drawn from under the feet of the poet. It is enough if Homer but say the sun sets. He is as serene as nature, and we can hardly detect the enthusiasm of the bard. It is as if nature spoke. He presents to us the simplest pictures of human life, so that childhood itself can understand them, and the man must not think twice to appreciate his naturalness. Each reader discovers for himself, that, with respect to the simpler features of nature, succeeding poets have done little else than copy his similes. His more memorable passages are as naturally bright, as gleams of sunshine in misty weather. Nature furnishes him not only with words, but with stereotyped lines and sentences from her mint.

"As from the clouds appears the full moon,
    All shining, and then again it goes behind the shadowy clouds,
    So Hector, at one time appeared among the foremost,
    And at another in the rear, commanding; and all with brass
    He shone, like to the lightning of ægis-bearing Zeus."

He conveys the least information, even the hour of the day, with such magnificence and vast expense of natural imagery, as if it were a message from the gods.

"While it was dawn, and sacred day was advancing,
  For that space the weapons of both flew fast, and the people fell;
  But when now the woodcutter was preparing his morning meal,
  In the recesses of the mountain, and had wearied his hands
  With cutting lofty trees, and satiety came to his mind,
  And the desire of sweet food took possession of his thoughts;
  Then the Danaans, by their valor, broke the phalanxes,
  Shouting to their companions from rank to rank."

When the army of the Trojans passed the night under arms, keeping watch lest the enemy should re-embark under cover of the dark,

'They, thinking great things, upon the neutral ground of war
  Sat all the night; and many fires burned for them.
  As when in the heavens the stars round the bright moon
  Appear beautiful, and the air is without wind;
  And all the heights, and the extreme summits,
  And the wooded sides of the mountains appear; and from the
    heavens an infinite ether is diffused,
  And all the stars are seen; and the shepherd rejoices in his heart;
  So between the ships and the streams of Xanthus
  Appeared the fires of the Trojans before Ilium.
  A thousand fires burned on the plain; and by each
  Sat fifty, in the light of the blazing fire;
  And horses eating white barley and corn,
  Standing by the chariots, awaited fair-throned Aurora."

The "white-armed goddess Juno," sent by the Father of gods and men for Iris and Apollo,

"Went down the Idæan mountains to far Olympus,
  As when the mind of a man, who has come over much earth,
  Sallies forth, and he reflects with rapid thoughts,
  There was I, and there, and remembers many things;
  So swiftly the august Juno hastening flew through the air,
  And came to high Olympus."

His scenery is always true, and not invented.
He does not leap in imagination from Asia to
Greece, through mid air,

—————— ἐπειὴ μάλα πολλὰ μεταξύ
"Ουρεά τε σκιοέντα, θαλάσσα τε ἠχήεσσα.
    for there are very many
Shady mountains and resounding seas between.

If his messengers repair but to the tent of
Achilles, we do not wonder how they got there,
but accompany them step by step along the
shore of the resounding sea.   Nestor's account
of the march of the Pylians against the Epeians
is extremely lifelike. —

"Then rose up to them sweet-worded Nestor, the shrill orator
  of the Pylians,
  And words sweeter than honey flowed from his tongue."

This time, however, he addresses Patroclus
alone. — "A certain river, Minyas by name,
leaps seaward near to Arene, where we Pylians
wait the dawn, both horse and foot.   Thence
with all haste we sped as on the morrow ere
't was noon-day, accoutred for the fight, even
to Alpheus' sacred source, &c."   We fancy that

we hear the subdued murmuring of the Minyas discharging its waters into the main the live-long night, and the hollow sound of the waves breaking on the shore, — until at length we are cheered at the close of a toilsome march by the gurgling fountains of Alpheus.

There are few books which are fit to be re-membered in our wisest hours, but the Iliad is brightest in the serenest days, and embodies still all the sunlight that fell on Asia Minor. No modern joy or ecstasy of ours can lower its height, or dim its lustre, but there it lies in the east of literature, as it were the earliest and latest production of the mind. The ruins of Egypt oppress and stifle us with their dust, foulness preserved in cassia and pitch, and swathed in linen; the death of that which never lived. But the rays of Greek poetry struggle down to us, and mingle with the sunbeams of the recent day. The statute of Memnon is cast down, but the shaft of the Iliad still meets the sun in his rising. —

> "Homer is gone; and where is Jove? and where
>   The rival cities seven?   His song outlives
>   Time, tower, and god, — all that then was save Heaven."

So too, no doubt, Homer had his Homer, and Orpheus his Orpheus, in the dim antiquity which preceded them. The mythological system of the ancients, and it is still the mythology of the

moderns, the poem of mankind, interwoven so
wonderfully with their astronomy, and match-
ing in grandeur and harmony the architecture
of the heavens themselves, seems to point to a
time when a mightier genius inhabited the earth.
But after all, man is the great poet, and not
Homer or Shakspeare; and our language itself,
and the common arts of life are his work. Poetry is so universally true and independent of
experience, that it does not need any particular biography to illustrate it, but we refer it
sooner or later to some Orpheus or Linus, and
after ages to the genius of humanity, and the
gods themselves.

It would be worth the while to select our
reading, for books are the society we keep; to
read only the serenely true; never statistics, nor
fiction, nor news, nor reports, nor periodicals,
but only great poems, and when they failed,
read them again, or perchance write more. Instead of other sacrifice, we might offer up our
perfect (τελεία) thoughts to the gods daily, in
hymns or psalms. For we should be at the helm
at least once a day. The whole of the day should
not be day-time; there should be one hour, if
no more, which the day did not bring forth.
Scholars are wont to sell their birthright for a
mess of learning. But is it necessary to know
what the speculator prints, or the thoughtless

study, or the idle read, the literature of the Russians and the Chinese, or even French philosophy and much of German criticism. Read the best books first, or you may not have a chance to read them at all. "There are the worshippers with offerings, and the worshippers with mortifications; and again the worshippers with enthusiastic devotion; so there are those, the wisdom of whose reading is their worship, men of subdued passions, and severe manners; — This world is not for him who doth not worship; and where, O Arjoon, is there another?" Certainly, we do not need to be soothed and entertained always like children. He who resorts to the easy novel, because he is languid, does no better than if he took a nap. The front aspect of great thoughts can only be enjoyed by those who stand on the side whence they arrive. Books, not which afford us a cowering enjoyment, but in which each thought is of unusual daring; such as an idle man cannot read, and a timid one would not be entertained by, which even make us dangerous to existing institutions, — such call I good books.

All that are printed and bound are not books; they do not necessarily belong to letters, but are oftener to be ranked with the other luxuries and appendages of civilized life. Base wares are palmed off under a thousand disguises. "The way to trade," as a pedler once told me, "is to

The Merrimack at Lawrence

put it right through," no matter what it is, anything that is agreed on. —

> "You grov'ling worldlings, you whose wisdom trades
> Where light ne'er shot his golden ray."

By dint of able writing and pen-craft, books are
cunningly compiled, and have their run and
success even among the learned, as if they were
the result of a new man's thinking, and their
birth were attended with some natural throes.
But in a little while their covers fall off, for no
binding will avail, and it appears that they are
not Books or Bibles at all.   There are new and
patented inventions in this shape, purporting
to be for the elevation of the race, which many
a pure scholar and genius who has learned to
read is for a moment deceived by, and finds
himself reading a horse-rake, or spinning jenny,
or wooden nutmeg, or oak-leaf cigar, or steam-
power press, or kitchen range, perchance, when
he was seeking serene and biblical truths. —

> "Merchants, arise,
> And mingle conscience with your merchandise."

Paper is cheap, and authors need not now erase
one book before they write another.   Instead
of cultivating the earth for wheat and potatoes,
they cultivate literature, and fill a place in the
Republic of Letters.   Or they would fain write
for fame merely, as others actually raise crops
of grain to be distilled into brandy.   Books are

for the most part wilfully and hastily written,
as parts of a system, to supply a want real or
imagined. Books of natural history aim commonly to be hasty schedules, or inventories of
God's property, by some clerk. They do not in
the least teach the divine view of nature, but
the popular view, or rather the popular method
of studying nature, and make haste to conduct
the persevering pupil only into that dilemma
where the professors always dwell. —

> "To Athens gown'd he goes, and from that school
> Returns unsped, a more instructed fool."

They teach the elements really of ignorance,
not of knowledge, for to speak deliberately and
in view of the highest truths, it is not easy to
distinguish elementary knowledge. There is a
chasm between knowledge and ignorance which
the arches of science can never span. A book
should contain pure discoveries, glimpses of
terra firma, though by shipwrecked mariners,
and not the art of navigation by those who have
never been out of sight of land. *They* must not
yield wheat and potatoes, but must themselves
be the unconstrained and natural harvest of
their author's lives. —

> "What I have learned is mine; I've had my thought,
> And me the Muses noble truths have taught."

We do not learn much from learned books,
but from true, sincere, human books, from frank

and honest biographies. The life of a good man will hardly improve us more than the life of a freebooter, for the inevitable laws appear as plainly in the infringement as in the observance, and our lives are sustained by a nearly equal expense of virtue of some kind. The decaying tree, while yet it lives, demands sun, wind, and rain no less than the green one. It secretes sap and performs the functions of health. If we choose, we may study the alburnum only. The gnarled stump has as tender a bud as the sapling.

At least let us have healthy books, a stout horse-rake or a kitchen range which is not cracked. Let not the poet shed tears only for the public weal. He should be as vigorous as a sugar maple, with sap enough to maintain his own verdure, beside what runs into the troughs, and not like a vine, which being cut in the spring bears no fruit, but bleeds to death in the endeavor to heal its wounds. The poet is he that hath fat enough, like bears and marmots, to suck his claws all winter. He hibernates in this world, and feeds on his own marrow. It is pleasant to think in winter, as we walk over the snowy pastures, of those happy dreamers that lie under the sod, of dormice and all that race of dormant creatures, which have such a superfluity of life enveloped in thick folds of fur, impervious to cold. Alas, the poet too is, in one sense, a sort of dormouse gone into winter quarters of deep and serene thoughts, insensible to surrounding circumstances; his words are the relation of his oldest and finest memory, a wisdom drawn from the remotest experience. Other men lead a starved existence, meanwhile, like hawks, that would fain keep on the wing, and trust to pick up a sparrow now and then.

There are already essays and poems, the growth of this land, which are not in vain, all which, however, we could conveniently have stowed in the till of our chest. If the gods permitted their own inspiration to be breathed in vain, these might be overlooked in the crowd, but the accents of truth are as sure to be heard at last on earth as in heaven. They already seem ancient, and in some measure have lost the traces of their modern birth. Here are they who

> —— "ask for that which is our whole life's light,
> For the perpetual, true, and clear insight."

I remember a few sentences which spring like the sward in its native pasture, where its roots were never disturbed, and not as if spread over a sandy embankment; answering to the poet's prayer,

> "Let us set so just
> A rate on knowledge, that the world may trust
> The poet's sentence, and not still aver
> Each art is to itself a flatterer."

But, above all, in our native port, did we not
frequent the peaceful games of the Lyceum,
from which a new era will be dated to New
England, as from the games of Greece. For if
Herodotus carried his history to Olympia to
read, after the cestus and the race, have we not
heard such histories recited there, which since
our countrymen have read, as made Greece
sometimes to be forgotten? — Philosophy, too,
has there her grove and portico, not wholly
unfrequented in these days.

Lately the victor, whom all Pindars praised,
has won another palm, contending with

> "Olympian bards who sung
> Divine ideas below,
> Which always find us young,
> And always keep us so." —

What earth or sea, mountain or stream, or
Muses' spring or grove, is safe from his all-
searching ardent eye, who drives off Phœbus'
beaten track, visits unwonted zones, makes the
gelid Hyperboreans glow, and the old polar serpent writhe, and many a Nile flow back and hide
his head! —

> That Phaeton of our day,
> Who'd make another milky way,
> And burn the world up with his ray;
>
> By us an undisputed seer, —
> Who'd drive his flaming car so near
> Unto our shuddering mortal sphere,

Disgracing all our slender worth,
And scorching up the living earth,
To prove his heavenly birth.

The silver spokes, the golden tire,
Are glowing with unwonted fire,
And ever nigher roll and nigher;

The pins and axle melted are,
The silver radii fly afar,
Ah, he will spoil his Father's car!

Who let him have the steeds he cannot steer?
Henceforth the sun will not shine for a year.
And we shall Ethiops all appear.

From *his*

—— "lips of cunning fell
The thrilling Delphic oracle."

And yet, sometimes,

We should not mind if on our ear there fell
Some less of cunning, more of oracle.

It is Apollo shining in your face. O rare Contemporary, let us have far off heats. Give us the
subtler, the heavenlier though fleeting beauty,
which passes through and through, and dwells
not in the verse; even pure water, which but
reflects those tints which wine wears in its
grain. Let epic trade-winds blow, and cease this
waltz of inspirations. Let us oftener feel even
the gentle south-west wind upon our cheeks

blowing from the Indians' heaven. What though
we lose a thousand meteors from the sky, if
skyey depths, if star-dust and undissolvable
nebulæ remain?   What though we lose a thousand wise responses of the oracle, if we may
have instead some natural acres of Ionian
earth?

Though we know well,

> 'That 't is not in the power of kings [or presidents] to raise
> A spirit for verse that is not born thereto,
> Nor are they born in every prince's days;"

yet spite of all they sang in praise of their
"Eliza's reign," we have evidence that poets
may be born and sing in *our* day, in the presi-
dency of James K. Polk,

> "And that the utmost powers of English rhyme,"
> *Were not* "within *her* peaceful reign confined."

The prophecy of Samuel Daniel is already how
much more than fulfilled!

> "And who in time knows whither we may vent
> The treasure of our tongue?   To what strange shores
> This gain of our best glory shall be sent,
> T' enrich unknowing nations with our stores?
> What worlds in th' yet unformed occident,
> May come refined with the accents that are ours."

Enough has been said in these days of the
charm of fluent writing. We hear it complained
of some works of genius, that they have fine

thoughts, but are irregular and have no flow.
But even the mountain peaks in the horizon
are, to the eye of science, parts of one range.
We should consider that the flow of thought is
more like a tidal wave than a prone river, and
is the result of a celestial influence, not of any
declivity in its channel. The river flows because
it runs down hill, and descends the faster as it
flows more rapidly. The reader who expects to
float down stream for the whole voyage, may
well complain of nauseating swells and choppings
of the sea when his frail shore-craft gets amidst
the billows of the ocean stream, which flows as
much to sun and moon as lesser streams to it.
But if we would appreciate the flow that is in
these books, we must expect to feel it rise from
the page like an exhalation, and wash away our
critical brains like burr millstones, flowing to
higher levels above and behind ourselves. There
is many a book which ripples on like a freshet,
and flows as glibly as a mill stream sucking under
a causeway; and when their authors are in the
full tide of their discourse, Pythagoras, and
Plato, and Jamblichus, halt beside them. Their
long, stringy, slimy sentences are of that consistency that they naturally flow and run together.
They read as if written for military men, for
men of business, there is such a despatch in them.
Compared with these, the grave thinkers and
philosophers seem not to have got their swad-

dling clothes off; they are slower than a Roman
army in its march, the rear camping to-night
where the van camped last night. The wise
Jamblichus eddies and gleams like a watery
slough.

> "How many thousand, never heard the name
> Of Sidney, or of Spenser, or their books?
> And yet brave fellows, and presume of fame,
> And seem to bear down all the world with looks."

The ready writer seizes the pen, and shouts,
Forward! Alamo and Fanning! and after rolls
the tide of war. The very walls and fences seem
to travel. But the most rapid trot is no flow
after all, — and thither you and I, at least,
reader, will not follow.

A perfectly healthy sentence, it is true, is
extremely rare. For the most part we miss the
hue and fragrance of the thought; as if we
could be satisfied with the dews of the morning
or evening without their colors, or the heavens
without their azure. The most attractive sentences are, perhaps, not the wisest, but the surest
and roundest. They are spoken firmly and con-
clusively, as if the speaker had a right to know
what he says, and if not wise, they have at least
been well learned. Sir Walter Raleigh might
well be studied if only for the excellence of his
style, for he is remarkable in the midst of so
many masters. There is a natural emphasis in

his style, like a man's tread, and a breathing
space between the sentences, which the best of
modern writing does not furnish. His chapters
are like English parks, or say rather like a
western forest, where the larger growth keeps
down the underwood, and one may ride on
horse-back through the openings. All the distinguished writers of that period, possess a
greater vigor and naturalness than the more
modern, — for it is allowed to slander our own
time, — and when we read a quotation from
one of them in the midst of a modern author,
we seem to have come suddenly upon a greener
ground, a greater depth and strength of soil.
It is as if a green bough were laid across the
page, and we are refreshed as by the sight of
fresh grass in mid-winter or early spring. You
have constantly the warrant of life and experience in what you read. The little that is said is
eked out by implication of the much that was
done. The sentences are verduous and blooming as evergreen and flowers, because they are
rooted in fact and experience, but our false
and florid sentences have only the tints of
flowers without their sap or roots. All men are
really most attracted by the beauty of plain
speech, and they even write in a florid style in
imitation of this. They prefer to be misunder-
stood rather than to come short of its exuberance.
Hussein Effendi praised the epistolary style of

Ibrahim Pasha to the French traveller Botta, because of "the difficulty of understanding it; there was," he said, "but one person at Jidda who was capable of understanding and explaining the Pasha's correspondence." A man's whole life is taxed for the least thing well done. It is its net result. Every sentence is the result of a long probation. Where shall we look for standard English, but to the words of a standard man? The word which is best said came nearest to not being spoken at all, for it is cousin to a deed which the speaker could have better done. Nay, almost it must have taken the place of a deed by some urgent necessity, even by some misfortune, so that the truest writer will be some captive knight, after all. And perhaps the fates had such a design, when, having stored Raleigh so richly with the substance of life and experience, they made him a fast prisoner, and compelled him to make his words his deeds, and transfer to his expression the emphasis and sincerity of his action.

Men have a respect for scholarship and learning greatly out of proportion to the use they commonly serve. We are amused to read how Ben Jonson engaged, that the dull masks with which the royal family and nobility were to be entertained, should be "grounded upon antiquity and solid learning." Can there be any greater reproach than an idle learning? Learn to split wood, at least. The necessity of labor and conversation with many men and things, to the scholar is rarely well remembered; steady labor with the hands, which engrosses the attention also, is unquestionably the best method of removing palaver and sentimentality out of one's style, both of speaking and writing. If he has worked hard from morning till night, though he may have grieved that he could not be watching the train of his thoughts during that time, yet the few hasty lines which at evening record his day's experience will be more musical and true than his freest but idle fancy could have furnished. Surely the writer is to address a world of laborers, and such therefore must be his own discipline. He will not idly dance at his work who has wood to cut and cord before nightfall in the short days of winter; but every stroke will be husbanded, and ring soberly through the wood; and so will the strokes of that scholar's pen, which at evening record the story of the day, ring soberly, yet cheerily, on the ear of the reader, long after the echoes of his axe have died away. The scholar may be sure that he writes the tougher truth for the calluses on his palms. They give firmness to the sentence. Indeed, the mind never makes a great and successful effort without a corresponding energy of the body. We are often struck by the force and precision of style to which hard-working men, unpractised in writing, easily attain, when required to make the effort. As if plainness, and vigor, and sincerity, the ornaments of style, were better learned on the farm and in the workshop than in the schools. The sentences written by such rude hands are nervous and tough, like hardened thongs, the sinews of the deer, or the roots of the pine. As for the graces of expression, a great thought is never found in a mean dress; but though it proceed from the lips of the Wol-offs, the nine Muses and the three Graces will have conspired to clothe it in fit phrase. Its education has always been liberal, and its implied wit can endow a college. The scholar might frequently emulate the propriety and emphasis of the farmer's call to his team, and confess that if that were written it would surpass his labored sentences. Whose are the truly *labored* sentences? From the weak and flimsy periods of the politician and literary man, we are glad to turn even to the description of work, the simple record of the month's labor in the farmer's almanac, to restore our tone and spirits. A sentence should read as if its author, had he held a plow instead of a pen, could have drawn a furrow deep and straight to the end. The scholar requires hard and serious labor to give an impetus to his thought. He will learn to grasp the pen firmly so, and wield it gracefully and effectively, as an axe or a sword. When we consider the weak and nerveless periods of some literary men, who perchance in feet and inches come up to the standard of their race, and are not deficient in girth also, we are amazed at the immense sacrifice of thews and sinews. What! these proportions, — these bones, — and this their work! Hands which could have felled an ox have hewed this fragile matter which would not have tasked a lady's fingers! Can this be a stalwart man's work, who has a marrow in his back and a tendon Achilles in his heel? They who set up the blocks of Stonehenge did somewhat, if they only laid out their strength for once, and stretched themselves.

Yet, after all, the truly efficient laborer will not crowd his day with work, but will saunter to his task surrounded by a wide halo of ease and leisure, and then do but what he loves best. He is anxious only about the fruitful kernels of time. Though the hen should sit all day, she could lay only one egg, and, besides, would not have picked up materials for another. Let a man take time enough for the most trivial deed, though it be but the paring of his nails. The buds swell imperceptibly, without hurry or confusion, as if the short spring days were an eternity. —

> Then spend an age in whetting thy desire,
> Thou need'st not *hasten* if thou dost *stand fast*.

Some hours seem not to be occasion for any deed, but for resolves to draw breath in. We do not directly go about the execution of the purpose that thrills us, but shut our doors behind us, and ramble with prepared mind, as if the half were already done. Our resolution is taking root or hold on the earth then, as seeds first send a shoot downward which is fed by their own albumen, ere they send one upward to the light.

There is a sort of homely truth and naturalness in some books which is very rare to find, and yet looks cheap enough. There may be nothing lofty in the sentiment, or fine in the expression, but it is careless country talk. Homeliness is almost as great a merit in a book as in a house, if the reader would abide there. It is next to beauty, and a very high art. Some have this merit only. The scholar is not apt to make his most familiar experience come gracefully to the aid of his expression. Very few men can speak of Nature, for instance, with any truth. They overstep her modesty, somehow or other, and confer no favor. They do not speak a good word for her. Most cry better than speak, and you can get more nature out of them by pinching than by addressing them. The surliness with which the woodchopper speaks of his woods, handling them as indifferently as his axe, is better than the mealy-

mouthed enthusiasm of the lover of Nature.
Better than the primrose by the river's brim be
a yellow primrose, and nothing more, than that
it be something less.   Aubrey relates of Thomas
Fuller that his was " a very working head, inso-
much that, walking and meditating before dinner,
he would eat up a penny loaf, not knowing that
he did it.   His natural memory was very great,
to which he added the art of memory.   He
would repeat to you forwards and backwards
all the signs from Ludgate to Charing-cross."
He says of Mr. John Hales, that "He loved
Canarie," and was buried "under an altar
monument of black marble —— with a too
long epitaph;" of Edmund Halley, that he,
"at sixteen could make a dial, and then, he said,
he thought himself a brave fellow;" of William
Holder, who wrote a book upon his curing one
Popham who was deaf and dumb, " he was beholding to no author; did only consult with
Nature."   For the most part, an author con-
sults only with all who have written before him
upon a subject, and his book is but the advice
of so many.   But a good book will never have
been forestalled, but the topic itself will in one
sense be new, and its author, by consulting with
Nature, will consult not only with those who
have gone before, but with those who may come
after.   There is always room and occasion
enough for a true book on any subject; as

there is room for more light the brightest day
and more rays will not interfere with the first.

We thus worked our way up this river, gradually adjusting our thoughts to novelties, beholding from its placid bosom a new nature and
new works of men, and as it were with increasing
confidence, finding Nature still habitable, genial,
and propitious to us; not following any beaten
path, but the windings of the river, as ever the
nearest way for us. Fortunately we had no
business in this country. The Concord had
rarely been a river or *rivus*, but barely *fluvius*, or
between *fluvius* and *lacus*. This Merrimack was
neither *rivus* nor *fluvius* nor *lacus*, but rather *am-
nis* here, a gently swelling and stately rolling flood
approaching the sea. We could even sympathize with its buoyant tide, going to seek its
fortune in the ocean, and anticipating the time
when "being received within the plain of its
freer water," it should "beat the shores for
banks," —

"campoque recepta
Liberioris aquæ, pro ripis litora pulsant."

At length we doubled a low shrubby islet,
called Rabbit Island, subjected alternately to
the sun and to the waves, as desolate as if it lay
some leagues within the icy sea, and found ourselves in a narrower part of the river, near the

sheds and yards for picking the stone known as the Chelmsford granite, which is quarried in Chelmsford and the neighboring towns. We passed Wicasuck Island, which contains seventy acres or more, on our right between Chelmsford and Tyngsboro'. This was a favorite residence of the Indians. According to the History of Dunstable, "About 1663, the eldest son of Passaconaway [Chief of the Penacooks] was thrown into jail for a debt of £45, due to John Tinker, by one of his tribe, and which he had promised verbally should be paid. To relieve him from his imprisonment, his brother Wannalancet and others, who owned Wicasuck Island, sold it and paid the debt." It was, however, restored to the Indians by the General Court in 1665. After the departure of the Indians in 1683, it was granted to Jonathan Tyng in payment for his services to the colony, in maintaining a garrison at his house. Tyng's house stood not far from Wicasuck Falls. Gookin, who, in his Epistle Dedicatory to Robert Boyle, apologizes for presenting his "matter clothed in a wilderness dress," says that on the breaking out of Philip's war in 1675, there were taken up by the Christian Indians and the English in Marlborough, and sent to Cambridge, seven "Indians belonging to Narragansett, Long Island, and Pequod, who had all been at work about seven weeks with one Mr. Jonathan

Southern end of Wicasuck or Tyng's Island

Tyng, of Dunstable, upon Merrimack River;
and hearing of the war, they reckoned with
their master, and getting their wages, conveyed
themselves away without his privity, and being
afraid, marched secretly through the woods,
designing to go to their own country." However, they were released soon after. Such were
the hired men in those days. Tyng was the
first permanent settler of Dunstable, which
then embraced what is now Tyngsboro' and
many other towns. In the winter of 1675, in
Philip's war, every other settler left the town,
but "he," says the historian of Dunstable,
"fortified his house; and although 'obliged to
send to Boston for his food,' sat himself down in
the midst of his savage enemies, alone, in the
wilderness, to defend his home. Deeming his
position an important one for the defence of the
frontiers, in Feb. 1676, he petitioned the Colony
for aid," humbly showing, as his petition runs,
that as he lived "in the uppermost house on
Merrimac River, lying open to ye enemy, yet
being so seated that it is, as it were, a watch-
house to the neighboring towns," he could render important service to his country if only he
had some assistance, "there being," he said,
"never an inhabitant left in the town but myself." Wherefore he requests that their "Hon-
ors would be pleased to order him *three or four
men* to help garrison his said house," which

they did. But methinks that such a garrison
would be weakened by the addition of a man.—

> "Make bandog thy scout watch to bark at a thief,
> Make courage for life, to be captain chief;
> Make trap-door thy bulwark, make bell to begin,
> Make gunstone and arrow shew who is within."

Thus he earned the title of first permanent
settler. In 1694 a law was passed "that every
settler who deserted a town for fear of the Indians,
should forfeit all his rights therein." But
now, at any rate, as I have frequently observed,
a man may desert the fertile frontier territories
of truth and justice, which are the State's best
lands, for fear of far more insignificant foes,
without forfeiting any of his civil rights therein.
Nay, townships are granted to deserters, and
the General Court, as I am sometimes inclined
to regard it, is but a deserters' camp itself.

As we rowed along near the shore of Wicasuck
Island, which was then covered with wood, in
order to avoid the current, two men, who looked
as if they had just run out of Lowell, where they
had been waylaid by the Sabbath, meaning to
go to Nashua, and who now found themselves
in the strange, natural, uncultivated and unsettled part of the globe which intervenes, full of
walls and barriers, a rough and uncivil place to
them, seeing our boat moving so smoothly up
the stream, called out from the high bank above

our heads to know if we would take them as passengers, as if this were the street they had missed; that they might sit and chat and drive away the time, and so at last find themselves in Nashua. This smooth way they much preferred. But our boat was crowded with necessary furniture, and sunk low in the water, and moreover required to be worked, for even *it* did not progress against the stream without effort; so we were obliged to deny them passage. As we glided away with even sweeps, while the fates scattered oil in our course, the sun now sinking behind the alders on the distant shore, we could still see them far off over the water, running along the shore and climbing over the rocks and fallen trees like insects, — for they did not know any better than we that they were on an island, — the unsympathizing river ever flowing in an opposite direction; until, having reached the entrance of the Island Brook, which they had probably crossed upon the locks below, they found a more effectual barrier to their progress. They seemed to be learning much in a little time. They ran about like ants on a burning brand, and once more they tried the river here, and once more there, to see if water still indeed was not to be walked on, as if a new thought inspired them, and by some peculiar disposition of the limbs they could accomplish it. At length sober common sense seemed to have resumed its sway, and they concluded that what they had so long heard must be true, and resolved to ford the shallower stream. When nearly a mile distant we could see them stripping off their clothes and preparing for this experiment; yet it seemed likely that a new dilemma would arise, they were so thoughtlessly throwing away their clothes on the wrong side of the stream, as in the case of the countryman with his corn, his fox, and his goose, which had to be transported one at a time. Whether they got safely through, or went round by the locks we never learned. We could not help being struck by the seeming, though innocent indifference of Nature to these men's necessities, while elsewhere she was equally serving others. Like a true benefactress, the secret of her service is unchangeableness. Thus is the busiest merchant, though within sight of his Lowell, put to pilgrim's shifts and soon comes to staff and scrip and scallop shell.

We, too, who held the middle of the stream, came near experiencing a pilgrim's fate, being tempted to pursue what seemed a sturgeon or larger fish, for we remembered that this was the Sturgeon river, its dark and monstrous back alternately rising and sinking in mid-stream. We kept falling behind, but the fish kept his back well out, and did not dive, and seemed to prefer to swim against the stream, so, at any rate, he would not escape us by going out to sea. At length, having got as near as was convenient, and looking out not to get a blow from his tail, now the bow-gunner delivered his charge, while the stern-man held his ground. But the halibut-skinned monster, in one of these swift-gliding pregnant moments, without ever ceasing his bobbing up and down, saw fit, without a chuckle or other prelude, to proclaim himself a huge imprisoned spar, placed there as a buoy, to warn sailors of sunken rocks. So, each casting some blame upon the other, we withdrew quickly to safer waters.

The Scene-shifter saw fit here to close the drama of this day, without regard to any unities which we mortals prize. Whether it might have proved tragedy, or comedy, or tragicomedy or pastoral, we cannot tell. This Sunday ended by the going down of the sun, leaving us still on the waves. But they who are on the water enjoy a longer and brighter twilight than they who are on the land, for here the water, as well as the atmosphere, absorbs and reflects the light, and some of the day seems to have sunk down into the waves. The light gradually forsook the deep water, as well as the deeper air, and the gloaming came to the fishes as well as to us, and more dim and gloomy to them, whose day is a perpetual twilight, though sufficiently bright for their weak and watery eyes.

Vespers had already rung in many a dim and watery chapel down below, where the shadows of the weeds were extended in length over the sandy floor. The vespertinal pout had already begun to flit on leathern fin, and the finny gossips withdrew from the fluvial street to creeks and coves, and other private haunts, excepting a few of stronger fin, which anchored in the stream, stemming the tide even in their dreams. Meanwhile, like a dark evening cloud, we were wafted over the cope of their sky, deepening the shadows on their deluged fields.

Having reached a retired part of the river where it spread out to sixty rods in width, we pitched our tent on the east side, in Tyngsboro', just above some patches of the beach plum, which was now nearly ripe, where the sloping bank was a sufficient pillow, and with the bustle of sailors making the land, we transferred such stores as were required from boat to tent, and hung a lantern to the tent-pole, and so our house was ready. With a buffalo spread on the grass, and a blanket for our covering, our bed was soon made. A fire crackled merrily before the entrance, so near that we could tend it without stepping abroad, and when we had supped, we put out the blaze, and closed the door, and with the semblance of domestic comfort, sat up to read the gazetteer, to learn our latitude and longitude, and write the journal of the voyage, or listened to the wind and the rippling of the river till sleep overtook us. There we lay under an oak on the bank of the stream, near to some farmer's corn-field, getting sleep, and forgetting where we were; a great blessing, that we are obliged to forget our enterprises every twelve hours. Minks, muskrats, meadow-mice, wood-chucks, squirrels, skunks, rabbits, foxes and weasles, all inhabit near, but keep very close while you are there. The river sucking and eddying away all night down toward the marts and the seaboard, a great work and freshet, and no small enterprise to reflect on. Instead of the Scythian vastness of the Billerica night, and its wild musical sounds, we were kept awake by the boisterous sport of some Irish laborers on the railroad, wafted to us over the water, still unwearied and unresting on this seventh day, who would not have done with whirling up and down the track with ever increasing velocity and still reviving shouts, till late in the night.

One sailor was visited in his dreams this night by the Evil Destinies, and all those powers that are hostile to human life, which constrain and oppress the minds of men, and make their path seem difficult and narrow, and beset with dangers, so that the most innocent and worthy enterprises appear insolent and a tempting of fate, and the gods go not with us. But the other happily passed serene and even ambrosial or immortal night, and his sleep was dreamless, or only the atmosphere of pleasant dreams remained, a happy natural sleep until the morning, and his cheerful spirit soothed and reassured his brother, for whenever they meet, the Good Genius is sure to prevail.

MONDAY

"I thynke for to touche also
The worlde whiche neweth everie daie,
So as I can, so as I maie."   — GOWER.

"Gazed on the Heavens for what he missed on Earth."
Britannia's Pastorals.

WHEN the first light dawned on the earth, and the birds awoke, and the brave river was heard rippling confidently seaward, and the nimble early rising wind rustled the oak leaves about our tent, all men, having reinforced their bodies and their souls with sleep, and cast aside doubt and fear, were invited to unattempted adventures.

One of us took the boat over to the opposite shore, which was flat and accessible, a quarter of a mile distant, to empty it of water and wash out the clay, while the other kindled a fire and got breakfast ready. At an early hour we were again on our way, rowing through the fog as before, the river already awake, and a million crisped waves come forth to meet the sun when he should show himself. The countrymen, recruited by their day of rest, were already stirring, and had begun to cross the ferry on the business

of the week. This ferry was as busy as a beaver
dam, and all the world seemed anxious to get
across the Merrimack River at this particular
point, waiting to get set over, — children with
their two cents done up in paper, jail-birds
broke loose and constable with warrant, travellers from distant lands to distant lands, men and
women to whom the Merrimack River was a
bar. There stands a gig in the gray morning,
in the mist, the impatient traveller pacing the
wet shore with whip in hand, and shouting
through the fog after the regardless Charon and
his retreating ark, as if he might throw that
passenger overboard and return forthwith for
himself; he will compensate him. He is to
break his fast at some unseen place on the opposite side. It may be Ledyard or the Wandering
Jew. Whence pray did he come out of the
foggy night? and whither through the sunny
day will he go? We observe only his transit;
important to us, forgotten by him, transiting
all day. There are two of them. May be,
they are Virgil and Dante. But when they
crossed the Styx, none were seen bound up or
down the stream, that I remember. It is only
a *transjectus*, a transitory voyage, like life itself, none but the long-lived gods bound up or
down the stream. Many of these Monday men
are ministers, no doubt, reseeking their parishes
with hired horses, with sermons in their valises

all read and gutted, the day after never with them. They cross each other's routes all the country over like woof and warp, making a garment of loose texture; vacation now for six days. They stop to pick nuts and berries, and gather apples by the wayside at their leisure. Good religious men, with the love of men in their hearts, and the means to pay their toll in their pockets. We got over this ferry chain without scraping, rowing athwart the tide of travel, — no toll from us that day.

The fog dispersed and we rowed leisurely along through Tyngsboro', with a clear sky and a mild atmosphere, leaving the habitations of men behind and penetrating yet further into the territory of ancient Dunstable. It was from Dunstable, then a frontier town, that the famous Capt. Lovewell, with his company, marched in quest of the Indians on the 18th of April, 1725. He was the son of "an ensign in the army of Oliver Cromwell, who came to this country, and settled at Dunstable, where he died at the great age of one hundred and twenty years." In the words of the old nursery tale, sung about a hundred years ago, —

"He and his valiant soldiers did range the woods full wide,
And hardships they endured to quell the Indian's pride."

In the shaggy pine forest of Pequawket they met the "rebel Indians," and prevailed, after a bloody

fight, and a remnant returned home to enjoy
the fame of their victory. A township called
Lovewell's Town, but now, for some reason, or
perhaps without reason, Pembroke, was granted
them by the State.

"Of all our valiant English, there were but thirty-four,
    And of the rebel Indians, there were about four score;
    And sixteen of our English did safely home return,
    The rest were killed and wounded, for which we all must mourn.

"Our worthy Capt. Lovewell among them there did die,
    They killed Lieut. Robbins, and wounded good young Frye,
    Who was our English Chaplin; he many Indians slew,
    And some of them he scalped while bullets round him flew."

   Our brave forefathers have exterminated all
the Indians, and their degenerate children no
longer dwell in garrisoned houses, nor hear
any war-whoop in their path.   It would be well,
perchance, if many an "English Chaplin" in
these days could exhibit as unquestionable trophies of this valor as did "good young Frye."
We have need to be as sturdy pioneers still as
Miles Standish, or Church, or Lovewell. We
are to follow on another trail, it is true, but one
as convenient for ambushes. What if the
Indians are exterminated, are not savages as
grim prowling about the clearings to-day? —

"And braving many dangers and hardships in the way,
    They safe arrived at Dunstable the thirteenth (?) day of May."

But they did not all "safe arrive in Dunstable the thirteenth," or the fifteenth, or the thirtieth "day of May." Eleazer Davis and Josiah Jones, both of Concord, for our native town had seven men in this fight, Lieutenant Farwell, of Dunstable, and Jonathan Frye, of Andover, who were all wounded, were left behind, creeping toward the settlements. "After travelling several miles, Frye was left and lost," though a more recent poet has assigned him company in his last hours. —

"A man he was of comely form,
    Polished and brave, well learned and kind;
Old Harvard's learned halls he left
    Far in the wilds a grave to find.

"Ah! now his blood-red arm he lifts;
    His closing lids he tries to raise;
And speak once more before he dies,
    In supplication and in praise.

"He prays kind Heaven to grant success,
    Brave Lovewell's men to guide and bless,
And when they've shed their heart-blood true,
    To raise them all to happiness." . . .

"Lieutenant Farwell took his hand,
    His arm around his neck he threw,
And said, 'brave Chaplain I could wish,
    That Heaven had made me die for you.'"

Farwell held out eleven days. "A tradition says," as we learn from the history of Concord, "that arriving at a pond with Lieut. Farwell,

Davis pulled off one of his moccasins, cut it in strings, on which he fastened a hook, caught some fish, fried and ate them. They refreshed him, but were injurious to Farwell, who died soon after." Davis had a ball lodged in his body, and his right hand shot off; but on the whole, he seems to have been less damaged than his companion. He came into Berwick after being out fourteen days. Jones also had a ball lodged in his body, but he likewise got into Saco after fourteen days, though not in the best condition imaginable. "He had subsisted," says an old journal, "on the spontaneous vegetables of the forest; and cranberries, which he had eaten, came out of wounds he had received in his body." This was also the case with Davis. The last two reached home at length, safe if not sound, and lived many years in a crippled state to enjoy their pension.

But alas! of the crippled Indians, and their adventures in the woods, —

"For as we are informed, so thick and fast they fell,
Scarce twenty of their number at night did get home well," —

how many balls lodged with them, how it fared with their cranberries, what Berwick or Saco they got into, and finally what pension or township was granted them, there is no journal to tell.

It is stated in the History of Dunstable, that just before his last march, Lovewell was warned to beware of the ambuscades of the enemy, but "he replied, 'that he did not care for them,' and bending down a small elm beside which he was standing into a bow, declared 'that he would treat the Indians in the same way.' This elm is still standing [in Nashua], a venerable and magnificent tree."

Meanwhile, having passed the Horseshoe Interval in Tyngsboro', where the river makes a sudden bend to the northwest, — for our reflections have anticipated our progress somewhat, — we were advancing further into the country and into the day, which last proved almost as golden as the preceding, though the slight bustle and activity of the Monday seemed to penetrate even to this scenery. Now and then we had to muster all our energy to get round a point, where the river broke rippling over rocks, and the maples trailed their branches in the stream, but there was generally a backwater or eddy on the side, of which we took advantage. The river was here about forty rods wide and fifteen feet deep. Occasionally one ran along the shore, examining the country, and visiting the nearest farm-houses, while the other followed the windings of the stream alone, to meet his companion at some distant point, and hear the report of his adventures; how the farmer praised the coolness of his well, and his

wife offered the stranger a draught of milk, or
the children quarrelled for the only transparency
in the window that they might get sight of the
man at the well.   For though the country seemed
so new, and no house was observed by us, shut
in between the high banks that sunny day, we
did not have to travel far to find where men
inhabited, like wild bees, and had sunk wells in
the loose sand and loam of the Merrimack.
There dwelt the subject of the Hebrew scriptures, and the Esprit des Lois, where a thin
vaporous smoke curled up through the noon.
All that is told of mankind, of the inhabitants
of the Upper Nile, and the Sunderbunds, and
Timbuctoo, and the Orinoko, was experience
here.   Every race and class of men was represented.   According to Belknap, the historian
of New Hampshire, who wrote sixty years ago,
here too, perchance, dwelt "new lights," and
free thinking men even then.   "The people in
general throughout the State," it is written,
"are professors of the Christian religion in some
form or other.   There is, however, a sort of *wise
men*, who pretend to reject it; but they have not
yet been able to substitute a better in its place."
   The other voyageur, perhaps, would in the
meanwhile have seen a brown hawk, or a woodchuck, or a musquash, creeping under the alders.
   We occasionally rested in the shade of a maple
or a willow, and drew forth a melon for our

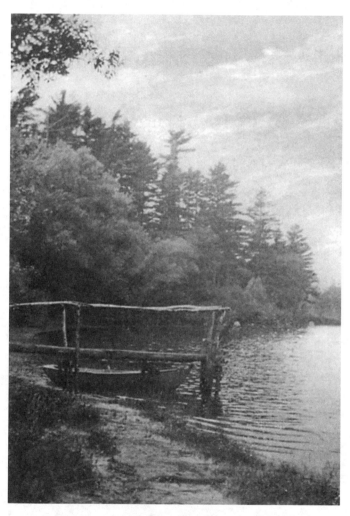

At the Horseshoe Bend

refreshment, while we contemplated at our leisure the lapse of the river and of human life; and as that current, with its floating twigs and leaves, so did all things pass in review before us, while far away in cities and marts on this very stream, the old routine was proceeding still. There is, indeed, a tide in the affairs of men, as the poet says, and yet as things flow they circulate, and the ebb always balances the flow. All streams are but tributary to the ocean, which itself does not stream, and the shores are unchanged but in longer periods than man can measure.   Go where we will, we discover infinite change in particulars only, not in generals. When I go into a museum, and see the mummies wrapped in their linen bandages, I see that the times began to need reform as long ago as when they walked the earth.   I come out into the streets, and meet men who declare that the time is near at hand for the redemption of the race.   But as men lived in Thebes, so do they live in Dunstable to-day.   "Time drinketh up the essence of every great and noble action, which ought to be performed, and is delayed in the execution," so says Veeshnoo Sarma; and we perceive that the schemers return again and again to common sense and labor.   Such is the evidence of history. —

"Yet I doubt not thro' the ages one increasing purpose runs,
    And the thoughts of men are widen'd with the process of the
        Suns."

There are secret articles in our treaties with the gods, of more importance than all the rest, which the historian can never know.

There are many skilful apprentices, but few master workmen. On every hand we observe a truly wise practice, in education, in morals, and in the arts of life, the embodied wisdom of many an ancient philosopher. Who does not see that heresies have some time prevailed, that reforms have already taken place? All this worldly wisdom might be regarded as the once unamiable heresy of some wise man. Some interests have got a footing on the earth which we have not made sufficient allowance for. Even they who first built these barns, and cleared the land thus, had some valor. The abrupt epochs and chasms are smoothed down in history as the inequalities of the plain are concealed by distance. But unless we do more than simply learn the trade of our time, we are but apprentices, and not yet masters of the art of life.

Now that we are casting away these melon seeds, how can we help feeling reproach? He who eats the fruit, should at least plant the seed; aye, if possible, a better seed than that whose fruit he has enjoyed. Seeds! there are seeds enough which need only to be stirred in with the soil where they lie, by an inspired voice or pen, to bear fruit of a divine flavor. O thou spendthrift! Defray thy debt to the world; eat not the seed of institutions, as the luxurious do, but plant it rather, while thou devourest the pulp and tuber for thy subsistence; that so, perchance, one variety may at last be found worthy of preservation.

There are moments when all anxiety and stated toil are becalmed in the infinite leisure and repose of nature. All laborers must have their nooning, and at this season of the day, we are all, more or less, Asiatics, and give over all work and reform. While lying thus on our oars by the side of the stream, in the heat of the day, our boat held by an osier put through the staple in its prow, and slicing the melons, which are a fruit of the east, our thoughts reverted to Arabia, Persia, and Hindostan, the lands of contemplation and dwelling places of the ruminant nations. In the experience of this noontide we could find some apology even for the instinct of the opium, betel, and tobacco chewers. Mount Sabér, according to the French traveller and naturalist, Botta, is celebrated for producing the Kát tree, of which "the soft tops of the twigs and tender leaves are eaten," says his reviewer, "and produce an agreeable soothing excitement, restoring from fatigue, banishing sleep, and disposing to the enjoyment of conversation." We thought that we might lead a dignified oriental life along this stream as well, and the maple and alders would be our Kát trees.

It is a great pleasure to escape sometimes from the restless class of Reformers. What if these grievances exist? So do you and I. Think you that sitting hens are troubled with ennui these long summer days, sitting on and on in the crevice of a hay-loft, without active employment? By the faint cackling in distant barns, I judge that dame Nature is interested to know how many eggs her hens lay. The Universal Soul, as it is called, has an interest in the stacking of hay, the foddering of cattle, and the draining of peat meadows. Away in Scythia, away in India, it makes butter and cheese. Suppose that all farms *are* run out, and we youths must buy old land and bring it to, still everywhere the relentless opponents of reform bear a strange resemblance to ourselves; or perchance, they are a few old maids and bachelors, who sit round the kitchen hearth, and listen to the singing of the kettle. "The oracles often give victory to our choice, and not to the order alone of the mundane periods. As, for instance, when they say, that our voluntary sorrows germinate in us as the growth of the particular life we lead." The reform which you talk about can be undertaken any morning before unbarring our doors. We need not call any convention. When two neighbors begin to eat corn bread, who before ate wheat, then the gods smile from ear to ear, for it is very pleasant to them. Why do you not try it? Don't let me hinder you.

There are theoretical reformers at all times, and all the world over, living on anticipation. Wolff, travelling in the deserts of Bokhara, says: "Another party of derveeshes came to me and observed, 'The time will come when there shall be no difference between rich and poor, between high and low, when property will be in common, even wives and children.'" But forever I ask of such, What then? The derveeshes in the deserts of Bokhara and the reformers in Marlboro' Chapel sing the same song. "There's a good time coming, boys," but, asked one of the audience in good faith, "Can you fix the date?" Said I, "Will you help it along?"

The nonchalance and *dolce-far-niente* air of nature and society hint at infinite periods in the progress of mankind. The States have leisure to laugh from Maine to Texas at some newspaper joke, and New England shakes at the double-entendres of Australian circles, while the poor reformer cannot get a hearing.

Men do not fail commonly for want of knowledge, but for want of prudence to give wisdom the preference. What we need to know in any case is very simple. It is but too easy to establish another durable and harmonious routine. Immediately all parts of nature consent

to it. Only make something to take the place
of something, and men will behave as if it were
the very thing they wanted. They *must* behave, at any rate, and will work up any material.
There is always a present and extant life, be it
better or worse, which all combine to uphold.
We should be slow to mend, my friends, as slow
to require mending, "Not hurling, according
to the oracle, a transcendent foot towards piety."
The language of excitement is at best picturesque merely. You must be calm before you
can utter oracles. What was the excitement of
the Delphic priestess compared with the calm wisdom of Socrates? — or whoever it was that was
wise. — Enthusiasm is a supernatural serenity.

> "Men find that action is another thing
>   Than what they in discoursing papers read;
> The world's affairs require in managing
>   More arts than those wherein you clerks proceed."

As in geology, so in social institutions, we may
discover the causes of all past change in the
present invariable order of society. The greatest appreciable physical revolutions arc the work
of the light-footed air, the stealthy-paced water,
and the subterranean fire. Aristotle said, "As
time never fails, and the universe is eternal,
neither the Tanais nor the Nile, can have flowed
forever." We are independent of the change
we detect. The longer the lever the less perceptible its motion. It is the slowest pulsation

which is the most vital. The hero then will
know how to wait, as well as to make haste. All
good abides with him who waiteth *wisely;* we
shall sooner overtake the dawn by remaining
here than by hurrying over the hills of the west.
Be assured that every man's success is in proportion to his *average* ability. The meadow
flowers spring and bloom where the waters
annually deposit their slime, not where they
reach in some freshet only. A man is not his
hope, nor his despair, nor yet his past deed. We
know not yet what we have done, still less what
we are doing. Wait till evening, and other parts
of our day's work will shine than we had thought
at noon, and we shall discover the real purport
of our toil. As when the farmer has reached
the end of the furrow and looks back, he can
best tell where the pressed earth shines most.

To one who habitually endeavors to contemplate the true state of things, the political state
can hardly be said to have any existence whatever.
It is unreal, incredible and insignificant to him,
and for him to endeavor to extract the truth
from such lean material is like making sugar
from linen rags, when sugar cane may be had.
Generally speaking, the political news, whether
domestic or foreign, might be written to-day for
the next ten years, with sufficient accuracy.
Most revolutions in society have not power to
interest, still less alarm us; but tell me that our

rivers are drying up, or the genus pine dying out in the country, and I might attend. Most events recorded in history are more remarkable than important, like eclipses of the sun and moon, by which all are attracted, but whose effects no one takes the trouble to calculate. But will the government never be so well administered, inquired one, that we private men shall hear nothing about it? "The king answered: At all events, I require a prudent and able man, who is capable of managing the state affairs of my kingdom. The ex-minister said, The criterion, O Sire! of a wise and competent man, is, that he will not meddle with such like matters." Alas, that the ex-minister should have been so nearly right.

In my short experience of human life, the *outward* obstacles, if there were any such, have not been living men, but the institutions of the dead. It is grateful to make one's way through this latest generation as through dewy grass. Men are as innocent as the morning to the unsuspicious. —

> "And round about good-morrows fly,
> As if day taught humanity."

Not being Reve of this Shire,

> "The early pilgrim blithe he hailed,
> That o'er the hills did stray,
> And many an early husbandman,
> That he met on his way;" —

thieves and robbers all nevertheless. I have not
so surely foreseen that any Cossack or Chippeway
would come to disturb the honest and simple
commonwealth, as that some monster institution
would at length embrace and crush its free members in its scaly folds; for it is not to be forgotten,
that while the law holds fast the thief and mur-
derer, it lets itself go loose. When I have not
paid the tax which the State d manded for that
protection which I did not want, itself has robbed
me; when I have asserted the liberty it presumed
to declare, itself has imprisoned me. Poor
creature! if it knows no better I will not blame
it. If it cannot live but by these means, I can.
I do not wish, it happens, to be associated with
Massachusetts, either in holding slaves or in
conquering Mexico. I am a little better than
herself in these respects. — As for Massachusetts,
that huge she Briareus, Argus, and Colchian
Dragon conjoined, set to watch the Heifer of
the Constitution and the Golden Fleece, we
would not warrant our respect for her, like some
compositions, to preserve its qualities through
all weathers. — Thus it has happened, that not
the Arch Fiend himself has been in my way, but
these toils which tradition says were originally
spun to obstruct him. They are cobwebs and
trifling obstacles in an earnest man's path, it is
true, and at length one even becomes attached
to his unswept and undusted garret. I love man

— kind, but I hate the institutions of the dead unkind. Men execute nothing so faithfully as the wills of the dead, to the last codicil and letter. *They* rule this world, and the living are but their executors. Such foundations too have our lectures and our sermons commonly. They are all *Dudleian;* and piety derives its origin still from that exploit of *pius Æneas,* who bore his father, Anchises, on his shoulders from the ruins of Troy. Or rather, like some Indian tribes, we bear about with us the mouldering relics of our ancestors on our shoulders. If, for instance, a man asserts the value of individual liberty over the merely political commonweal, his neighbor still tolerates him, that is he who is *living near* him, sometimes even sustains him, but never the State. Its officer, as a living man, may have human virtues and a thought in his brain, but as the tool of an institution, a jailor or constable it may be, he is not a whit superior to his prison key or his staff. Herein is the tragedy; that men doing outrage to their proper natures, even those called wise and good, lend themselves to perform the office of inferior and brutal ones. Hence come war and slavery in; and what else may not come in by this opening? But certainly there are modes by which a man may put bread into his mouth which will not prejudice him as a companion and neighbor.

"Now turn again, turn again, said the pindèr,
For a wrong way you have gone,
For you have forsaken the king's highway,
And made a path over the corn."

Undoubtedly, countless reforms are called for, because society is not animated, or instinct enough with life, but in the condition of some snakes which I have seen in early spring, with alternate portions of their bodies torpid and flexible, so that they could wriggle neither way. All men are partially buried in the grave of custom, and of some we see only the crown of the head above ground. Better are the physically dead, for they more lively rot. Even virtue is no longer such if it be stagnant. A man's life should be constantly as fresh as this river. It should be the same channel, but a new water every instant. —

—— "Virtues as rivers pass,
But still remains that virtuous man there was."

Most men have no inclination, no rapids, no cascades, but marshes, and alligators, and miasma instead. We read that when in the expedition of Alexander, Onesicritus was sent forward to meet certain of the Indian sect of Gymnosophists, and he had told them of those new philosophers of the west, Pythagoras, Socrates, and Diogenes, and their doctrines, one of them named Dandamis answered, that "They appeared to him to have been men of genius, but to have lived with too passive a regard for the laws." The philosophers of the west are liable to this rebuke still. "They say that Lieou-hia-hoei, and Chao-lien did not sustain to the end their resolutions, and that they dishonored their character. Their language was in harmony with reason and justice; while their acts were in harmony with the sentiments of men."

Chateaubriand said, "There are two things which grow stronger in the breast of man, in proportion as he advances in years; the love of country and religion. Let them be never so much forgotten in youth, they sooner or later present themselves to us arrayed in all their charms, and excite in the recesses of our hearts, an attachment justly due to their beauty." It may be so. But even this infirmity of noble minds marks the gradual decay of youthful hope and faith. It is the allowed infidelity of age. There is a saying of the Yoloffs, "He who was born first has the greatest number of old clothes," consequently M. Chateaubriand has more old clothes than I have. It is comparatively a faint and reflected beauty that is admired, not an essential and intrinsic one. It is because the old are weak, feel their mortality, and think that they have measured the strength of man. They will not boast; they will be frank and humble. Well, let them have the few poor comforts they can keep.   Humility is still a very human virtue.   They look back on life, and so see not into the future.   The prospect of the young is forward and unbounded, mingling the future with the present.   In the declining day the thoughts make haste to rest in darkness, and hardly look forward to the ensuing morning. The thoughts of the old prepare for night and slumber.   The same hopes and prospects are not for him who stands upon the rosy mountain-tops of life, and him who expects the setting of his earthly day.

I must conclude that Conscience, if that be the name of it, was not given us for no purpose, or for a hindrance.   However flattering order and experience may look, it is but the repose of a lethargy, and we will choose rather to be awake, though it be stormy, and maintain ourselves on this earth and in this life, as we may, without signing our death-warrant.   Let us see if we cannot stay here where He has put us, on his own conditions.   Does not his law reach as far as his light?   The expedients of the nations clash with one another, only the absolutely right is expedient for all.

There are some passages in the Antigone of Sophocles, well known to scholars, of which I am reminded in this connection.   Antigone has resolved to sprinkle sand on the dead body of her brother, Polynices, notwithstanding the

edict of King Creon condemning to death that
one who should perform this service, which the
Greeks deemed so important, for the enemy of
his country; but Ismene, who is of a less resolute
and noble spirit, declines taking part with her
sister in this work, and says, —

" I, therefore, asking those under the earth to
consider me, that I am compelled to do thus, will
obey those who are placed in office; for to do extreme things is not wise."

ANTIGONE.

" I would not ask you, nor would you, if you
still wished, do it joyfully with me. Be such as
seems good to you. But I will bury him. It
is glorious for me doing this to die. I beloved
will lie with him beloved, having, like a criminal,
done what is holy; since the time is longer which
it is necessary for me to please those below, than
those here, for there I shall always lie. But if
it seems good to you, hold in dishonor things
which are honored by the gods."

ISMENE.

" I indeed do not hold them in dishonor; but
to act in opposition to the citizens I am by
nature unable."

Antigone being at length brought before King Creon, he asks,

"Did you then dare to transgress these laws?"

ANTIGONE.

"For it was not Zeus who proclaimed these to me, nor Justice who dwells with the gods below; it was not they who established these laws among men.   Nor did I think that your proclamations were so strong, as, being a mortal, to be able to transcend the unwritten and immovable, to be able to transcend the unwritten and immovable laws of the gods.   For not something now and yesterday, but forever these live, and no one knows from what time they appeared.   I was not about to pay the penalty of violating these to the gods, fearing the presumption of any man. For I well know that I should die, and why not? even if you had not proclaimed it."

This was concerning the burial of a dead body.

The wisest conservatism is that of the Hindoos. "Immemorial custom is transcendent law," says Menu.   That is, it was the custom of the gods before men used it.   The fault of our New England custom is that it is memorial.   What is morality but immemorial custom?   Conscience is the chief of conservatives.   "Perform the settled functions," says Kreeshna in the

Bhagvat-Geeta, "action is preferable to inaction. The journey of thy mortal frame may not succeed from inaction." — "A man's own calling, with all its faults, ought not to be forsaken. Every undertaking is involved in its faults as the fire in its smoke." — "The man who is acquainted with the whole, should not drive those from their works who are slow of comprehension, and less experienced than himself." — "Wherefore, O Arjoon, resolve to fight," — is the advice of the God to the irresolute soldier who fears to slay his best friends. It is a sublime conservatism; as wide as the world, and as unwearied as time; preserving the universe with Asiatic anxiety, in that state in which it appeared to their minds. These philosophers dwell on the inevitability and unchangeableness of laws, on the power of temperament and constitution, the three *goon* or qualities, and the circumstances of birth and affinity. The end is an immense consolation; eternal absorption in Brahma. Their speculations never venture beyond their own table lands, though they are high and vast as they. Buoyancy, freedom, flexibility, variety, possibility, which also are qualities of the Unnamed, they deal not with. The undeserved reward is to be earned by an everlasting moral drudgery; the incalculable promise of the morrow is, as it were, weighed. And who will say that their conservatism has not been effectual. "Assuredly," says a French translator, speaking of the antiquity and durability of the Chinese and Indian nations, and of the wisdom of their legislators, "there are there some vestiges of the eternal laws which govern the world."

Christianity, on the other hand, is humane, practical, and, in a large sense, radical. So many years and ages of the gods those eastern sages sat contemplating Brahm, uttering in silence the mystic "Om," being absorbed into the essence of the Supreme Being, never going out of themselves, but subsiding further and deeper within; so infinitely wise, yet infinitely stagnant; until, at last, in that same Asia, but in the western part of it, appeared a youth, wholly unforetold by them,— not being absorbed into Brahm, but bringing Brahm down to earth and to mankind; in whom Brahm had awaked from his long sleep, and exerted himself, and the day began, — a new avatar. The Brahman had never thought to be a brother of mankind as well as a child of God. Christ is the prince of Reformers and Radicals. Many expressions in the New Testament come naturally to the lips of all protestants, and it furnishes the most pregnant and practical text. There is no harmless dreaming, no wise speculation in it, but everywhere a substratum of good sense. It never *reflects*, but it *repents*. There is no poetry in it, we may say, nothing regarded in the light of pure beauty, but moral truth is its object. All mortals are convicted by its conscience.

The New Testament is remarkable for its pure morality; the best of the Hindoo Scripture, for its pure intellectuality. The reader is nowhere raised into and sustained in a higher, purer, or *rarer* region of thought than in the Bhagvat-Geeta. Warren Hastings, in his sensible letter recommending the translation of this book to the Chairman of the East India Company, declares the original to be "of a sublimity of conception, reasoning, and diction, almost unequalled," and that the writings of the Indian philosophers "will survive when the British dominion in India shall have long ceased to exist, and when the sources which it once yielded to wealth and power are lost to remembrance." It is unquestionably one of the noblest and most sacred scriptures that have come down to us. Books are to be distinguished by the grandeur of their topics, even more than by the manner in which they are treated. The oriental philosophy approaches, easily, loftier themes than the modern aspires to; and no wonder if it sometimes prattle about them. *It* only assigns their due rank respectively to Action and Contemplation, or rather does full justice to the latter. Western philosophers have not conceived of the significance of Contemplation in their sense.

Speaking of the spiritual discipline to which the Brahmans subjected themselves, and the wonderful power of abstraction to which they attained, instances of which had come under his notice, Hastings says: —

"To those who have never been accustomed to the separation of the mind from the notices of the senses, it may not be easy to conceive by what means such a power is to be attained; since even the most studious men of our hemisphere will find it difficult so to restrain their attention, but that it will wander to some object of present sense or recollection; and even the buzzing of a fly will sometimes have the power to disturb it.   But if we are told that there have been men who were successively, for ages past, in the daily habit of abstracted contemplation, begun in the earliest period of youth, and continued in many to the maturity of age, each adding some portion of knowledge to the store accumulated by his predecessors; it is not assuming too much to conclude, that as the mind ever gathers strength, like the body, by exercise, so in such an exercise it may in each have acquired the faculty to which they aspired, and that their collective studies may have led them to the discovery of new tracks and combinations of sentiment, totally different from the doctrines with which the learned of other nations are acquainted; doctrines which, however speculative and subtle, still, as they possess the advantage of being derived from a source so free from every adventitious mixture, may be equally founded in truth with the most simple of our own."

"The forsaking of works" was taught by Kreeshna to the most ancient of men, and handed down from one to another, "until at length, in the course of time the mighty art was lost.

"In wisdom is to be found every work without exception," says Kreeshna.

"Although thou wert the greatest of all offenders, thou shalt be able to cross the gulf of sin with the bark of wisdom."

"There is not anything in this world to be compared with wisdom for purity."

"The action stands at a distance inferior to the application of wisdom."

The wisdom of a Moonee "is confirmed, when, like the tortoise, he can draw in all his members, and restrain them from their wonted purposes."

"Children only, and not the learned, speak of the speculative and the practical doctrines as two. They are but one. For both obtain the self-same end, and the place which is gained by the followers of the one, is gained by the followers of the other."

"The man enjoyeth not freedom from action, from the non-commencement of that which he hath to do; nor doth he obtain happiness from a total inactivity. No one ever resteth a moment inactive. Every man is involuntarily urged to act by those principles which are inherent in his nature. The man who restraineth his active faculties, and sitteth down with his mind attentive to the objects of his senses, is called one of an astrayed soul, and the practiser of deceit. So the man is praised, who, having subdued all his passions, performeth with his active faculties all the functions of life, unconcerned about the event."

"Let the motive be in the deed and not in the event. Be not one whose motive for action is the hope of regard. Let not thy life be spent in inaction."

"For the man who doeth that which he hath to do, without affection, obtaineth the Supreme."

"He who may behold, as it were inaction in action, and action in inaction, is wise amongst mankind. He is a perfect performer of all duty."

"Wise men call him a *Pandeet*, whose every undertaking is free from the idea of desire, and whose actions are consumed by the fire of wisdom. He abandoneth the desire of a reward of his actions; he is always contented and independent; and although he may be engaged in a work, he, as it were, doeth nothing."

"He is both a Yogee and a Sannyasee who performeth that which he hath to do independent of the fruit thereof; not he who liveth without the sacrificial fire and without action."

"He who enjoyeth but the Amreeta which is left of his offerings, obtaineth the eternal spirit of Brahm, the Supreme."

What after all does the practicalness of life amount to? The things immediate to be done are very trivial. I could postpone them all to hear this locust sing. The most glorious fact in our experience is not anything that we have done or may hope to do, but a transient thought, or vision, or dream, which we have had. I would give all the wealth of the world, and all the deeds of all the heroes, for one true vision. But how can I communicate with the gods who am a pencil-maker on the earth, and not be insane?

"I am the same to all mankind," says Kreeshna; "there is not one who is worthy of my love or hatred."

This teaching is not practical in the sense in which the New Testament is. It is not always sound sense in practice. The Brahman never proposes courageously to assault evil, but patiently to starve it out. His active faculties are paralyzed by the idea of caste, of impassable limits, of destiny, and the tyranny of time.

Kreeshna's argument, it must be allowed, is defective. No sufficient reason is given why Arjoon should fight. Arjoon may be convinced, but the reader is not, for his judgment is *not* "formed upon speculative doctrines of the *Sankhya Sastra.*" "Seek an asylum in wisdom alone," — but what is wisdom to a western mind? He speaks of duty, but the duty of which he speaks, is it not an arbitrary one? When was it established? The Brahman's virtue consists not in doing right, but arbitrary things. What is that which a man "hath to do"? What is "action"? What are the "settled functions"? What is "a man's own religion," which is so much better than another's? What is "a man's own particular calling"? What are the duties which are appointed by one's birth? It is in fact a defence of the institution of caste, of what is called the "natural duty" of the Kshetree, or soldier, "to attach himself to the discipline," "not to flee from the field," and the like. But they who are unconcerned about the consequences of their actions, are not therefore unconcerned about their actions. — Yet we know not where we should look for a loftier speculative faith.

Behold the difference between the oriental and the occidental. The former has nothing to do in this world; the latter is full of activity. The one look in the sun till his eyes are put out; the other follows him prone in his westward course. There is such a thing as caste, even in the West; but it is comparatively faint. It is conservatism here. It says forsake not your calling, outrage no institution, use no violence, rend no bonds. The State is thy parent. Its virtue or manhood is wholly filial. There is a struggle between the oriental and occidental in every nation; some who would be forever contemplating the sun, and some who are hastening toward the sunset. The former class says to the latter, When you have reached the sunset, you will be no nearer to the sun. To which the latter replies, But we so prolong the day. The former "walketh but in that night, when all things go to rest, the night of *time*. The contemplative Moonee sleepeth but in the day of *time* when all things wake."

To conclude these extracts, I can say, in the words of Sanjay, "As, O mighty Prince! I recollect again and again this holy and wonderful dialogue of Kreeshna and Arjoon, I continue more and more to rejoice; and as I recall to my memory the more than miraculous form of Haree, my astonishment is great, and I marvel and rejoice again and again! Wherever Kreeshna the God of devotion may be, wherever Arjoon the mighty bowman may be, there too, without doubt, are fortune, riches, victory, and good conduct. This is my firm belief.''

I would say to the readers of Scriptures, if they wish for a good book to read, read the Bhagvat-Geeta, an episode to the Mahabharat, said to have been written by Kreeshna Dwy-payen Veias, — known to have been written by ——, more than four thousand years ago, — it matters not whether three or four, or when, — translated by Charles Wilkins. It deserves to be read with reverence even by Yankees, as a part of the sacred writings of a devout people; and the intelligent Hebrew will rejoice to find in it a moral grandeur and sublimity akin to those of his own Scriptures.

To an American reader, who, by the advantage of his position, can see over that strip of Atlantic coast to Asia and the Pacific, who, as it were, sees the shore slope upward over the Alps to the Himmaleh mountains, the comparatively recent literature of Europe often appears partial and clannish, and, notwithstanding the limited range of his own sympathies and studies, the European writer who presumes that he is speaking for the world, is perceived by him to speak only for that corner of it which he inhabits. One of the rarest of England's scholars and critics, in his classification of the worthies of the world, be-trays the narrowness of his European culture and the exclusiveness of his reading. None

of her children has done justice to the poets
and philosophers of Persia or of India. They
have been better known to her merchant scholars than to her poets and thinkers by profession.
You may look in vain through English poetry
for a single memorable verse inspired by these
themes. Nor is Germany to be excepted, though
her philological industry is indirectly serving the
cause of philosophy and poetry. Even Goethe,
one would say, wanted that universality of genius which could have appreciated the philosophy of India, if he had more nearly approached
it. His genius was more practical, dwelling
much more in the regions of the understanding,
and less native to contemplation, than the genius
of those sages. It is remarkable that Homer
and a few Hebrews are the most oriental names
which modern Europe, whose literature has
taken its rise since the decline of the Persian, has
admitted into her list of Worthies, and perhaps
the *worthiest* of mankind, and the fathers of
modern thinking, — for the contemplations of
those Indian sages have influenced the intellec-
tual development of mankind, — whose works
even yet survive in wonderful completeness, are,
for the most part, not recognized as ever having
existed. If the lions had been the painters it
would have been otherwise. In every one's
youthful dreams philosophy is still vaguely but
inseparably, and with singular truth, associated

Mt. Uncannunuc

with the East, nor do after years discover its local habitation in the Western world. In comparison with the philosophers of the East we may say that modern Europe has yet given birth to none. Beside the vast and cosmogonal philosophy of the Bhagvat-Geeta, even our Shakespeare seems sometimes youthfully green and practical merely. Some of these sublime sentences, as the Chaldæan oracles of Zoroaster, for instance, still surviving after a thousand revolutions and translations, make us doubt if the poetic form and dress are not transitory, and not essential to the most effective and enduring expression of thought. *Ex oriente lux* may still be the motto of scholars, for the Western world has not yet derived from the East all the light which it is destined to receive thence.

It would be worthy of the age to print together the collected Scriptures or Sacred Writings of the several nations, the Chinese, the Hindoos, the Persians, the Hebrews, and others, as the Scripture of mankind. The New Testament is still, perhaps, too much on the lips and in the hearts of men to be called a Scripture in this sense. Such a juxtaposition and comparison might help to liberalize the faith of men. This is a work which Time will surely edit, reserved to crown the labors of the printing press. This would be the Bible, or Book of Books, which

let the missionaries carry to the uttermost parts
of the earth.

While engaged in these reflections, thinking
ourselves the only navigators of these waters,
suddenly a canal boat, with its sail set, glided
round a point before us, like some huge river
beast, and changed the scene in an instant;
and then another and another glided into sight,
and we found ourselves in the current of commerce once more. So we threw our rinds into
the water for the fishes to nibble, and added our
breath to the life of living men. Little did we
think in the distant garden in which we had
planted the seed and reared this fruit, where it
would be eaten. Our melons lay at home on
the sandy bottom of the Merrimack, and our
potatoes in the sun and water at the bottom of
the boat looked like a fruit of the country.
Soon, however, we were delivered from this
fleet of junks, and possessed the river in solitude, rowing steadily upward through the noon,
between the territories of Nashua on the one
hand, and Hudson, once Nottingham, on the
other; from time to time scaring up a king-fisher
or a summer duck, the former flying rather by
vigorous impulses, than by steady and patient
steering with that short rudder of his, sounding
his rattle along the fluvial street.
Ere long another scow hove in sight, creeping

down the river, and hailing it, we attached ourselves to its side, and floated back in company,
chatting with the boatmen, and obtaining a
draught of cooler water from their jug. They
appeared to be green hands from far among the
hills, who had taken this means to get to the
seaboard, and see the world; and would possibly
visit the Falkland Isles, and the China seas,
before they again saw the waters of the Merrimack, or perchance, not return this way forever.
They had already embarked the private interests of the landsman in the larger venture of
the race, and were ready to mess with mankind,
reserving only the till of a chest to themselves.
But they too were soon lost behind a point, and
we went croaking on our way alone. What
grievances has its root among the New Hampshire hills? we asked; what is wanting to human
life here, that these men should make such haste
to the antipodes? We prayed that their bright
anticipations might not be rudely disappointed.

> Though all the fates should prove unkind,
> Leave not your native land behind.
> The ship, becalmed, at length stands still;
> The steed must rest beneath the hill;
> But swiftly still our fortunes pace,
> To find us out in every place.
>
> The vessel, though her masts be firm,
> Beneath her copper bears a worm;
> Around the cape, across the line,
> Till fields of ice her course confine;

> It matters not how smooth the breeze,
> How shallow or how deep the seas,
> Whether she bears Manilla twine,
> Or in her hold Madeira wine,
> Or China teas, or Spanish hides,
> In port or quarantine she rides;
> Far from New England's blustering shore,
> New England's worm her hulk shall bore,
> And sink her in the Indian seas,
> Twine, wine, and hides, and China teas.

We passed a small desert here on the east bank, between Tyngsboro' and Hudson, which was interesting and even refreshing to our eyes in the midst of the almost universal greenness. This sand was indeed somewhat impressive and beautiful to us. A very old inhabitant, who was at work in a field on the Nashua side, told us that he remembered when corn and grain grew there, and it was a cultivated field. But at length the fishermen, for this was a fishing place, pulled up the bushes on the shore, for greater convenience in hauling their seines, and when the bank was thus broken, the wind began to blow up the sand from the shore, until at length it had covered about fifteen acres several feet deep. We saw near the river, where the sand was blown off down to some ancient surface, the foundation of an Indian wigwam exposed, a perfect circle of burnt stones four or five feet in diameter, mingled with fine charcoal and the bones of small animals, which had been preserved in the sand. The surrounding sand was sprinkled with other burnt stones on which their fires had been built, as well as with flakes of arrow-head stone, and we found one perfect arrow-head. In one place we noticed where an Indian had sat to manufacture arrow-heads out of quartz, and the sand was sprinkled with a quart of small glass-like ships about as big as a fourpence, which he had broken off in his work. Here, then, the Indians must have fished before the whites arrived. There was another similar sandy tract about half a mile above this.

Still the noon prevailed, and we turned the prow aside to bathe, and recline ourselves under some buttonwoods by a ledge of rocks, in a retired pasture, sloping to the water's edge, and skirted with pines and hazels, in the town of Hudson. Still had India, and that old noontide philosophy, the better part of our thoughts.

It is always singular, but encouraging, to meet with common sense in very old books, as the Heetopades of Veeshnoo Sarma; a playful wisdom which has eyes behind as well as before, and oversees itself. It asserts their health and independence of the experience of later times. This pledge of sanity cannot be spared in a book, that it sometimes pleasantly reflect upon itself. The story and fabulous portion of this book winds loosely from sentence to sentence as so

many oases in a desert, and is as indistinct as a
camel's track between Mourzouk and Darfour.
It is a comment on the flow and freshet of modern books. The reader leaps from sentence
to sentence, as from one stepping-stone to another,
while the stream of the story rushes past un-
regarded. The Bhagvat-Geeta is less senten-
tious and poetic, perhaps, but still more wonderfully sustained and developed. Its sanity and
sublimity have impressed the minds even of
soldiers and merchants. It is the characteristic
of great poems that they will yield of their
sense in due proportion to the hasty and the
deliberate reader. To the practical they will
be common sense, and to the wise wisdom; as
either the traveller may wet his lips, or an army
may fill its water casks at a full stream.

One of the most attractive of those ancient
books that I have met with is the Laws of Menu.
According to Sir William Jones, "Vyasa, the son
of Parasara, has decided that the Veda, with its
Angas, or the six compositions deduced from it,
the revealed system of medicine, the Puranas,
or sacred histories, and the code of Menu, were
four works of supreme authority, which ought
never to be shaken by arguments merely human."
The last is believed by the Hindoos "to have
been promulgated in the beginning of time, by
Menu, son or grandson of Brahma," and "first
of created beings"; and Brahma is said to have

"taught his laws to Menu in a hundred thousand verses, which Menu explained to the primitive world in the very words of the book now translated." Others affirm that they have undergone successive abridgments for the convenience of mortals, "while the gods of the lower haven, and the band of celestial musicians, are engaged in studying the primary code." — "A number of glosses or comments on Menu were composed by the Munis, or old philosophers, whose treatises, together with that before us, constitute the Dherma Sastra, in a collective sense, or Body of Law." Culluca Bhatta was one of the more modern of these.

Every sacred book, successively, seems to have been accepted in the faith that it was to be the final resting-place of the sojourning soul; but after all, it is but a caravansary which supplies refreshment to the traveller, and directs him farther on his way to Isphahan or Bagdat. Thank God, no Hindoo tyranny prevailed at the framing of the world, but we are freemen of the universe, and not sentenced to any caste.

I know of no book which has come down to us with grander pretensions than this, and it is so impersonal and sincere that it is never offensive nor ridiculous. Compare the modes in which modern literature is advertised with the prospectus of this book, and think what a reading public it addresses, what criticism it expects.

It seems to have been uttered from some eastern summit, with a sober morning prescience in the dawn of time, and you cannot read a sentence without being elevated as upon the table-land of the Ghauts. It has such a rhythm as the winds of the desert, such a tide as the Ganges, and is as superior to criticism as the Himmaleh mountains. Its tone is of such unrelaxed fibre, that even at this late day, unworn by time, it wears the English and the Sanscrit dress indifferently, and its fixed sentences keep up their distant fires still like the stars, by whose dissipated rays this lower world is illumined. The whole book by noble gestures and inclinations seems to render many words unnecessary. English sense has toiled, but Hindoo wisdom never perspired. The sentences open, as we read them, unexpensively, and, at first, almost unmeaningly, as the petals of a flower, yet they sometimes startle us with that rare kind of wisdom which could only have been learned from the most trivial experience; but it comes to us as refined as the porcelain earth which subsides to the bottom of the ocean. They are clean and dry as fossil truths, which have been exposed to the elements for thousands of years, so impersonally and scientifically true that they are the ornament of the parlor and the cabinet. Any *moral* philosophy is exceedingly rare. This of Menu addresses our privacy more than most. It is a

more private and familiar, and, at the same
time, a more public and universal word than is
spoken in parlor or pulpit now-a-days. As
our domestic fowls are said to have their original
in the wild pheasant of India, so our domestic
thoughts have their prototypes in the thoughts
of her philosophers. We seem to be dabbling
in the very elements of our present conventional
and actual life; as if it were the primeval con-
venticle where how to eat and to drink and to
sleep, and maintain life with adequate dignity
and sincerity, were the questions to be decided.
It is later and more intimate even than the
advice of our nearest friends. And yet it is
true for the widest horizon, and read out of
doors has relation to the dim mountain line, and
is native and aboriginal there. Most books
belong to the house and street only, and in the
fields their leaves feel very thin. They are bare
and obvious, and have no halo nor haze about
them. Nature lies far and fair behind them all.
But this, as it proceeds from, so does it address
what is deepest and most abiding in man. It
belongs to the noontide of the day, the mid-
summer of the year, and after the snows have
melted, and the waters evaporated in the spring,
still its truth speaks freshly to our experience.
It helps the sun to shine, and his rays fall on
its page to illustrate it. It spends the mornings
and the evenings, and makes such an impres-

sion on us over night as to awaken us before
dawn, and its influence lingers around us like
a fragrance late into the day. It conveys a
new gloss to the meadows and the depths of the
wood. Its spirit, like a more subtile ether,
sweeps along with the prevailing winds of a
country, and the very locusts and crickets of a
summer day are but later or earlier glosses on
the Dherma Sastra of the Hindoos, a continua-
tion of the sacred code. As we have said, there
is an orientalism in the most restless pioneer,
and the farthest west is but the farthest east.
This fair modern world is only a reprint of the
Laws of Menu with the gloss of Culluca. Tried
by a New England eye, or the mere practical
wisdom of modern times, they are the oracles
of a race already in its dotage, but held up to
the sky, which is the only impartial and incor-
ruptible ordeal, they are of a piece with its
depth and serenity, and I am assured that they
will have a place and significance as long as
there is a sky to test them by.

Give me a sentence which no intelligence can
understand. There must be a kind of life and
palpitation to it, and under its words a kind
of blood must circulate forever. It is wonderful that this sound should have come down to
us from so far, when the voice of man can be
heard so little way, and we are not now within
ear-shot of any contemporary. The wood-

cutters have here felled an ancient pine forest, and brought to light to these distant hills a fair lake in the south-west; and now in an instant it is distinctly shown to these woods as if its image had travelled hither from eternity. Perhaps these old stumps upon the knoll remember when anciently this lake gleamed in the horizon. One wonders if the bare earth itself did not experience emotion at beholding again so fair a prospect. That fair water lies there in the sun thus revealed, so much the prouder and fairer because its beauty needed not to be seen. It seems yet lonely, sufficient to itself, and superior to observation. — So are these old sentences like serene lakes in the south-west, at length revealed to us, which have so long been reflecting our own sky in their bosom.

The great plain of India lies as in a cup between the Himmaleh and the ocean on the north and south, and the Brahmapootra and Indus, on the east and west, wherein the primeval race was received. We will not dispute the story. We are pleased to read in the natural history of the country, of the "pine, larch, spruce, and silver fir," which cover the southern face of the Himmaleh range; of the "gooseberry, raspberry, strawberry," which from an imminent temperate zone overlook the torrid plains. So did this active modern life have even then a foothold and lurking place in the midst of the stateliness and contemplativeness of those eastern plains. In another era the "lily-of-the-valley, cowslip, dandelion," were to work their way down into the plain, and bloom in a level zone of their own reaching round the earth. Already has the era of the temperate zone arrived, the era of the pine and the oak, for the palm and the banian do not supply the wants of this age. The lichens on the summits of the rocks will perchance find their level ere long.

As for the tenets of the Brahmans, we are not so much concerned to know what doctrines they held, as that they were held by any. We can tolerate all philosophies, Atomists, Pneumatologists, Atheists, Theists, — Plato, Aristotle, Leucippus, Democritus, Pythagorus, Zoroaster, and Confucius. It is the attitude of these men, more than any communication which they make, that attracts us. Between these and their commentators, it is true, there is an endless dispute. But if it comes to this that you compare notes, then you are all wrong. As it is, each takes us up into the serene heavens, whither the smallest bubble rises as surely as the largest, and paints earth and sky for us. Any sincere thought is irresistible. The very austerity of the Brahmans is tempting to the devotional soul, as a more refined and nobler luxury. Wants so easily and gracefully satisfied seem like a more refined pleasure. Their conception of creation is peaceful as a dream. "When that power awakes, then has this world its full expansion; but when he slumbers with a tranquil spirit, then the whole system fades away." In the very indistinctness of their theogony a sublime truth is implied. It hardly allows the reader to rest in any supreme first cause, but directly it hints at a supremer still which created the last, and the Creator is still behind increate.

Nor will we disturb the antiquity of this Scripture; "From fire, from air, and from the sun," it was "milked out." One might as well investigate the chronology of light and heat. Let the sun shine. Menu understood this matter best, when he said, "Those best know the divisions of days and nights who understand that the day of Brahma, which endures to the end of a thousand such ages, [infinite ages, nevertheless, according to mortal reckoning,] gives rise to virtuous exertions; and that his night endures as long as his day." Indeed, the Mussulman and Tartar dynasties are beyond all dating. Methinks I have lived under them myself. In every man's brain is the Sanscrit. The Vedas and their Angas are not so ancient as serene contemplation. Why will we be imposed on by antiquity? Is the babe young? When I behold it, it seems more venerable than the oldest man; it is more ancient than Nestor or the Sibyls, and bears the wrinkles of father

Saturn himself. And do we live but in the present? How broad a line is that? I sit now on a stump whose rings number centuries of growth. If I look around I see that the soil is composed of the remains of just such stumps, ancestors to this. The earth is covered with mould. I thrust this stick many æons deep into its surface, and with my heel make a deeper furrow than the elements have plowed here for a thousand years. If I listen, I hear the peep of frogs which is older than the slime of Egypt, and the distant drumming of a partridge on a log, as if it were the pulse beat of the summer air. I raise my fairest and freshest flowers in the old mould. Why, what we would fain call new is not skin deep; the earth is not yet stained by it. It is not the fertile ground which we walk on, but the leaves that flutter over our heads. The newest is but the oldest made visible to our senses. When we dig up the soil from a thousand feet below the surface, we call it new, and the plants which spring from it; and when our vision pierces deeper into space, and detects a remoter star, we call that new also. The place where we sit is called Hudson, — once it was Nottingham, — once —

We should read history as little critically as we consider the landscape, and be more interested by the atmospheric tints and various lights

and shades which the intervening spaces create,
than by its groundwork and composition. It
is the morning now turned evening and seen in
the west, — the same sun, but a new light and
atmosphere. Its beauty is like the sunset; not
a fresco painting on a wall, flat and bounded, but
atmospheric and roving or free. In reality,
history fluctuates as the face of the landscape
from morning to evening. What is of moment
is its hue and color. Time hides no treasures;
we want not its *then*, but its *now*. We do not complain that the mountains in the horizon are blue
and indistinct; they are the more like the heavens.

Of what moment are facts that can be lost, —
which need to be commemorated? The monument of death will outlast the memory of the
dead. The pyramids do not tell us the tale
that was confided to them; the living fact com-
memorates itself. Why look in the dark for
light? Strictly speaking, the historical societies
have not recovered one fact from oblivion, but
are themselves, instead of the fact, that is lost.
The researcher is more memorable than the
researched. The crowd stood admiring the
mist and the dim outlines of the trees seen
through it, when one of their number advanced
to explore the phenomenon, and with fresh
admiration all eyes were turned on his dimly
retreating figure. It is astonishing with how
little coöperation of the societies the past is

remembered. Its story has indeed had another
muse than has been assigned it. There is a
good instance of the manner in which all history
began, in Alwákidis' Arabian Chronicle, "I was
informed by *Ahmed Almatin Aljorhami*, who
had it from *Rephâa Ebn Kais Alámiri*, who had
it from *Saiph Ebn Fabalah Alchâtquarmi*, who
had it from *Thabet Ebn Alkamah*, who said he
was present at the action." These fathers of
history were not anxious to preserve, but to
learn the fact; and hence it was not forgotten.
Critical acumen is exerted in vain to uncover
the past; the *past* cannot be *presented;* we cannot
know what we are not. But one veil hangs over
past, present, and future, and it is the province
of the historian to find out, not what was, but
what is. Where a battle has been fought, you
will find nothing but the bones of men and beasts;
where a battle is being fought, there are hearts
beating. We will sit on a mound and muse, and
not try to make these skeletons stand on their legs
again. Does Nature remember, think you, that
they *were* men, or not rather that they *are* bones?

Ancient history has an air of antiquity. It
should be more modern. It is written as if
the spectator should be thinking of the back-
side of the picture on the wall, or as if the author
expected that the dead would be his readers,
and wished to detail to them their own experience.
Men seem anxious to accomplish an orderly

retreat through the centuries, earnestly rebuilding the works behind, as they are battered down by the encroachments of time; but while they loiter, they and their works both fall a prey to the arch enemy. History has neither the venerableness of antiquity, nor the freshness of the modern. It does as if it would go to the beginning of things, which natural history might with reason assume to do; but consider the Universal History, and then tell us — when did burdock and plantain sprout first? It has been so written for the most part, that the times it describes are with remarkable propriety called *dark ages*. They are dark, as one has observed, because we are so in the dark about them. The sun rarely shines in history, what with the dust and confusion; and when we meet with any cheering fact which implies the presence of this luminary, we excerpt and modernize it. As when we read in the history of the Saxons that Edwin of Northumbria "caused stakes to be fixed in the highways where he had seen a clear spring," and "brazen dishes were chained to them, to refresh the weary sojourner, whose fatigues Edwin had himself experienced." This is worth all Arthur's twelve battles.

"Through the shadow of the world we sweep into the younger
        day:
    Better fifty years of Europe than a cycle of Cathay.
    Than fifty years of Europe better one New England ray!"

Biography, too, is liable to the same objection; it should be autobiography. Let us not, as the Germans advise, endeavor to go abroad and vex our bowels that we may be somebody else to explain him. If I am not I, who will be?

But it is fit that the Past should be dark; though the darkness is not so much a quality of the past as of tradition. It is not a distance of time, but a distance of relation, which makes thus dusky its memorials. What is near to the heart of this generation is fair and bright still. Greece lies outspread fair and sunshiny in floods of light, for there is the sun and daylight in her literature and art. Homer does not allow us to forget that the sun shone, — nor Phidias, nor the Parthenon. Yet no era has been wholly dark, nor will we too hastily submit to the historian, and congratulate ourselves on a blaze of light. If we could pierce the obscurity of those remote years, we should find it light enough; only *there* is not our day. Some creatures are made to see in the dark. There has always been the same amount of light in the world. The new and missing stars, the comets and eclipses, do not affect the general illumination, for only our glasses appreciate them. The eyes of the oldest fossil remains, they tell us, indicate that the same laws of light prevailed then as now. Always the laws of light are the same, but the modes and degrees of seeing vary. The gods

are partial to no era, but steadily shines their
light in the heavens, while the eye of the beholder is turned to stone.   There was but
the sun and the eye from the first.   The ages
have not added a new ray to the one, nor altered
a fibre of the other.

If we will admit time into our thoughts at all,
the mythologies, those vestiges of ancient poems,
wrecks of poems, so to speak, the world's in-
heritance, still reflecting some of their original
splendor, like the fragments of clouds tinted by
the rays of the departed sun; reaching into the
latest summer day, and allying this hour to the
morning of creation; as the poet sings: —

> "Fragments of the lofty strain
> Float down the tide of years,
> As buoyant on the stormy main
> A parted wreck appears; " —

these are the materials and hints for a history of
the rise and progress of the race; how, from the
condition of ants, it arrived at the condition of
men, and arts were gradually invented.   Let
a thousand surmises shed some light on this
story.   We will not be confined by historical,
even geological periods, which would allow us
to doubt of a progress in human affairs.   If we
rise above this wisdom for the day, we shall
expect that this morning of the race, in which
it has been supplied with the simplest necessaries,

with corn, and wine, and honey, and oil, and fire, and articulate speech, and agricultural and other arts, reared up, by degrees, from the condition of ants, to men, will be succeeded by a day of equally progressive splendor; that, in the lapse of the divine periods, other divine agents and godlike men will assist to elevate the race as much above its present condition. But we do not know much about it.

Thus did one voyageur waking dream, while his companion slumbered on the bank. Suddenly, a boatman's horn was heard, echoing from shore to shore, to give notice of his approach to the farmer's wife, with whom he was to take his dinner, though in that place only muskrats and king-fishers seemed to hear. The current of our reflections and our slumbers being thus disturbed, we weighed anchor once more.

As we proceeded on our way in the afternoon, the western bank became lower, or receded further from the channel in some places, leaving a few trees only to fringe the water's edge; while the eastern rose abruptly here and there into wooded hills fifty or sixty feet high. The bass, *tilia Americana*, also called the lime or linden, which was a new tree to us, overhung the water with its broad and rounded leaf, interspersed with clusters of small hard berries, now nearly ripe, and made an agreeable shade for us sailors.

The inner bark of this genus is the bast, the material of the fisherman's matting, and the ropes, and peasant's shoes, of which the Russians make so much use, and also of nets and a coarse cloth in some places. According to poets, this was once Philyra, one of the Oceanides. The ancients are said to have used its bark for the roofs of cottages, for baskets, and for a kind of paper called Philyra. They also made bucklers of its wood, "on account of its flexibility, lightness, and resiliency." It was once much used for carving, and is still in demand for panels of carriages, and for various uses for which toughness and flexibility are required. Its sap affords sugar, and the honey made from its flowers is said to be preferred to any other. Its leaves are in some countries given to cattle, a kind of chocolate has been made of its fruit, a medicine has been prepared from an infusion of its flowers, and finally, the charcoal made of its wood is greatly valued for gunpowder.

The sight of this tree reminded us that we had reached a strange land to us. As we sailed under this canopy of leaves we saw the sky through its chinks, and, as it were, the meaning and idea of the tree stamped in a thousand hieroglyphics on the heavens. The universe is so aptly fitted to our organization, that the eye wanders and reposes at the same time. On every side there is something to soothe and refresh this sense.

Look up at the tree-tops and see how finely Nature finishes off her work there. See how the pines spire without end higher and higher, and make a graceful fringe to the earth. And who shall count the finer cobwebs that soar and float away from their utmost tops, and the myriad insects that dodge between them. Leaves are of more various forms than the alphabets of all languages put together; of the oaks alone there are hardly two alike, and each expresses its own character.

In all her products Nature only develops her simplest germs. One would say that it was no great stretch of invention to create birds. The hawk, which now takes his flight over the top of the wood, was at first perchance only a leaf which fluttered in its aisles. From rustling leaves she came in the course of ages to the loftier flight and clear carol of the bird.

Salmon Brook comes in from the west under the railroad, a mile and a half below the village of Nashua. We rode up far enough into the meadows which border it, to learn its piscatorial history from a hay-maker on its banks. He told us that the silver eel was formerly abundant here, and pointed to some sunken creels at its mouth. This man's memory and imagination were fertile in fishermen's tales of floating isles in bottomless ponds, and of lakes mysteriously stocked with fishes, and would have kept us till night-fall to listen, but we could not afford to loiter in this roadstead, and so stood out to our sea again. Though we never trod in these meadows, but only touched their margin with our hands, we still retain a pleasant memory of them.

Salmon Brook, whose name is said to be a translation from the Indian, was a favorite haunt of the aborigines. Here too the first white settlers of Nashua planted, and some dents in the earth, where their houses stood, and the wrecks of ancient apple trees, are still visible. About one mile up this stream stood the house of old John Lovewell, who was an ensign in the army of Oliver Cromwell, and the father of "famous Captain Lovewell." He settled here before 1690, and died about 1754, at the age of one hundred and twenty years. He is thought to have been engaged in the famous Narragansett swamp fight, which took place in 1675, before he came here. The Indians are said to have spared him in succeeding wars on account of his kindness to them. Even in 1700 he was so old and gray-headed that his scalp was worth nothing, since the French Governor offered no bounty for such. I have stood in the dent of his cellar on the bank of the brook, and talked there with one whose grandfather had, whose father might have, talked with Lovewell. Here also he had a mill in his old age, and kept a small store. He was remembered by some who

were recently living, as a hale old man who drove
the boys out of his orchard with his cane. —
Consider the triumphs of the mortal man, and
what poor trophies it would have to show, to
wit: He cobbled shoes without glasses at a
hundred, and cut a handsome swathe at a hundred and five! — Lovewell's house is said to
have been the first which Mrs. Dustin reached
on her escape from the Indians. Here probably
the hero of Pequawket was born and bred.
Close by may be seen the cellar and the grave-
stone of Joseph Hassell, who, as was elsewhere
recorded, with his wife Anna and son Benjamin,
and Mary Marks, "were slain by our Indian
enemies on Sept. 2d [1691] in the evening."
As Gookin observed on a previous occasion,
"The Indian rod upon the English backs had
not yet done God's errand."   Salmon Brook
near its mouth is still a solitary stream, meandering through woods and meadows, while the then
uninhabited mouth of the Nashua now resounds
with the din of a manufacturing town.

A stream from Otternic pond in Hudson comes
in just above Salmon Brook, on the opposite
side.   There was a good view of Uncannunuc,
the most conspicuous mountain in these parts,
from the bank here, seen rising over the west end
of the bridge above.   We soon after passed the
village of Nashua, on the river of the same name,
where there is a covered bridge over the Merri-

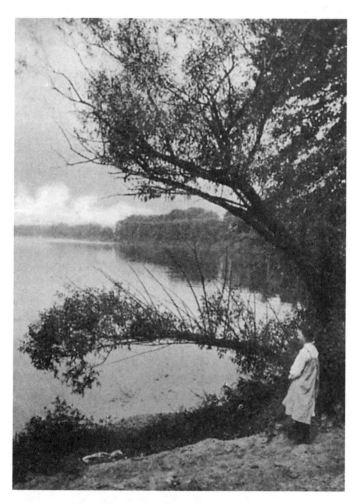

On the Hudson shore opposite Nashua

mack. The Nashua, which is one of the largest
tributaries, flows from Wachusett mountain,
through Lancaster, Groton, and other towns,
where it has formed well-known elm-shaded
meadows, but near its mouth it is obstructed
by falls and factories, and did not tempt us to
explore it.

Far away from here, in Lancaster, with another
companion, I have crossed the broad valley of
the Nashua, over which we had so long looked
westward from the Concord hills without seeing it
to the blue mountains in the horizon. So many
streams, so many meadows and woods and
quiet dwellings of men had lain concealed between
us and those Delectable Mountains; — from yonder hill on the road to Tyngsboro' you may get
a good view of them. — There where it seemed
uninterrupted forest to our youthful eyes, between two neighboring pines in the horizon, lay
the valley of the Nashua, and this very stream
was even then winding at its bottom, and then,
as now, it was here silently mingling its waters
with the Merrimack. The clouds which floated
over its meadows and were born there, seen far
in the west, gilded by the rays of the setting sun,
had adorned a thousand evening skies for us.
But as it were by a turf wall this valley was concealed, and in our journey to those hills it was
first gradually revealed to us. Summer and
winter our eyes had rested on the dim outline

of the mountains, to which distance and indistinctness lent a grandeur not their own, so that they served to interpret all the allusions of poets and travellers. Standing on the Concord Cliffs we thus spoke our mind to them:—

> With frontier strength ye stand your ground,
> With grand content ye circle round,
> Tumultuous silence for all sound,
> Ye distant nursery of rills,
> Monadnock and the Peterboro' hills;—
> Firm argument that never stirs,
> Outcircling the philosophers,—
> Like some vast fleet,
> Sailing through rain and sleet,
> Through winter's cold and summer's heat;
> Still holding on upon your high emprise,
> Until ye find a shore amid the skies;
> Not skulking close to land,
> With cargo contraband,
> For they who sent a venture out by ye
> Have set the Sun to see
> Their honesty.
>
> Ships of the line, each one,
> Ye westward run,
> Convoying clouds,
> Which cluster in your shrouds,
> Always before the gale,
> Under a press of sail,
> With weight of metal all untold,—
> I seem to feel ye in my firm seat here,
> Immeasurable depth of hold,
> And breadth of beam, and length of running gear.
>
> Methinks ye take luxurious pleasure
> In your novel western leisure;

So cool your brows and freshly blue,
As Time had naught for ye to do;
For ye lie at your length,
An unappropriated strength,
Unhewn primeval timber,
For knees so stiff, for masts so limber;
The stock of which new earths are made,
One day to be our *western* trade,
Fit for the stanchions of a world
Which through the seas of space is hurled.

While we enjoy a lingering ray,
Ye still o'ertop the western day,
Reposing yonder on God's croft
Like solid stacks of hay;
So bold a line as ne'er was writ
On any page by human wit;
The forest glows as if
An enemy's camp-fires shone
Along the horizon,
Or the day's funeral pyre
Were lighted there;
Edged with silver and with gold,
The clouds hang o'er in damask fold,
And with such depth of amber light
The west is dight,
Where still a few rays slant,

That even Heaven seems extravagant.
Watatic Hill
Lies on the horizon's sill
Like a child's toy left over night,
And other duds to left and right,
On the earth's edge, mountains and trees,
Stand as they were on air graven,
Or as the vessels in a haven
Await the morning breeze.

I fancy even
Through your defiles windeth the way to Heaven;
And yonder still, in spite of history's page,
Linger the golden and the silver age;
Upon the laboring gale
The news of future centuries is brought,
And of new dynasties of thought,
From your remotest vale.

But special I remember thee,
Wachusett, who like me
Standest alone without society.
Thy far blue eye,
A remnant of the sky,
Seen through the clearing or the gorge,
Or from the windows of the forge,
Doth leaven all it passes by.
Nothing is true
But stands 'tween me and you,
Thou western pioneer.
Who know'st not shame nor fear,
By venturous spirit driven
Under the eaves of Heaven;
And can'st expand thee there,
And breathe enough of air ?
Even beyond the West
Thou migratest,
Into unclouded tracts,
Without a pilgrim's axe,
Cleaving thy road on high
With thy well-tempered brow,
And mak'st thyself a clearing in the sky.
Upholding Heaven, holding down earth,
Thy pastime from thy birth;
Not steadied by the one, nor leaning on the other,
May I approve myself thy worthy brother!

At length, like Rasselas and other inhabitants
of happy valleys, we had resolved to scale the

blue wall which bounded the western horizon,
though not without misgivings that thereafter
no visible fairy land would exist for us. But
it would be long to tell of our adventures, and
we have no time this afternoon, transporting
ourselves in imagination up this hazy Nashua
valley, to go over again that pilgrimage. We
have since made many similar excursions to the
principal mountains of New England and New
York, and even far in the wilderness, and have
passed a night on the summit of many of them.
And now when we look again westward from
our native hills, Wachusett and Monadnock
have retreated once more among the blue and
fabulous mountains in the horizon, though our
eyes rest on the very rocks on both of them,
where we have pitched our tent for a night, and
boiled our hasty-pudding amid the clouds.

As late as 1724 there was no house on the
north side of the Nashua, but only scattered
wigwams and gristly forests between this frontier and Canada. In September of that year,
two men who were engaged in making turpentine on that side, for such were the first enterprises in the wilderness, were taken captive
and carried to Canada by a party of thirty
Indians. Ten of the inhabitants of Dunstable
going to look for them, found the hoops of their
barrel cut, and the turpentine spread on the

ground. I have been told by an inhabitant of Tyngsboro', who had the story from his ancestors, that one of these captives, when the Indians were about to upset his barrel of turpentine, seized a pine knot and, flourishing it, swore so resolutely that he would kill the first who touched it, that they refrained, and when at length he returned from Canada he found it still standing. Perhaps there was more than one barrel. — However this may have been, the scouts knew by marks on the trees, made with coal mixed with grease, that the men were not killed, but taken prisoners. One of the company, named Farwell, perceiving that the turpentine had not done spreading, concluded that the Indians had been gone but a short time, and they accordingly went in instant pursuit. Contrary to the advice of Farwell, following directly on their trail up the Merrimack, they fell into an ambuscade near Thornton's Ferry, in the present town of Merrimack, and nine were killed, only one, Farwell, escaping after a vigorous pursuit. The men of Dunstable went out and picked up their bodies, and carried them all down to Dunstable and buried them. It is almost word for word as in the Robin Hood ballad: —

"They carried these foresters into fair Nottingham,
  As many there did know,
They digg'd them graves in their churchyard,
  And they buried them all a-row."

Nottingham is only the other side of the river, and they were not exactly all a-row. You may read in the churchyard at Dunstable, under the "Memento Mori," and the name of one of them, how they "departed this life," and

> "This man with seven more that lies in
> this grave was slew all in a day by
> the Indians."

The stones of some others of the company stand around the common grave with their separate inscriptions. Eight were buried here, but nine were killed, according to the best authorities.

> "Gentle river, gentle river,
>   Lo, thy streams are stained with gore,
> Many a brave and noble captain
>   Floats along thy willowed shore.
>
> All beside thy limpid waters,
>   All beside thy sands so bright,
> *Indian* Chiefs and Christian warriors
>   Joined in fierce and mortal fight."

It is related in the history of Dunstable, that on the return of Farwell the Indians were engaged by a fresh party, which they compelled to retreat, and pursued as far as the Nashua, where they fought across the stream at its mouth. After the departure of the Indians, the figure of an Indian's head was found carved by them on a large tree by the shore, which circumstance

has given its name to this part of the village of
Nashville, — the "Indian Head." "It was observed by some judicious," says Gookin, referring to Philip's war, "that at the beginning of
the war, the English soldiers made a nothing of
the Indians, and many spake words to this effect;
that one Englishman was sufficient to chase ten
Indians; many reckoned it was no other but
Veni, vidi, vici." But we may conclude that
the judicious would by this time have made a
different observation.

Farwell appears to have been the only one
who had studied his profession, and understood
the business of hunting Indians. He lived to
fight another day, for the next year he was Lovewell's Lieutenant at Pequawket, but that time,
as we have related, left his bones in the wilderness. His name still reminds us of twilight days
and forest scouts on Indian trails, with an uneasy
scalp; — an indispensable hero to New England.
As the more recent poet of Lovewell's fight has
sung, halting a little but bravely still; —

> "Then did the crimson streams that flowed,
>   Seem like the waters of the brook,
> That brightly shine, that loudly dash,
>   Far down the cliffs of Agiochook."

These battles sound incredible to us. I think
posterity will doubt if such things ever were;
if our bold ancestors who settled this land were

not struggling rather with the forest shadows,
and not with a copper-colored race of men.
They were vapors, fever and ague of the unsettled
woods.   Now, only a few arrow-heads are turned
up by the plow.   In the Pelasgic, the Etruscan,
or the British story, there is nothing so shadowy
and unreal.

It is a wild and antiquated looking grave-yard,
overgrown with bushes, on the high road, about
a quarter of a mile from and overlooking the
Merrimack, with deserted mill stream bounding
it on one side, where lie the earthly remains of
the ancient inhabitants of Dunstable.   We passed it three or four miles below here.   You may
read there the names of Lovewell, Farwell, and
many others whose families were distinguished
in Indian warfare.   We noticed there two large
masses of granite more than a foot thick and
rudely squared, lying flat on the ground over the
remains of the first pastor and his wife.

It is remarkable that the dead lie everywhere
under stones, —

"Strata jacent passim *suo* quæque sub" *lapide* —

corpora, we might say, if the measure allowed.
When the stone is a slight one, and stands upright, pointing to the skies, it does not oppress

the spirits of the traveller to meditate by it;
but these did seem a little heathenish to us; and
so are all large monuments over men's bodies,
from the pyramids down. A monument should
at least be "star-y-pointing," to indicate whither
the spirit is gone, and not prostrate, like the
body it has deserted. There have been some
nations who could do nothing but construct
tombs, and these are the only traces which they
have left. They are the heathen. But why
these stones, so upright and emphatic, like ex-
clamation points! What was there so remarkable that lived? Why should the monument be
so much more enduring than the fame which
it is designed to commemorate, — a stone to a
bone? "Here lies," — "Here lies"; — why do
they not sometimes write, There rises? Is
it a monument to the body only that is intended?
"Having reached the term of his *natural* life;"
— would it not be truer to say, Having reached
the term of his *unnatural* life? The rarest
quality in an epitaph is truth. If any character
is given it should be as severely true as the de-
cision of the three judges below, and not the
partial testimony of friends. Friends and contemporaries should supply only the name and
date, and leave it to posterity to write the
epitaph.

> Here lies an honest man,
> Rear-Admiral Van.

The old Dunstable graveyard

Faith, then ye have
Two in one grave,
For in his favor,
Here too lies the Engraver.

Fame itself is but an epitaph; as late, as false, as true.   But they only are the true epitaphs which Old Mortality retouches.

A man might well pray that he may not taboo or curse any portion of Nature by being buried in it.   For the most   part, the man's spirit makes a fearful sprite to haunt his grave, and it is therefore much to the credit of Little John, the famous follower of Robin Hood, that his grave was "long celebrous for the yielding of excellent whetstones."   I confess that I have but little love for such collections as they have at the Catacombs, Père la Chaise, Mount Auburn, and even this Dunstable grave-yard.   At any rate, nothing but great antiquity can make grave-yards interesting to me.   I have no friends there.   It may be that I am not competent to write the poetry of the grave.   The farmer who has skimmed his farm might perchance leave his body to Nature to be plowed in, and in some measure restore its fertility.   We should not retard but forward her economies.

Soon the village of Nashua was out of sight, and the woods were gained again, and we rowed slowly on before sunset, looking for a solitary

place in which to spend the night. A few evening clouds began to be reflected in the water,
and the surface was dimpled only here and there
by a muskrat crossing the stream. We camped
at length near Penichook Brook, on the confines
of Nashville, by a deep ravine, under the skirts
of a pine wood, where the dead pine leaves were
our carpet, and their tawny boughs stretched
over head. But fire and smoke soon tamed the
scene; the rocks consented to be our walls, and
the pines our roof. A woodside was already
the fittest locality for us.

The wilderness is near, as well as dear, to every
man. Even the oldest villages are indebted
to the border of wild wood which surrounds
them, more than to the gardens of men. There
is something indescribably inspiriting and beautiful in the aspect of the forest skirting and occasionally jutting into the midst of new towns,
which, like the sand-heaps of fresh fox burrows,
have sprung up in their midst. The very up-
rightness of the pines and maples asserts the
ancient rectitude and vigor of nature. Our
lives need the relief of such a background, where
the pine flourishes and the jay still screams.

We had found a safe harbor for our boat,
and as the sun was setting carried up our furniture, and soon arranged our house upon the bank,
and while the kettle steamed at the tent door,
we chatted of distant friends, and of the sights

we were to behold, and wondered which way the towns lay from us.   Our cocoa was soon boiled, and supper set upon our chest, and we lengthened out this meal, like old voyageurs, with our talk.   Meanwhile we spread the map on the ground, and read in the gazetteer when the first settlers came here and got a township granted. Then, when supper was done, and we had written the journal of our voyage, we wrapped our buffaloes about us, and lay down with our heads pillowed on our arms, listening awhile to the distant baying of a dog, or the murmurs of the river, or to the wind, which had not gone to rest,—

> The western wind came lumbering in,
> Bearing a faint Pacific din,
> Our evening mail, swift at the call
> Of its Post-Master General;
> Laden with news from Californ',
> Whate'er transpired hath since morn,
> How wags the world by brier and brake
> From hence to Athabasca lake; —

or half awake and half asleep, dreaming of a star which glimmered through our cotton roof. Perhaps at midnight one was awakened by a cricket shrilly singing on his shoulder, or by a hunting spider in his eye, and was lulled asleep again by some streamlet purling its way along at the bottom of a wooded and rocky ravine in our neighborhood.   It was pleasant to lie with our heads so low in the grass, and hear what a tinkling ever-busy laboratory it was. A thousand little artisans beat on their anvils all night long.

Far in the night, as we were falling asleep on the bank of the Merrimack, we heard some tyro beating a drum incessantly, in preparation for a country muster, as we learned, and we thought of the line,

"When the drum beat at dead of night."

We could have assured him that his beat would be answered, and the forces be mustered. Fear not, thou drummer of the night, we too will be there. And still he drummed on in the silence and the dark. This stray sound from a far-off sphere came to our ears from time to time, far, sweet, and significant, and we listened with such an unprejudiced sense as if for the first time we heard at all. No doubt he was an insignificant drummer enough, but his music afforded us a prime and leisure hour, and we felt that we were in season wholly. These simple sounds related us to the stars. Aye, there was a logic in them so convincing that the combined sense of mankind could never make me doubt their conclusions. I stop my habitual thinking, as if the plow had suddenly run deeper in its furrow through the crust of the world. How can I go on, who have just stepped over such a bottomless

skylight in the bog of my life. Suddenly old
Time winked at me, — Ah, you know me, you
rogue, — and news had come that IT was well.
That ancient universe is in such capital health,
I think undoubtedly it will never die. Heal
yourselves, doctors; by God I live. —

> Then idle Time ran gadding by
> And left me with Eternity alone;
> I hear beyond the range of sound,
> I see beyond the verge of sight, —

I see, smell, taste, hear, feel, that everlasting
Something to which we are allied, at once our
maker, our abode, our destiny, our very Selves;
the one historic truth, the most remarkable
fact which can become the distinct and unin-
vited subject of our thought, the actual glory of
the universe; the only fact which a human being
cannot avoid recognizing, or in some way forget or dispense with. —

> It doth expand my privacies
> To all, and leave me single in the crowd.

I have seen how the foundations of the world
are laid, and I have not the least doubt that it
will stand a good while.

> Now chiefly is my natal hour,
> And only now my prime of life.
> I will not doubt the love untold,
> Which not my worth nor want hath brought,
> Which wooed me young and wooes me old,
> And to this evening hath me brought.

What are ears? what is Time? that this particular series of sounds called a strain of music,
an invisible and fairy troop which never brushed
the dew from any mead, can be wafted down
through the centuries from Homer to me, and
he have been conversant with that same aerial
and mysterious charm which now so tingles my
ears? What a fine communication from age to
age, of the fairest and noblest thoughts, the aspirations of ancient men, even such as were never
communicated by speech! It is the flower of
language, thought colored and curved, fluent and
flexible, its crystal fountain tinged with the sun's
rays, and its purling ripples reflecting the grass
and the clouds. A strain of music reminds me of
a passage of the Vedas, and I associate with it
the idea of infinite remoteness, as well as beauty
and serenity, for to the senses that is furthest
from us which addresses the greatest depth
within us. It teaches us again and again to
trust the remotest and finest as the divinest
instinct, and makes a dream our only real experience. As polishing expresses the vein in
marble and grain in wood, so music brings out
what of heroic lurks anywhere. The hero is the
sole patron of music. That harmony which
exists naturally between the hero's moods and
the universe the soldier would fain imitate with
drum and trumpet. When we are in health
all sounds fife and drum for us; we hear the notes

of music in the air, or catch its echoes dying away when we awake in the dawn. Marching is when the pulse of the hero beats in unison with the pulse of Nature, and he steps to the measure of the universe; then there is true courage and invincible strength.

Plutarch says that "Plato thinks the gods never gave men music, the science of melody and harmony, for mere delectation or to tickle the ear; but that the discordant parts of the circulations and beauteous fabric of the soul, and that of it that roves about the body, and many times, for want of tune and air, breaks forth into many extravagances and excesses, might be sweetly recalled and artfully wound up to their former consent and agreement."

Music is the sound of the universal laws promulgated. It is the only assured tone. There are in it such strains as far surpass any man's faith in the loftiness of his destiny. Things are to be learned which it will be worth the while to learn. Formerly I heard these

RUMORS FROM AN ÆOLIAN HARP

There is a vale which none hath seen,
Where foot of man has never been,
Such as here lives with toil and strife,
An anxious and a sinful life.

There every virtue has its birth,
Ere it descends upon the earth,

And thither every deed returns,
Which in the generous bosom burns.

There love is warm, and youth is young,
And poetry is yet unsung,
For Virtue still adventures there,
And freely breathes her native air.

And ever, if you hearken well,
You still may hear its vesper bell,
And tread of high-souled men go by,
Their thoughts conversing with the sky.

According to Jamblichus, "Pythagoras did
not procure for himself a thing of this kind
through instruments or the voice, but employing
a certain ineffable divinity, and which it is
difficult to apprehend, he extended his ears and
fixed his intellect in the sublime symphonies of
the world, he alone hearing and understanding,
as it appears, the universal harmony and con-
sonance of the spheres, and the stars that are
moved through them, and which produce a
fuller and more intense melody than anything
effected by mortal sounds."

Travelling on foot very early one morning due
east from here about twenty miles, from Caleb
Harriman's tavern in Hampstead toward Haverhill, when I reached the railroad in Plaistow, I
heard at some distance a faint music in the air
like an Æolian harp, which I immediately suspected to proceed from the cord of the telegraph vibrating in the just awakening morning

wind, and applying my ear to one of the posts I was convinced that it was so. It was the telegraph harp singing its message through the country, its message sent not by men but by gods. Perchance, like the statue of Memnon, it resounds only in the morning when the first rays of the sun fall on it. It was like the first lyre or shell heard on the sea-shore,—that vibrating cord high in the air over the shores of earth. So have all things their higher and their lower uses. I heard a fairer news than the journals ever print. It told of things worthy to hear, and worthy of the electric fluid to carry the news of, not of the price of cotton and flour, but it hinted at the price of the world itself and of things which are priceless, of absolute truth and beauty.

Still the drum rolled on, and stirred our blood to fresh extravagance that night. The clarion sound and clang of corselet and buckler were heard from many a hamlet of the soul, and many a knight was arming for the fight behind the encamped stars. —

> " Before each van
> Prick forth the aery knights, and couch their spears
> Till thickest legions close; with feats of arms
> From either end of Heaven the welkin burns."

———

> Away! away! away! away!
>   Ye have not kept your secret well,
> I will abide that other day,
>   Those other lands ye tell.

Has time no leisure left for these,
    The acts that ye rehearse?
Is not eternity a lease
    For better deeds than verse?

'T is sweet to hear of heroes dead,
    To know them still alive,
But sweeter if we earn their bread,
    And in us they survive.

Our life should feed the springs of fame
    With a perennial wave,
As ocean feeds the babbling founts
    Which find in it their grave.

Ye skies drop gently round my breast,
    And be my corselet blue,
Ye earth receive my lance in rest,
    My faithful charger you;

Ye stars my spear-heads in the sky,
    My arrow-tips ye are, —
I see the routed foemen fly,
    My bright spears fixed are.

Give me an angel for a foe,
    Fix now the place and time,
And straight to meet him I will go
    Above the starry chime.

And with our clashing bucklers' clang
    The heavenly spheres shall ring,
While bright the northern lights shall hang
    Beside our tourneying.

And if she lose her champion true,
    Tell Heaven not despair,
For I will be her champion new,
    Her fame I will repair.

There was a high wind this night, which we afterwards learned had been still more violent elsewhere, and had done much injury to the corn-fields far and near; but we only heard it sigh from time to time, as if it had no license to shake the foundations of our tent; the pines murmured, the water rippled, and the tent rocked a little, but we only laid our ears closer to the ground while the blast swept on to alarm other men, and long before sunrise we were ready to pursue our voyage as usual.

TUESDAY

"On either side the river lie
Long fields of barley and of rye,
That clothe the wold and meet the sky;
And thro' the fields the road runs by
To many-towered Camelot."
— TENNYSON.

LONG before daylight we ranged abroad with hatchet in hand, in search of fuel, and made the yet slumbering and dreaming wood resound with our blows. Then with our fire we burned up a portion of the loitering night, while the kettle sang its homely strain to the morning star. We tramped about the shore, waked all the muskrats, and scared up the bittern and birds that were asleep upon their roosts; we hauled up and upset our boat, and washed it and rinsed out the clay, talking aloud as if it were broad day, until at length, by three o'clock, we had completed our preparations and were ready to pursue our voyage as usual; so, shaking the clay from our feet, we pushed into the fog.

Though we were enveloped in mist as usual, we trusted that there was a bright day behind it.

Ply the oars! away! away!
In each dew-drop of the morning
Lies the promise of a day.
Rivers from the sunrise flow,
Springing with the dewy morn;
Voyageurs 'gainst time do row,
Idle noon nor sunset know,
Ever even with the dawn,

Belknap, the historian of this State, says that "In the neighborhood of fresh rivers and ponds, a whitish fog in the morning, lying over the water, is a sure indication of fair weather for that day; and when no fog is seen, rain is expected before night." That which seemed to us to invest the world, was only a narrow and shallow wreath of vapor stretched over the channel of the Merrimack from the sea-board to the mountains. More extensive fogs, however, have their own limits. I once saw the day break from the top of Saddle-back Mountain in Massachusetts, above the clouds. As we cannot distinguish objects through this dense fog, let me tell this story more at length.

I had come over the hills on foot and alone in serene summer days, plucking the raspberries by the wayside, and occasionally buying a loaf of bread at a farmer's house, with a knapsack on my back, which held a few traveller's books and a change of clothing, and a staff in my hand. I had that morning looked down from the Hoosack Mountain, where the road crosses it, on the village of North Adams in the valley, three miles away under my feet, showing how uneven the earth may sometimes be, and making it seem an accident that it should ever be level and convenient for the feet of man. Putting a little rice and sugar and a tin cup into my knapsack at this village, I began in the afternoon to ascend the mountain, whose summit is three thousand six hundred feet above the level of the sea, and was seven or eight miles distant by the path. My route lay up a long and spacious valley called the Bellows, because the winds rush up or down it with violence in storms, sloping up to the very clouds between the principal range and a lower mountain. There were a few farms scattered along at different elevations, each commanding a fine prospect of the mountains to the north, and a stream ran down the middle of the valley, on which near the head there was a mill. It seemed a road for the pilgrim to enter upon who would climb to the gates of heaven. Now I crossed a hay-field, and now over the brook on a slight bridge, still gradually ascending all the while, with a sort of awe, and filled with indefinite expectations as to what kind of inhabitants and what kind of nature I should come to at last. It now seemed some advantage that the earth was uneven, for one could not imagine a more noble position for a

farm-house than this vale afforded, further from
or nearer to its head, from a glen-like seclusion
overlooking the country at a great elevation
between these two mountain walls.

It reminded me of the homesteads of the
Huguenots on Staten Island, off the coast of
New Jersey. The hills in the interior of this
island, though comparatively low, are penetrated
in various directions by similar sloping valleys
on a humble scale, gradually narrowing and rising to the centre, and at the head of these
the Huguenots, who were the first settlers,
placed their houses, quite within the land, in
rural and sheltered places, in leafy recesses where
the breeze played with the poplar and the gum
tree, from which, with equal security in calm
and storm, they looked out through a widening
vista, over miles of forest and stretching salt
marsh, to the Huguenots' Tree, an old elm on
the shore at whose root they had landed, and
across the spacious outer bay of New York to
Sandy Hook and the Highlands of Neversink,
and thence over leagues of the Atlantic, perchance
to some faint vessel in the horizon, almost a
day's sail on her voyage to that Europe whence
they had come. When walking in the interior
there, in the midst of rural scenery, where there
was as little to remind me of the ocean as amid
the New Hampshire hills, I have suddenly,
through a gap, a cleft or "clove road," as the

Dutch settlers called it, caught sight of a ship under full sail, over a field of corn, twenty or thirty miles at sea. The effect was similar, since I had no means of measuring distances, to seeing a painted ship passed backwards and forwards through a magic lantern.

But to return to the mountain. It seemed as if he must be the most singular and heavenly-minded man whose dwelling stood highest up the valley. The thunder had rumbled at my heels all the way, but the shower passed off in another direction, though if it had not, I half believed that I should get above it. I at length reached the last house but one, where the path to the summit diverged to the right, while the summit itself rose directly in front. But I determined to follow up the valley to its head, and then find my own route up the steep, as the shorter and more adventurous way. I had thoughts of returning to this house, which was well kept and so nobly placed, the next day, and perhaps remaining a week there, if I could have entertainment. Its mistress was a frank and hospitable young woman, who stood before me in a dishabille, busily and unconcernedly combing her long black hair while she talked, giving her head the necessary toss with each sweep of the comb, with lively, sparkling eyes, and full of interest in that lower world from which I had come, talking all the while as familiarly as if she had known me for years, and reminding me of a cousin of mine. She at first had taken me for a student from Williamstown, for they went by in parties, she said, either riding or walking, almost every pleasant day, and were a pretty wild set of fellows; but they never went by the way I was going. As I passed the last house, a man called out to know what I had to sell, for seeing my knapsack, he thought that I might be a pedler, who was taking this unusual route over the ridge of the valley into South Adams. He told me that it was still four or five miles to the summit by the path which I had left, though not more than two in a straight line from where I was, but nobody ever went this way; there was no path, and I should find it as steep as the roof of a house. But I knew that I was more used to woods and mountains than he, and went along through his cow-yard, while he, looking at the sun, shouted after me that I should not get to the top that night. I soon reached the head of the valley, but as I could not see the summit from this point, I ascended a low mountain on the opposite side, and took its bearing with my compass. I at once entered the woods, and began to climb the steep side of the mountain in a diagonal direction, taking the bearing of a tree every dozen rods. The ascent was by no means difficult or unpleasant, and occupied much less time than it would have taken to follow the path.   Even country people, I have observed, magnify the difficulty of travelling in the forest, and especially among mountains. They seem to lack their usual common sense in this.   I have climbed several higher mountains without guide or path, and have found, as might be expected, that it takes only more time and patience commonly than to travel the smoothest highway.   It is very rare that you meet with obstacles in this world, which the humblest man has not faculties to surmount. It is true, we may come to a perpendicular precipice, but we need not jump off, nor run our heads against it.   A man may jump down his own cellar stairs, or dash his brains out against his chimney, if he is mad.   So far as my experience goes, travellers generally exaggerate the difficulties of the way.   Like most evil, the difficulty is imaginary; for what's the hurry? If a person lost would conclude that after all he is not lost, he is not beside himself, but standing in his own old shoes on the very spot where he is, and that for the time being he will live there; but the places that have known him, *they* are lost, — how much anxiety and danger would vanish.   I am not alone if I stand by myself. Who knows where in space this globe is rolling? Yet we will not give ourselves up for lost, let it go where it will.

I made my way steadily upward in a straight

line through a dense undergrowth of mountain laurel, until the trees began to have a scraggy and infernal look, as if contending with frost goblins, and at length I reached the summit, just as the sun was setting. Several acres here had been cleared, and were covered with rocks and stumps, and there was a rude observatory in the middle which overlooked the woods. I had one fair view of the country before the sun went down, but I was too thirsty to waste any light in viewing the prospect, and set out directly to find water. First, going down a well-beaten path for half a mile through the low scrubby wood, till I came to where the water stood in the tracks of the horses which had carried travellers up, I lay down flat, and drank these dry one after another, a pure, cold, spring-like water, but yet I could not fill my dipper, though I contrived little syphons of grass stems and ingenious aqueducts on a small scale; it was too slow a process. Then remembering that I had passed a moist place near the top on my way up, I returned to find it again, and here with sharp stones and my hands, in the twilight, I made a well about two feet deep, which was soon filled with pure cold water, and the birds too came and drank at it. So I filled my dipper, and making my way back to the observatory, collected some dry sticks and made a fire on some flat stones, which had been placed on the floor for that purpose, and so I soon cooked my supper of rice, having already whittled a wooden spoon to eat it with.

I sat up during the evening, reading by the light of the fire the scraps of newspapers in which some party had wrapped their luncheon; the prices current in New York and Boston, the advertisements, and the singular editorials which some had seen fit to publish, not foreseeing under what critical circumstances they would be read. I read these things at a vast advantage there, and it seemed to me that the advertisements, or what is called the business part of a paper, were greatly the best, the most useful, natural, and respectable. Almost all the opinions and sentiments expressed were so little considered, so shallow and flimsy, that I thought the very texture of the paper must be weaker in that part and tear the more easily. The advertisements and the prices current were more closely allied to nature, and were respectable in some measure as tide and meteorological tables are; but the reading matter, which I remembered was most prized down below, unless it was some humble record of science, or an extract from some old classic, struck me as strangely whimsical and crude, and one-idea'd, like a school-boy's theme, such as youths write and after burn. The opinions were of that kind that are doomed to wear a different aspect to-morrow, like last year's fashions; as if mankind were very green indeed, and would be ashamed of themselves in a few years, when they had outgrown this verdant period. There was, moreover, a singular disposition to wit and humor, but rarely the slightest real success; and the apparent success was a terrible satire on the attempt; as if the Evil Genius of man laughed the loudest at his best jokes. The advertisements, as I have said, such as were serious, and not of the modern quack kind, suggested pleasing and poetic thoughts; for commerce is really as interesting as nature. The very names of the commodities were poetic, and as suggestive as if they had been inserted in a pleasing poem. — Lumber, Cotton, Sugar, Hides, Guano, and Logwood. Some sober, private, and original thought would have been grateful to read here, and as much in harmony with the circumstances as if it had been written on a mountain top; for it is of a fashion which never changes, and as respectable as hides and log-wood, or any natural product. What an inestimable companion such a scrap of paper would have been, containing some fruit of a mature life. What a relic! What a recipe! It seemed a divine invention, by which not mere shining coin, but shining and current thoughts, could be brought up and left there.

As it was cold, I collected quite a pile of wood and lay down on a board against the side of the building, not having any blanket to cover me, with my head to the fire, that I might look after it, which is not the Indian rule. But as it grew colder towards midnight, I at length encased myself completely in boards, managing even to put a board on top of me, with a large stone on it, to keep it down, and so slept comfortably. I was reminded, it is true, of the Irish children, who inquired what their neighbors did who had no door to put over them in winter nights as they had; but I am convinced that there was nothing very strange in the inquiry. Those who have never tried it can have no idea how far a door, which keeps the single blanket down, may go toward making one comfortable. We are constituted a good deal like chickens, which taken from the hen, and put in a basket of cotton in the chimney corner, will often peep till they die nevertheless, but if you put in a book, or anything heavy, which will press down the cotton, and feel like the hen, they go to sleep directly. My only companions were the mice, which came to pick up the crumbs that had been left in those scraps of paper; still, as everywhere, pensioners on man, and not unwisely improving this elevated track for their habitation. They nibbled what was for them; I nibbled what was for me. Once or twice in the night, when I looked up, I saw a white cloud drifting through the windows, and filling the whole upper story.

This observatory was a building of considerable size, erected by the students of Williamstown College, whose buildings might be seen by
daylight gleaming far down in the valley.   It
would really be no small advantage if every
college were thus located at the base of a mountain, as good at least as one well-endowed pro-
fessorship.   It were as well to be educated in
the shadow of a mountain as in more classical
shades.   Some will remember, no doubt, not
only that they went to the college, but that
they went to the mountain.   Every visit to its
summit would, as it were, generalize the particular information gained below, and subject it
to more catholic tests.

I was up early and perched upon the top of
this tower to see the daybreak, for some time
reading the names that had been engraved there
before I could distinguish more distant objects.
An " untamable fly " buzzed at my elbow with
the same nonchalance as on a molasses hogs-
head at the end of Long Wharf.   Even there I
must attend to his stale humdrum.   But now
I come to the pith of this long digression. —
As the light increased I discovered around me
an ocean of mist, which reached up by chance
exactly to the base of the tower, and shut out
every vestige of the earth, while I was left
floating on this fragment of the wreck of a world,
on my carved plank in cloudland; a situation

which required no aid from the imagination
to render it impressive. As the light in the east
steadily increased, it revealed to me more clearly
the new world into which I had risen in the
night, the new terra-firma perchance of my
future life. There was not a crevice left through
which the trivial places we name Massachusetts,
or Vermont, or New York, could be seen, while
I still inhaled the clear atmosphere of a July
morning, — if it were July there. All around
beneath me was spread for a hundred miles
on every side, as far as the eye could reach, an
undulating country of clouds, answering in the
varied swell of its surface to the terrestrial world
it veiled. It was such a country as we might
see in dreams, with all the delights of paradise.
There were immense snowy pastures apparently
smooth-shaven and firm, and shady vales between the vaporous mountains, and far in the
horizon I could see where some luxurious misty
timber jutted into the prairie, and trace the
windings of a water course, some unimagined
Amazon or Orinoko, by the misty trees on its
brink. As there was wanting the symbol, so
there was not the substance of impurity, no spot
nor stain. It was a favor for which to be forever silent to be shown this vision. The earth
beneath had become such a flitting thing of
lights and shadows as the clouds had been before.
It was not merely veiled to me, but it had

passed away like the phantom of a shadow,
σκιᾶς ὄναρ, and this new platform was gained.
As I had climbed above storm and cloud, so by
successive days' journeys I might reach the
region of eternal day beyond the tapering shadow
of the earth; aye,

> "Heaven itself shall slide
> And roll away, like melting stars that glide
> Along their oily threads."

But when its own sun began to rise on this pure
world, I found myself a dweller in the dazzling
halls of Aurora, into which poets have had but
a partial glance over the eastern hills, — drifting
amid the saffron-colored clouds, and playing
with the rosy fingers of the Dawn, in the very
path of the Sun's chariot, and sprinkled with
its dewy dust, enjoying the benignant smile,
and near at hand the far-darting glances of the
god. The inhabitants of earth behold commonly
but the dark and shadowy under-side of heaven's
pavement; it is only when seen at a favorable
angle in the horizon, morning or evening, that
some faint streaks of the rich lining of the clouds
are revealed. But my muse would fail to convey
an impression of the gorgeous tapestry by which
I was surrounded, such as men see faintly reflected afar off in the chambers of the east.
Here, as on earth, I saw the gracious god.

"Flatter the mountain tops with sovereign eye, . . .
Gilding pale streams with heavenly alchemy."

But never here did "Heaven's sun" stain himself. But alas, owing as I think to some unworthiness in myself, my private sun did stain himself, and

" Anon permit the basest clouds to ride
With ugly wrack on his celestial face," —

for before the god had reached the zenith the heavenly pavement rose and embraced my wavering virtue, or rather I sank down again into that "forlorn world," from which the celestial Sun had hid his visage. —

" How may a worm, that crawls along the dust,
Clamber the azure mountains, thrown so high,
And fetch from thence thy fair idea just,
That in those sunny courts doth hidden lie,
Cloth'd with such light, as blinds the angel's eye?
How may weak mortal ever hope to file
His unsmooth tongue, and his deprostrate style?
O, raise thou from his corse thy now entombed exile ! "

In the preceding evening I had seen the summits of new and yet higher mountains, the Catskills, by which I might hope to climb to heaven again, and had set my compass for a fair lake in the south-west, which lay in my way, for which I now steered, descending the mountain by my own route, on the side opposite to that by which I had ascended, and soon found myself in the region of cloud and drizzling rain, and the inhabitants affirmed that it had been a cloudy and drizzling day wholly.

But now we must make haste back before the fog disperses to the blithe Merrimack water. —

> Since that first "away! away!"
> Many a lengthy reach we've rowed,
> Still the sparrow on the spray
> Hastes to usher in the day
> With her simple stanza'd ode.

We passed a canal boat before sunrise, groping its way to the seaboard, and though we could not see it on account of the fog, the few dull, thumping, stertorous sounds which we heard, impressed us with a sense of weight and irresistible motion.   One little rill of commerce already awake on this distant New Hampshire river. The fog, as it required more skill in the steering, enhanced the interest of our early voyage, and made the river seem indefinitely broad. A slight mist, through which objects are faintly visible, has the effect of expanding even ordinary streams, by a singular mirage, into arms of the sea or inland lakes. In the present instance it was even fragrant and invigorating, and we enjoyed it as a sort of earlier sunshine, or dewy and embryo light.

> Low-anchored cloud,
> Newfoundland air,

Fountain-head and source of rivers,
Dew cloth, dream drapery,
And napkin spread by fays;
Drifting meadow of the air,
Where bloom the daisied banks and violets,
And in whose fenny labyrinth
The bittern booms and heron wades;
Spirit of lakes and seas and rivers,
Bear only perfumes and the scent
Of healing herbs to just men's fields.

The same pleasant and observant historian whom we quoted above says, that " In the mountainous parts of the country, the ascent of vapors, and their formation into clouds, is a curious and entertaining object.   The vapors are seen rising in small columns like smoke from many chimneys. When risen to a certain height, they spread, meet, condense, and are attracted to the mountains, where they either distil in gentle dews, and replenish the springs, or descend in showers, accompanied with thunder.   After short intermissions, the process is repeated many times in the course of a summer day, affording to travellers a lively illustration of what is observed in the book of Job, 'They are wet with the showers of the mountains.' "

Fogs and clouds which conceal the overshadowing mountains lend the breath of the plains to mountain vales.   Even a small featured country acquires some grandeur in stormy weather, when clouds are seen drifting between the beholder and the neighboring hills. When in travelling toward Haverhill through Hampstead in this State, on the height of land between the Merrimack and the Piscataqua or the sea, you commence the descent eastward, the view toward the coast is so distant and unexpected, though the sea is invisible, that you at first suppose the unobstructed atmosphere to be a fog in the lowlands concealing hills of corresponding elevation to that you are upon; but it is the mist of prejudice alone, which the winds will not disperse. The most stupendous scenery ceases to be sublime when it becomes distinct, or in other words limited, and the imagination is no longer encouraged to exaggerate it. The actual height and breadth of a mountain or a water-fall are always ridiculously small; they are the imagined only that content us. Nature is not made after such a fashion as we would have her. We piously exaggerate her wonders as the scenery around our home.

Such was the heaviness of the dews along this river, that we were generally obliged to leave our tent spread over the bows of the boat till the sun had dried it, to avoid mildew. We passed the mouth of Penichook Brook, a wild salmon stream, in the fog without seeing it. At length the sun's rays struggled through the mist and showed us the pines on shore dripping with dew, and springs trickling from the moist banks, —

"And now the taller sons, whom Titan warms,
    Of unshorn mountains blown with easy winds,
    Dandle the morning's childhood in their arms,
    And if they chanced to slip the prouder pines
    The under corylets did catch their shines,
    To gild their leaves."

We rowed for some hours between glistening banks before the sun had dried the grass and leaves, or the day had established its character. Its serenity at last seemed the more profound and secure for the denseness of the morning's fog. The river became swifter, and the scenery more pleasing than before. The banks were steep and clayey for the most part, and trickling with water, and where a spring oozed out a few feet above the river, the boatmen had cut a trough out of a slab with their axes, and placed it so as to receive the water and fill their jugs conveniently. Sometimes this purer and cooler water, bursting out from under a pine or a rock, was collected into a basin close to the edge of, and level with the river, a fountain-head of the Merrimack. So near along life's stream are the fountains of innocence and youth making fertile its sandy margin; and the voyageur will do well to replenish his vessels often at these uncontaminated sources. Some youthful spring, perchance, still empties with tinkling music into the oldest river, even when it is falling into the sea, and we imagine that its music is distinguished by the river gods from the general lapse of the stream, and falls sweeter on their ears in proportion as it is nearer to the ocean. As the evaporations of the river feed thus these unsuspected springs which filter through its banks, so, perchance, our aspirations fall back again in springs on the margin of life's stream to refresh and purify it. The yellow and tepid river may float his scow, and cheer his eye with its reflections and its ripples, but the boatman quenches his thirst at this small rill alone. It is this purer and cooler element that chiefly sustains his life. The race will long survive that is thus discreet.

Our course this morning lay between the territories of Merrimack, on the west, and Litchfield, once called Brenton's Farm, on the east, which townships were anciently the Indian Naticook. Brenton was a fur trader among the Indians, and these lands were granted to him in 1656. The latter township contains about five hundred inhabitants, of whom, however, we saw none, and but few of their dwellings. Being on the river, whose banks are always high and generally conceal the few houses, the country appeared much more wild and primitive than to the traveller on the neighboring roads. The river is by far the most attractive highway, and those boatmen who have spent twenty or twenty-five years on it, must have had a much fairer, more wild and memorable experience than the dusty and jarring one of the teamster, who has driven, during the same time, on the roads which run parallel with the stream. As one ascends the Merrimack, he rarely sees a village, but for the most part, alternate wood and pasture lands, and sometimes a field of corn or potatoes, of rye or oats or English grass, with a few straggling apple trees, and, at still longer intervals, a farmer's house. The soil, excepting the best of the interval, is commonly as light and sandy as a patriot could desire. Sometimes, this forenoon, the country appeared in its primitive state, and as if the Indian still inhabited it; and again, as if many free new settlers occupied it, their slight fences straggling down to the water's edge, and the barking of dogs, and even the prattle of children, were heard, and smoke was seen to go up from some hearthstone, and the banks were divided into patches of pasture, mowing, tillage, and woodland. But when the river spread out broader, with an uninhabited islet, or a long low sandy shore which ran on single and devious, not answering to its opposite, but far off as if it were seashore or single coast, and the land no longer nursed the river in its bosom, but they conversed as equals, the rustling leaves with rippling waves, and few fences were seen, but high oak woods on one side, and large herds of cattle, and all tracks seemed a point to one centre, behind some

In Litchfield village

statelier grove, — we imagined that the river flowed through an extensive manor, and that the few inhabitants were retainers to a lord, and a feudal state of things prevailed.

When there was a suitable reach, we caught sight of the Goffstown Mountain, the Indian Uncannunuc, rising before us on the west side. It was a calm and beautiful day, with only a slight zephyr to ripple the surface of the water, and rustle the woods on shore, and just warmth enough to prove the kindly disposition of Nature to her children. With buoyant spirits and vigorous impulses we tossed our boat rapidly along into the very middle of this forenoon. The fish-hawk sailed and screamed overhead. The chipping, or striped squirrel, *sciurus striatus*, sat upon the end of some Virginia fence or rider reaching over the stream, twirling a green nut with one paw, as in a lathe, while the other held it fast against its incisors as chisels. Like an independent russet leaf, with a will of its own, rustling whither it could; now under the fence, now over it, now peeping at the voyageurs through a crack with only its tail visible, now at its lunch deep in the toothsome kernel, and now a rod off playing at hide-and-seek, with the nut stowed away in its chops, where were half a dozen more beside, extending its cheeks to a ludicrous breadth. As if it were devising through what safe valve of frisk or

somerset to let its superfluous life escape; the
stream passing harmlessly off, even while it
sits, in constant electric flashes through its
tail; and now with a chuckling squeak it dives
into the root of a hazel, and we see no more of it.
Or the larger red squirrel or chickaree, sometimes
called the Hudson Bay squirrel, *striurus Hud-
sonius*, gave warning of our approach by that
peculiar alarum of his, like the winding up of
some strong clock, in the top of a pine tree,
and dodged behind its stem, or leaped from tree
to tree, with such caution and adroitness as if
much depended on the fidelity of his scout,
running along the white pine boughs sometimes twenty rods by our side, with such speed,
and by such unerring routes as if it were some
well-worn familiar path to him; and presently,
when we have passed, he returns to his work of
cutting off the pine cones, and letting them fall
to the ground.

We passed Cromwell's Falls, the first we met
with on this river, this forenoon, by means of
locks, without using our wheels. These falls
are the Nesenkeag of the Indians. Great Nesenkeag Stream comes in on the right just above,
and Little Nesenkeag some distance below,
both in Litchfield. We read in the gazetteer,
under the head of Merrimack, that "The first
house in this town was erected on the margin
of the river [soon after 1665] for a house of traffic

with the Indians. For some time one Cromwell carried on a lucrative trade with them, weighing their furs with his foot, till, enraged at his supposed or real deception, they formed the resolution to murder him. This intention being communicated to Cromwell, he buried his wealth and made his escape. Within a few hours after his flight, a party of the Penacook tribe arrived, and not finding the object of their resentment, burnt his habitation." Upon the top of the high bank here, close to the river, was still to be seen his cellar, now overgrown with trees. It was a convenient spot for such a traffic, at the foot of the first falls above the settlements, and commanding a pleasant view up the river, where he could see the Indians coming down with their furs. The lock-man told us that his shovel and tongs had been plowed up here, and also a stone with his name on it. But we will not vouch for the truth of this story. These were the traces of the white trader. On the opposite bank, where it jutted over the stream cape-wise, we picked up four arrow-heads and a small Indian tool made of stone, as soon as we had climbed it, where plainly there had once stood a wigwam of the Indians with whom Cromwell traded, and who fished and hunted here before he came.

As usual the gossips have not been silent respecting Cromwell's buried wealth, and it is said that some years ago a farmer's plow, not far from here, slid over a flat stone which emitted a hollow sound, and on its being raised a sum of money was found. The lock-man told us another similar story about a farmer in a neighboring town, who had been a poor man, but who suddenly bought a good farm, and was well to do in the world; and, when he was questioned, did not give a satisfactory account of the matter; — how few alas, could! This caused his hired man to remember, that one day as they were plowing together the plow struck something, and his employer going back to look, concluded not to go round again, saying that the sky looked rather louring, and so put up his team. The like urgency has caused many things to be remembered which never transpired. The truth is, there is money buried everywhere, and you have only to go work to find it.

Not far from these falls stands an oak tree on the interval, about a quarter of a mile from the river, on the farm of a Mr. Lund, which was pointed out to us as the spot where French, the leader of the party which went in pursuit of the Indians from Dunstable, was killed. Farwell dodged them in the thick woods near. It did not look as if men had ever had to run for their lives on this now open and peaceful interval.

Here too was another extensive desert by the side of the road in Litchfield, visible from the bank of the river. The sand was blown off in some places to the depth of ten or twelve feet, leaving small grotesque hillocks of that height where there was a clump of bushes firmly rooted. Thirty or forty years ago, as we were told, it was a sheep pasture, but the sheep being worried by the fleas, began to paw the ground, till they broke the sod, and so the sand began to blow, till now it had extended over forty or fifty acres. This evil might easily have been remedied at first, by spreading birches with their leaves on over the sand, and fastening them down with stakes, to break the wind. The flies bit the sheep, and the sheep bit the ground, and the sore had spread to this extent. It is astonishing what a great sore a little scratch breedeth. Who knows but Sahara, where caravans and cities are buried, began with the bite of an African flea. This poor globe, how it must itch in many places! Will no god be kind enough to spread a salve of birches over its sores? — Here too we noticed where the Indians had gathered a heap of stones, perhaps for their council fire, which by their weight having prevented the sand under them from blowing away, were left on the summit of a mound. They told us that arrow-heads, and also bullets of lead and iron, had been found here. We noticed several other sandy tracts in our voyage; and the course of the Merrimack can be traced from the nearest mountain by its

yellow sandbanks, though the river itself is
for the most part invisible. Lawsuits, as we
hear, have in some cases grown out of these
causes. Railroads have been made through
certain irritable districts, breaking their sod,
and so have set the sand to blowing, till it has
converted fertile farms into deserts, and the
Company has had to pay the damages.

This sand seemed to us the connecting link
between land and water. It was a kind of water
on which you could walk, and you could see the
ripple marks on its surface, produced by the
winds, precisely like those at the bottom of a
brook or lake. We had read that Mussulmans
are permitted by the Koran to perform their
ablutions in sand when they cannot get water,
a necessary indulgence in Arabia, and we now
understood the propriety of this provision.

Plum Island, at the mouth of this river, to
whose formation, perhaps, these very banks
have sent their contribution, is a similar desert
of drifting sand, of various colors, blown into
graceful curves by the wind. It is a mere sand-
bar exposed, stretching nine miles parallel to
the coast, and, exclusive of the marsh on the
inside, rarely more than half a mile wide. There
are but half a dozen houses on it, and it is almost
without a tree, or a sod, or any green thing
with which a countryman is familiar. The

Plum Island

thin vegetation stands half buried in sand, as in drifting snow. The only shrub, the beach plum, which gives the island its name, grows but a few feet high; but this is so abundant that parties of a hundred at once come from the main land and down the Merrimack in September, and pitch their tents, and gather the plums, which are good to eat raw and to preserve. The graceful and delicate beach pea too grows abundantly amid the sand; and several strange moss-like and succulent plants. The island for its whole length is scolloped into low hills, not more than twenty feet high, by the wind, and excepting a faint trail on the edge of the marsh, is as trackless as Sahara. There are dreary bluffs of sand and valleys plowed by the wind, where you might expect to discover the bones of a caravan. Schooners come from Boston to load with the sand for masons' uses, and in a few hours the wind obliterates all traces of their work. Yet you have only to dig a foot or two anywhere to come to fresh water; and you are surprised to learn that woodchucks abound here, and foxes are found, though you see not where they can burrow or hide themselves. I have walked down the whole length of its broad beach at low tide, at which time alone you can find a firm ground to walk on, and probably Massachusetts does not furnish a more grand and dreary walk. On the sea side there are only a distant sail and

a few coots to break the grand monotony. A
solitary stake stuck up, or a sharper sand-hill
than usual, is remarkable as a land-mark for
miles; while for music you hear only the cease-
less sound of the surf, and the dreary peep of
the beach birds.

There were several canal boats at Cromwell's
Falls, passing through the locks, for which we
waited. In the forward part of one stood a
brawny New Hampshire man, leaning on his
pole, bareheaded and in shirt and trousers only,
a rude Apollo of a man, coming down from that
" vast uplandish country " to the main; of name-
less age, with flaxen hair, and vigorous, weather-
bleached countenance, in whose wrinkles the
sun still lodged, as little touched by the heats
and frosts and withering cares of life, as a mountain maple; an undressed, unkempt, uncivil man,
with whom we parleyed a while, and parted not
without a sincere interest in one another. His
humanity was genuine and instinctive, and his
rudeness only a manner. He inquired, just as
we were passing out of earshot, if we had killed
anything, and we shouted after him that we had
shot a *buoy*, and could see him for a long while
scratching his head in vain, to know if he had
heard aright.
There is reason in the distinction of civil and
uncivil. The manners are sometimes so rough

a rind, that we doubt whether they cover any core or sapwood at all. We sometimes meet uncivil men, children of Amazons, who dwell by mountains paths, and are said to be inhospitable to strangers; whose salutation is as rude as the grasp of their brawny hands, and who deal with men as unceremoniously as they are wont to deal with the elements. They need only to extend their clearings, and let in more sunlight, to seek out the southern slopes of the hills, from which they may look down on the civil plain or ocean, and temper their diet duly with the cereal fruits, consuming less wild meat and acorns, to become like the inhabitants of cities. A true politeness does not result from any hasty and artificial polishing, it is true, but grows naturally in characters of the right grain and quality, through a long fronting of men and events, and rubbing on good and bad fortune. Perhaps I can tell a tale to the purpose while the lock is filling, — for our voyage this forenoon furnishes but few incidents of importance.

Early one summer morning I had left the shores of the Connecticut, and for the livelong day travelled up the bank of a river, which came in from the west; now looking down on the stream, foaming and rippling through the forest a mile off, from the hills over which the road led, and now sitting on its rocky brink and dipping my feet in its rapids, or bathing adventurously in mid-channel. The hills grew more and more frequent, and gradually swelled into mountains as I advanced, hemming in the course of the river, so that at last I could not see where it came from, and was at liberty to imagine the most wonderful meanderings and descents. At noon I slept on the grass in the shade of a maple, where the river had found a broader channel than usual, and was spread out shallow, with frequent sand-bars exposed. In the names of the towns I recognized some which I had long ago read on teamsters' wagons, that had come from far up country, quiet, uplandish towns, of mountainous fame. I walked along musing, and enchanted by rows of sugar-maples, through the small and uninquisitive villages, and sometimes was pleased with the sight of a boat drawn up on a sand-bar, where there appeared no inhabitants to use it. It seemed, however, as essential to the river as a fish, and to lend a certain dignity to it. It was like the trout of mountain streams to the fishes of the sea, or like the young of the land crab born far in the interior, who have never yet heard the sound of the ocean's surf. The hills approached nearer and nearer to the stream, until at last they closed behind me, and I found myself, just before night-fall, in a romantic and retired valley, about half a mile in length, and barely wide enough for the stream at its bottom. I thought that there could be no finer site for a cottage among mountains. You could anywhere run across the stream on the rocks, and its constant murmuring would quiet the passions of mankind forever. Suddenly the road, which seemed aiming for the mountain side, turned short to the left, and another valley opened, concealing the former, and of the same character with it. It was the most remarkable and pleasing scenery I had ever seen. I found here a few mild and hospitable inhabitants, who, as the day was not quite spent, and I was anxious to improve the light, directed me four or five miles further on my way to the dwelling of a man whose name was Rice, who occupied the last and highest of the valleys that lay in my path, and who, they said, was a rather rude and uncivil man. But, "What is a foreign country to those who have science? Who is a stranger to those who have the habit of speaking kindly?"

At length, as the sun was setting behind the mountains in a still darker and more solitary vale, I reached the dwelling of this man. Except for the narrowness of the plain, and that the stones were solid granite, it was the counterpart of that retreat to which Belphœbe bore the wounded Timias; —

"in a pleasant glade,
With mountains round about environed,
And mighty woods, which did the valley shade,
And like a stately theatre it made,
Spreading itself into a spacious plain;
And in the midst a little river played
Amongst the pumy stones, which seemed to plain,
With gentle murmur, that his course they did restrain."

I observed, as I drew near, that he was not
so rude as I had anticipated, for he kept many
cattle, and dogs to watch them, and I saw where
he had made maple sugar on the sides of the
mountains, and above all distinguished the
voices of children mingling with the murmur
of the torrent before the door. As I passed
his stable I met one whom I supposed to be a
hired man, attending to his cattle, and inquired
if they entertained travellers at that house.
"Sometimes we do," he answered, gruffly, and
immediately went to the farthest stall from me,
and I perceived that it was Rice himself whom I
had addressed. But pardoning this incivility
to the wildness of the scenery, I bent my steps
to the house. There was no sign-post before it,
nor any of the usual invitations to the traveller, though I saw by the road that many went
and came there, but the owner's name only was
fastened to the outside, a sort of implied and
sullen invitation, as I thought. I passed from
room to room without meeting any one, till I
came to what seemed the guests' apartment,

which was neat, and even had an air of refinement about it, and I was glad to find a map against the wall which would direct me on my journey on the morrow. At length I heard a step in a distant apartment, which was the first I had entered, and went to see if the landlord had come in; but it proved to be only a child, one of those whose voices I had heard, probably his son, and between him and me stood in the door-way a large watch-dog, which growled at me, and looked as if he would presently spring, but the boy did not speak to him; and when I asked for a glass of water, he briefly said, "It runs in the corner."   So I took a mug from the counter and went out of doors, and searched round the corner of the house, but could find neither well nor spring, nor any water but the stream which ran all along the front. I came back, therefore, and setting down the mug, asked the child if the stream was good to drink; whereupon he seized the mug and going to the corner of the room, where a cool spring which issued from the mountain behind trickled through a pipe into the apartment, filled it, and drank and gave it to me empty again, and calling to the dog, rushed out of doors. Ere long some of the hired men made their appearance, and drank at the spring, and lazily washed themselves and combed their hair in silence, and some sat down as if weary, and fell asleep in their seats.

But all the while I saw no women, though I sometimes heard a bustle in that part of the house from which the spring came.

At length Rice himself came in, for it was now dark, with an ox whip in his hand, breathing hard, and he too soon settled down into his seat not far from me, as if now that his day's work was done he had no further to travel, but only to digest his supper at his leisure. When I asked him if he could give me a bed, he said there was one ready, in such a tone as implied that I ought to have known it, and the less said about that the better. So far so good. And yet he continued to look at me as if he would fain have me say something further like a traveller. I remarked, that it was a wild and rugged country he inhabited, and worth coming many miles to see. "Not so very rough neither," said he, and appealed to his men to bear witness to the breadth and smoothness of his fields, which consisted in all of one small interval, and to the size of his crops; "and if we have some hills," added he, "there's no better pasturage anywhere." I then asked if this place was the one I had heard of, calling it by a name I had seen on the map, or if it was a certain other; and he answered, gruffly, that it was neither the one nor the other; that he had settled it and cultivated it, and made it what it was, and I could know nothing about it. Observing some guns

and other implements of hunting hanging on
brackets around the room, and his hounds now
sleeping on the floor, I took occasion to change
the discourse, and inquired if there was much
game in that country, and he answered this
question more graciously, having some glim-
mering of my drift; but when I inquired if there
were any bears, he answered impatiently, that
he was no more in danger of losing his sheep than
his neighbors, he had tamed and civilized that
region. After a pause, thinking of my journey
on the morrow, and the few hours of daylight
in that hollow and mountainous country which
would require me to be on my way betimes, I
remarked that the day must be shorter by an
hour there than on the neighboring plains; at
which he gruffly asked what I knew about it,
and affirmed that he had as much daylight as his
neighbors; he ventured to say the days were
longer there than where I lived, as I should
find if I stayed; that in some way, I could not
be expected to understand how, the sun came
over the mountains half an hour earlier, and
stayed half an hour later there than on the neighboring plains. — And more of like sort he said.
He was, indeed, as rude as a fabled satyr. But
I suffered him to pass for what he was, for why
should I quarrel with nature? and was even
pleased at the discovery of such a singular natural
phenomenon. I dealt with him as if to me all

manners were indifferent, and he had a sweet wild way with him. I would not question Nature, and I would rather have him as he was, than as I would have him. For I had come up here not for sympathy, or kindness, or society, but for novelty and adventure, and to see what Nature had produced here. I therefore did not repel his rudeness, but quite innocently welcomed it all, and knew how to appreciate it, as if I were reading in an old drama a part well sustained. He was indeed a coarse and sensual man, and, as I have said, uncivil, but he had his just quarrel with nature and mankind, I have no doubt, only he had no artificial covering to his ill humors. He was earthy enough, but yet there was good soil in him, and even a long-suffering Saxon probity at bottom. If you could represent the case to him, he would not let the race die out in him, like a red Indian.

At length I told him that he was a fortunate man, and I trusted that he was grateful for so much light, and rising, said I would take a lamp, and that I would pay him then for my lodging, for I expected to recommence my journey, even as early as the sun rose in his country; but he answered in haste, and this time civilly, that I should not fail to find some of his household stirring, however early, for they were no sluggards, and I could take my breakfast with them before I started if I chose; and as he lighted the

Looking up the River from Cromwell's Falls

lamp I detected a gleam of true hospitality and ancient civility, a beam of pure and even gentle humanity from his bleared and moist eyes. It was a look more intimate with me, and more explanatory, than any words of his could have been if he had tried to his dying day. It was more significant than any Rice of those parts could even comprehend, and long anticipated this man's culture, — a glance of his pure genius, which did not much enlighten him, but did impress and rule him for the moment, and faintly constrain his voice and manner. He cheerfully led the way to my apartment, stepping over the limbs of his men who were asleep on the floor in an intervening chamber, and showed me a clean and comfortable bed. For many pleasant hours, after the household was asleep, I sat at the open window, for it was a sultry night, and heard the little river

" Amongst the pumy stones, which seemed to plain,
    With gentle murmur, that his course they did restrain."

But I arose as usual by starlight the next morning, before my host, or his men, or even his dogs, were awake; and having left a ninepence on the counter, was already half way over the mountain with the sun, before they had broken their fast.

Before I had left the country of my host, while the first rays of the sun slanted over

the mountains, as I stopped by the wayside
to gather some raspberries, a very old man, not
far from a hundred, came along with a milking
pail in his hand, and turning aside began to
pluck the berries near me; —

—— " his reverend locks
In comelye curles did wave;
And on his aged temples grew
The blossoms of the grave." —

But when I inquired the way, he answered in a
low, rough voice, without looking up or seeming
to regard my presence, which I imputed to his
years; and presently, muttering to himself,
he proceeded to collect his cows in a neighboring
pasture; and when he had again returned near
to the wayside, he suddenly stopped, while his
cows went on before, and, uncovering his head,
prayed aloud in the cool morning air, as if he
had forgotten this exercise before, for his daily
bread, and also that He who letteth his rain fall
on the just and on the unjust, and without whom
not a sparrow falleth to the ground, would not
neglect the stranger (meaning me), and with even
more direct and personal applications, though
mainly according to the long established formula
common to lowlanders and the inhabitants of
mountains.   When he had done praying, I made
bold to ask him if he had any cheese in his hut
which he would sell me, but he answered without

looking up, and in the same low and repulsive voice
as before, that they did not make any, and went
to milking. It is written, "The stranger who
turneth away from a house with disappointed
hopes, leaveth there his own offences, and de-
parteth, taking with him all the good actions of
the owner."

Being now fairly in the stream of this week's
commerce, we began to meet with boats more
frequently, and hailed them from time to time
with the freedom of sailors. The boatmen appeared to lead an easy and contented life, and
we thought that we should prefer their employment ourselves to many professions which are
much more sought after. They suggested how
few circumstances are necessary to the well-
being and serenity of man, how indifferent all
employments are, and that any may seem noble
and poetic to the eyes of men, if pursued with
sufficient buoyancy and freedom. With liberty
and pleasant weather, the simplest occupation,
any unquestioned country mode of life which
detains us in the open air, is alluring. The man
who picks peas steadily for a living is more than
respectable, he is even envied by his shop-worn
neighbors. We are as happy as the birds when
our Good Genius permits us to pursue any out-
door work without a sense of dissipation. Our
pen-knife glitters in the sun; our voice is echoed

by yonder wood; if an oar drops, we are fain to let it drop again.

The canal boat is of very simple construction, requiring but little ship timber, and, as we were told, costs about two hundred dollars. They are managed by two men. In ascending the stream they use poles fourteen or fifteen feet long, shod with iron, walking about one third the length of the boat from the forward end. Going down, they commonly keep in the middle of the stream, using an oar at each end; or if the wind is favorable they raise their broad sail, and have only to steer. They commonly carry down bricks or wood,—fifteen or sixteen thousand bricks, and as many cords of wood, at a time,—and bring back stores for the country, consuming two or three days each way between Concord and Charlestown. They sometimes pile the wood so as to leave a shelter in one part where they may retire from the rain. One can hardly imagine a more healthful employment, or one more favorable to contemplation and the observation of nature. Unlike the mariner, they have the constantly varying panorama of the shore to relieve the monotony of their labor, and it seemed to us that as they thus glided noiselessly from town to town, with all their furniture about them, for their very homestead is a-movable, they could comment on the character of the inhabitants with greater advantage

and security to themselves than the traveller in
a coach, who would be unable to indulge in such
broadsides of wit and humor in so small a vessel,
for fear of the recoil.   They are not subject to
great exposure, like the lumberers of Maine,
in any weather, but inhale the healthfullest
breezes, being slightly encumbered with clothing, frequently with the head and feet bare.
When we met them at noon as they were leisurely descending the stream, their busy commerce did not look like toil, but rather like some
ancient oriental game still played on a large
scale, as the game of chess, for instance, handed
down to this generation.   From morning till
night, unless the wind is so fair that his single
sail will suffice without other labor than steering, the boatman walks backwards and forwards
on the side of his boat, now stooping with his
shoulder to the pole, then drawing it back slowly
to set it again, meanwhile moving steadily forward through an endless valley and an ever-
changing scenery, now distinguishing his course
for a mile or two, and now shut in by a sudden
turn of the river in a small woodland lake. All the
phenomena which surround him are simple and
grand, and there is something impressive, even
majestic, in the very motion he causes, which will
naturally be communicated to his own character,
and he feels the slow irresistible movement under him with pride, as if it were his own energy.

The news spread like wild fire among us youths, when formerly, once in a year or two, one of these boats came up the Concord River, and was seen stealing mysteriously through the meadows and past the village. It came and departed as silently as a cloud, without noise or dust, and was witnessed by few. One summer day this huge traveller might be seen moored at some meadow's wharf, and another summer day it was not there. Where precisely it came from, or who these men were who knew the rocks and soundings better than we who bathed there, we could never tell. We knew some river's bay only, but they took rivers from end to end. They were a sort of fabulous river-men to us. It was inconceivable by what sort of mediation any mere landsman could hold communication with them. Would they heave to to gratify his wishes? No, it was favor enough to know faintly of their destination, or the time of their possible return. I have seen them in the summer, when the stream ran low, mowing the weeds in mid-channel, and with hayers' jests cutting broad swathes in three feet of water, that they might make a passage for their scow, while the grass in long windrows was carried down the stream, undried by the rarest hay weather. We used to admire unweariedly how their vessel would float, like a huge chip, sustaining so many casks of lime, and thousands of bricks, and such heaps of iron ore, with wheel-barrows aboard, — and that when we stepped on it, it did not yield to the pressure of our feet. It gave us confidence in the prevalence of the law of buoyancy, and we imagined to what infinite uses it might be put. The men appeared to lead a kind of life on it, and it was whispered that they slept aboard. Some affirmed that it carried sail, and that such winds blew here as filled the sails of vessels on the ocean; which again others much doubted. They had been seen to sail across our Fair-Haven bay by lucky fishers who were out, but unfortunately others were not there to see. We might then say that our river was navigable, — why not? In after years I read in print, with no little satisfaction, that it was thought by some that with a little expense in removing rocks and deepening the channel, " there might be a profitable inland navigation." *I* then lived somewhere to tell of.

Such is Commerce, which shakes the cocoa-nut and bread-fruit tree in the remotest isle, and sooner or later dawns on the duskiest and most simple-minded savage. If we may be par-doned the digression, — who can help being affected at the thought of the very fine and slight, but positive relation, in which the savage in-habitants of some remote isle stand to the myste-rious white mariner, the child of the sun? — As if *we* were to have dealings with an animal higher

in the scale of being than ourselves. It is a
barely recognized fact to the natives that he
exists, and has his home far away somewhere,
and is glad to buy their fresh fruits with his superfluous commodities. Under the same catholic
sun glances his white ship over Pacific waves
into their smooth bays, and the poor savage's
paddle gleams in the air.

> Man's little acts are grand,
> Beheld from land to land,
> There as they lie in time,
> Within their native clime.
> > Ships with the noon-tide weigh,
> > And glide before its ray,
> > To some retired bay,
> > Their haunt,
> > Whence, under tropic sun,
> > Again they run,
> > Bearing gum Senegal and Tragicant.
> For this was ocean meant,
> For this the sun was sent,
> And moon was lent,
> And winds in distant caverns pent.

Since our voyage the railroad on the bank has
been extended, and there is now but little boating
on the Merrimack. All kinds of produce and
stores were formerly conveyed by water, but
now nothing is carried up the stream, and almost wood and bricks alone are carried down,
and these are also carried on the railroad. The
locks are fast wearing out, and will soon be

impassable, since the tolls will not pay the expense of repairing them, and so in a few years there will be an end of boating on this river. The boating, at present, is principally between Merrimack and Lowell, or Hooksett and Manchester. They make two or three trips from Merrimack to Lowell and back, about twenty-five miles each way, in a week, according to wind and weather. The boatman comes singing in to shore late at night, and moors his empty boat, and gets his supper and lodging in some house near at hand, and again early in the morning, by starlight, perhaps, he pushes away up stream, and, by a shout, or the fragment of a song, gives notice of his approach to the lock-man, with whom he is to take his breakfast. If he gets up to his wood-pile before noon he proceeds to load his boat, with the help of his single "hand" and is on his way down again before night. When he gets to Lowell he unloads his boat, and gets his receipt for his cargo, and having heard the news at the public house at Middlesex or elsewhere, goes back with his empty boat and his receipt in his pocket to the owner, and to get a new load. We were frequently advertised of their approach by some faint sound behind us, and looking round saw them a mile off, creeping stealthily up the side of the stream like alligators. It was pleasant to hail these sailors of the Merrimack from time to time, and learn the news which circulated with them. We imagined that the sun shining on their bare heads had stamped a liberal and public character on their most private thoughts.

The open and sunny interval still stretched away from the river, sometimes by two or more terraces, to the distant hill country, and when we climbed the bank we commonly found an irregular copse-wood skirting the river, the primitive having floated down stream long ago to ——the "King's navy." Sometimes we saw the river road a quarter or half a mile distant, and the particolored Concord stage, with its cloud of dust, its van of earnest travelling faces, and its rear of dusty trunks, reminding us that the country had its places of rendezvous for restless Yankee men. There dwelt along at considerable distances on this interval a quiet agricultural and pastoral people, with every house its well, as we sometimes proved, and every household, though never so still and remote it appeared in the noontide, its dinner about these times. There they lived on, those New England people, farmer lives, father and grand-father and great-grandfather, on and on without noise, keeping up tradition, and expecting, beside fair weather and abundant harvests, we did not learn what. They were contented

to live, since it was so contrived for them, and
where their lines had fallen. —

> Our uninquiring corpses lie more low
> Than our life's curiosity doth go.

Yet these men had no need to travel to be as
wise as Solomon in all his glory, so similar are
the lives of men in all countries, and fraught
with the same homely experiences. One half
the world *knows* how the other half lives.

About noon we passed a small village in Merrimack at Thornton's Ferry, and tasted of the
waters of Naticook Brook on the same side,
where French and his companions, whose grave
we saw in Dunstable, were ambuscaded by the
Indians. The humble village of Litchfield, with
its steepleless meeting-house, stood on the opposite or east bank, near where a dense grove of
willows backed by maples skirted the shore.
There also we noticed some shagbark trees,
which, as they do not grow in Concord, were as
strange a sight to us as the palm would be, whose
fruit only we have seen. Our course now curved
gracefully to the north, leaving a low flat shore
on the Merrimack side, which forms a sort of
harbor for canal boats. We observed some fair
elms and particularly large and handsome white-
maples standing conspicuously on this interval,
and the opposite shore, a quarter of a mile
below, was covered with young elms and maples

six inches high, which had probably sprung from the seeds which had been washed across.

Some carpenters were at work here mending a scow on the green and sloping bank. The strokes of their mallets echoed from shore to shore, and up and down the river, and their tools gleamed in the sun a quarter of a mile from us, and we realized that boat-building was as ancient and honorable an art as agriculture, and that there might be a naval as well as a pastoral life. The whole history of commerce was made manifest in that scow turned bottom upward on the shore. Thus did men begin to go down upon the sea in ships. We thought that it would be well for the traveller to build his boat on the bank of a stream, instead of finding a ferry or a bridge. In the Adventures of Henry the fur-trader, it is pleasant to read that when with his Indians he reached the shore of Ontario, they consumed two days in making two canoes of the bark of the elm tree, in which to transport themselves to Fort Niagara. It is a worthy incident in a journey, a delay as good as much rapid travelling. A good share of our interest in Xenophon's story of his retreat is in the manœuvres to get the army safely over the rivers, whether on rafts of logs or fagots, or on sheep-skins blown up. And where could they better afford to tarry meanwhile than on the banks of a river?

At Thornton's Ferry

As we glided past at a distance, these outdoor workmen appeared to have added some dignity to their labor by its very publicness. It was a part of the industry of nature, like the work of hornets and mud-wasps. —

> The waves slowly beat,
> Just to keep the noon sweet,
> And no sound is floated o'er,
> Save the mallet on shore,
> Which echoing on high,
> Seems a-caulking the sky.

The haze, the sun's dust of travel, had a lethean influence on the land and its inhabitants, and all creatures resigned themselves to float upon the inappreciable tides of nature.

> Woof of the sun, ethereal gauze,
> Woven of Nature's richest stuffs,
> Visible heat, air-water, and dry sea,
> Last conquest of the eye;
> Toil of the day displayed, sun-dust,
> Aerial surf upon the shores of earth,
> Ethereal estuary, frith of light,
> Breakers of air, billows of heat,
> Fine summer spray on inland seas;
> Bird of the sun, transparent-winged,
> Owlet of noon, soft-pinioned,
> From heath or stubble rising without song;
> Establish thy serenity o'er the fields.

The routine which is in the sunshine and the finest days, as that which has conquered and prevailed, commends itself to us by its very

antiquity and apparent solidity and necessity.
Our weakness needs it, and our strength uses
it.   We cannot draw on our boots without brac-
ing ourselves against it.   If there were but one
erect and solid standing tree in the woods, all
creatures would go to rub against it and make
sure of their footing.   During the many hours
which we spend in this waking sleep, the hand
stands still on the face of the clock, and we
grow like corn in the night.   Men are as busy
as the brooks or bees, and postpone everything
to their busyness; as carpenters discuss poli-
tics between the strokes of the hammer while
they are shingling a roof.

This noontide was a fit occasion to make
some pleasant harbor, and there read the journal
of some voyageur like ourselves, not too moral
nor inquisitive, and which would not disturb
the noon; or else some old classic, the very flower
of all reading, which we had postponed to such
a season

" Of Syrian peace, immortal leisure."

But, alas, our chest, like the cabin of a coaster,
contained only its well-thumbed Navigator for
all literature, and we were obliged to draw on
our memory for these things.   We naturally
remembered Alexander Henry's Adventures here
as a sort of classic among books of American

travel. It contains scenery and rough sketching of men and incidents enough to inspire poets for many years, and to my fancy is as full of sounding names as any page of history, — Lake Winnipeg, Hudson's Bay, Ottaway, and portages innumerable; Chipeways, Gens de Terres, Les Pilleurs, The Weepers; with reminiscences of Hearne's journey, and the like; an immense and shaggy but sincere country summer and winter, adorned with chains of lakes and rivers, covered with snows, with hemlocks and fir trees. There is a naturalness, an unpretending and cold life in this traveller, as in a Canadian winter, what life was preserved through low temperatures and frontier dangers by furs within a stout heart. He has truth and moderation worthy of the father of history, which belong only to an intimate experience, and he does not defer too much to literature. The unlearned traveller may quote his single line from the poets with as good right as the scholar. He too may speak of the stars, for he sees them shoot perhaps when the astronomer does not. The good sense of this author is very conspicuous. He is a traveller who does not exaggerate, but writes for the information of his readers, for science and for history. His story is told with as much good faith and directness as if it were a report to his brother traders, or the Directors of the Hudson Bay Company, and is fitly dedicated to Sir Joseph Banks. It reads like the argument to a great poem on the primitive state of the country and its inhabitants, and the reader imagines what in each case with the invocation of the Muse might be sung, and leaves off with suspended interest, as if the full account were to follow. In what school was this fur-trader educated? He seems to travel the immense snowy country with such purpose only as the reader who accompanies him, and to the latter's imagination, it is, as it were, momentarily created to be the scene of his adventures. What is most interesting and valuable in it, however, is not the materials for the history of Pontiac, of Braddock, or the North West, which it furnishes; not the *annals* of the country, but the natural facts, or *perennials*, which are ever without date. When out of history the truth shall be extracted, it will have shed its dates like withered leaves.

The Souhegan, or *Crooked* river, as some translate it, comes in from the west about a mile and a half above Thornton's Ferry. Babboosuck Brook empties into it near its mouth. There are said to be some of the finest water privileges in the country still unimproved on the former stream, at a short distance from the Merrimack. One spring morning, March 22, in the year 1677, an incident occurred on the banks of the river here, which is interesting to us as a slight memorial of an interview between two ancient tribes of men, one of which is now extinct, while the other, though it is still represented by a miserable remnant, has long since disappeared from its ancient hunting grounds. A Mr. James Parker at "Mr. Hinchmanne's farme ner Meremack," wrote thus "to the Honred Governer and Council at Bostown, *Hast, Post Hast.*"

"Sagamore Wanalancet come this morning to informe me, and then went to Mr. Tyng's to informe him, that his son being on ye other sid of Meremack river over against Souhegan upon the 22 day of this instant, about tene of the clock in the morning, he discovered 15 Indians on this sid the river, which he soposed to be Mohokes by ther spech. He called to them; they answered, but he could not understand ther spech; and he having a conow ther in the river, he went to breck his conow that they might not have ani ues of it. In the mean time they shot about thirty guns at him, and he being much frighted fled, and come home forthwith to Nashamcock, [Pawtucket Falls or Lowell] wher ther wigowames now stand."

Penacooks and Mohawks! *ubique gentium sunt?* Where are they now? — In the year 1670, a Mohawk warrior scalped a Naamkeak or Wamesit Indian maiden near where Lowell now stands. She, however, recovered. Even as late as 1685, John Hogkins, a Penacook Indian, who describes his grand-father as having lived "at place called Malamake rever, other name chef Natukkog and Panukkog, that one rever great many names," wrote thus to the governor: —

"May 15th, 1685.
"Honor governor my friend, —
"You my friend I desire your worship and your power, because I hope you can do som great matters this one. I am poor and naked and I have no men at my place because I afraid all-wayes Mohogs he will kill me every day and night. If your worship when please pray help me you no let Mohogs kill me at my place at Malamake river called Pannukkog and Natukkog, I will submit your worship and your power. — And now I want pouder and such alminishon shatt and guns, because I have forth at my hom and I plant theare.
"This all Indian hand, but pray you do consider your humble servant, JOHN HOGKINS."

Signed also by Simon Detogkom, King Hary, Sam Linis, Mr. Jorge Rodunnonukgus, John Owamosimmin, and nine other Indians, with their marks against their names.

But now, one hundred and fifty-four years having elapsed since the date of this letter, we went unalarmed on our way, without "brecking" our "conow," reading the New England Gazetteer, and seeing no traces of "Mohogs" on the banks.

The Souhegan, though a rapid river, seemed to-day to have borrowed its character from the noon.

> Where gleaming fields of haze
> Meet the voyageur's gaze,
> And above, the heated air
> Seems to make a river there,
> The pines stand up with pride
> By the Souhegan's side,
> And the hemlock and the larch
> With their triumphal arch
> Are waving o'er its march
>   To the sea.
> No wind stirs its waves,
> But the spirits of the braves
>   Hov'ring o'er,
> Whose antiquated graves
> Its still water laves
>   On the shore.
> With an Indian's stealthy tread
> It goes sleeping in its bed,
> Without joy or grief,
> Or the rustle of a leaf,
> Without a ripple or a billow,
> Or the sigh of a willow,
> From the Lyndeboro' hills
> To the Merrimack mills.
> With a louder din
> Did its current begin,

When melted the snow
On the far mountain's brow,
And the drops came together
In that rainy weather.
Experienced river,
Hast thou flowed forever?
Souhegan soundeth old,
But the half is not told,
What names hast thou borne
In the ages far gone,
When the Xanthus and Meander
Commenced to wander,
Ere the black bear haunted
  Thy red forest-floor,
Or Nature had planted
  The pines by thy shore.

During the heat of the day, we rested on a large island a mile above the mouth of this river, pastured by a herd of cattle, with steep banks and scattered elms and oaks, and a sufficient channel for canal boats on each side. When we made a fire to boil some rice for our dinner, the flames spreading amid the dry grass, and the smoke curling silently upward and casting grotesque shadows on the ground seemed phenomena of the noon, and we fancied that we progressed up the stream without effort, and as naturally as the wind and tide went down, not outraging the calm days by unworthy bustle or impatience. The woods on the neighboring shore were alive with pigeons, which were moving south looking for mast, but now, like ourselves, spending their noon in the shade. We could hear the slight wiry winnowing sound of their wings as they changed their roosts from time to time, and their gentle and tremulous cooing. They sojourned with us during the noontide, greater travellers far than we. You may frequently discover a single pair sitting upon the lower branches of the white pine in the depths of the wood, at this hour of the day, so silent and solitary, and with such a hermit-like appearance, as if they had never strayed beyond its skirts, while the acorn which was gathered in the forests of Maine is still undigested in their crops. We obtained one of these handsome birds, which lingered too long upon its perch, and plucked and broiled it here with some other game, to be carried along for our supper; for beside the provisions which we carried with us, we depended mainly on the river and forest for our supply. It is true, it did not seem to be putting this bird to its right use, to pluck off its feathers, and extract its entrails, and broil its carcass on the coals; but we heroically persevered, nevertheless, waiting for farther information. The same regard for Nature which excited our sympathy for her creatures, nerved our hands to carry through what we had begun. For we would be honorable to the party we deserted; we would fulfil fate, and so at length, perhaps, detect the secret

innocence of these incessant tragedies which
Heaven allows. —

> " Too quick resolves do resolution wrong,
> What, part so soon to be divorced so long?
> Things to be done are long to be debated;
> Heaven is not day'd, Repentance is not dated."

We are double-edged blades, and every time we
whet our virtue the return stroke straps our
vice. Where is the skilful swordsman who
can give clean wounds, and not rip up his work
with the other edge?

Nature herself has not provided the most
graceful end for her creatures. What becomes
of all these birds that people the air and forest
for our solacement? The sparrows seem always
chipper, never infirm. We do not see their
bodies lie about; yet there is a tragedy at the
end of each one of their lives. They must
perish miserably; not one of them is translated.
True, " not a sparrow falleth to the ground without our Heavenly Father's knowledge," but
they do fall, nevertheless.

The carcasses of some poor squirrels, however,
the same that frisked so merrily in the morning,
which we had skinned and embowelled for our
dinner, we abandoned in disgust, with tardy
humanity, as too wretched a resource for any
but starving men. It was to perpetuate the
practice of a barbarous era. If they had been

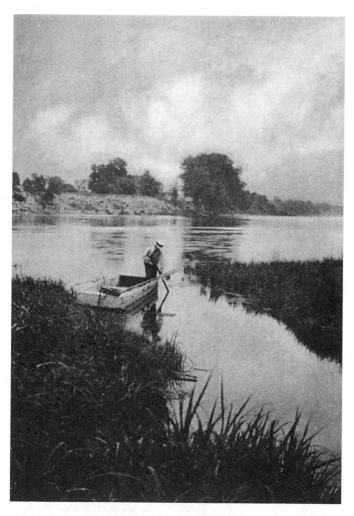

The mouth of Nanticook Brook

larger, our crime had been less. Their small red bodies, little bundles of red tissue, mere gobbets of venison, would not have "fattened fire." With a sudden impulse we threw them away, and washed our hands, and boiled some rice for our dinner. "Behold the difference between the one who eateth flesh, and him to whom it belonged! The first hath a monentary enjoyment, whilst the latter is deprived of existence!"—"Who could commit so great a crime against a poor animal, who is fed only by the herbs which grow wild in the woods, and whose belly is burnt up with hunger?" We remembered a picture of mankind in the hunter age, chasing hares down the mountains, O me miserable! Yet sheep and oxen are but larger squirrels, whose hides are saved and meat is salted, whose souls perchance are not so large in proportion to their bodies.

There should always be some flowering and maturing of the fruits of nature in the cooking process. Some simple dishes recommend themselves to our imaginations as well as palates. In parched corn, for instance, there is a manifest sympathy between the bursting seed and the more perfect developments of vegetable life. It is a perfect flower with its petals, like the houstonia or anemone. On my warm hearth these cerealian blossoms expanded; here is the bank whereon they grew. Perhaps some such visible blessing would always attend the simple and wholesome repast.

Here was that "pleasant harbor" which we had sighed for, where the weary voyageur could read the journal of some other sailor, whose bark had plowed, perchance, more famous and classic seas. At the tables of the gods, after feasting follow music and song; we will recline now under these island trees, and for our minstrel call on

ANACREON

"Nor has he ceased his charming song, but still that lyre,
Though he is dead, sleeps not in Hades."
Simonides' Epigram on Anacreon.

I lately met with an old volume from a London bookshop, containing the Greek Minor Poets, and it was a pleasure to read once more only the words, — Orpheus, — Linus, — Musæus, — those faint poetic sounds and echoes of a name, dying away on the ears of us modern men; and those hardly more substantial sounds, Mimnermus — Ibycus — Alcæus — Stesichorus — Menander. They lived not in vain. We can converse with these bodiless fames without reserve or personality.

I know of no studies so composing as those of the classical scholar. When we have sat down to them, life seems as still and serene as if it were very far off, and I believe it is not habitually seen from any common platform so truly and unexaggerated as in the light of literature. In serene hours we contemplate the tour of the Greek and Latin authors with more pleasure than the traveller does the fairest scenery of Greece or Italy. Where shall we find a more refined society? That highway down from Homer and Hesiod to Horace and Juvenal is more attractive than the Appian. Reading the classics, or conversing with those old Greeks and Latins in their surviving works, is like walking amid the stars and constellations, a high and by way serene to travel. Indeed, the true scholar will be not a little of an astronomer in his habits. Distracting cares will not be allowed to obstruct the field of his vision, for the higher regions of literature, like astronomy, are above storm and darkness.

But passing by these rumors of bards, let us pause for a moment at the Teian poet.

There is something strangely modern about him. He is very easily turned into English. Is it that our lyric poets have resounded only that lyre, which would sound only light subjects, and which Simonides tells us does not sleep in Hades? His odes are like gems of pure ivory. They possess an ethereal and evanescent beauty like summer evenings, ὅ χρή σε νοεῖν νόου ἄνθει, *which you must perceive with the flower of the mind,* — and show how slight a beauty could be expressed. You have to consider them, as the stars of lesser magnitude, with the side of the eye, and look aside from them to behold them. They charm us by their serenity and freedom from exaggeration and passion, and by a certain flowerlike beauty, which does not propose itself, but must be approached and studied like a natural object. But perhaps their chief merit consists in the lightness and yet security of their tread;

> "The young and tender stalk
> Ne'er bends when *they* do walk."

True, our nerves are never strung by them; — it is too constantly the sound of the lyre, and never the note of the trumpet; but they are not gross, as has been presumed, but always elevated above the sensual.

Perhaps these are the best that have come down to us.

ON HIS LYRE

I wish to sing the Atridæ,
And Cadmus I wish to sing;
But my lyre sounds
Only love with its chords.
Lately I changed the strings
And all the lyre;
And I began to sing the labors
Of Hercules; but my lyre
Resounded loves.

Farewell, henceforth, for me,
Heroes, for my lyre
Sings only loves.

———

TO A SWALLOW

Thou indeed, dear swallow,
Yearly going and coming,
In summer weavest thy nest,
And in winter go'st disappearing
Either to Nile or to Memphis.
But Love always weaveth
His nest in my heart.***

———

ON A SILVER CUP

Turning the silver,
Vulcan, make for me,
Not indeed a panoply,
For what are battles to me?
But a hollow cup,
As deep as thou canst.
And make for me in it
Neither stars, nor wagons,
Nor sad Orion;
What are the Pleiades to me?
What the shining Bootes?
Make vines for me,
And clusters of grapes in it,
And of gold Love and Bathyllus
Treading the grapes
With the fair Lyæus.

———

ON HIMSELF

Thou sing'st the affairs of Thebes
And he the battles of Troy,

But I of my own defeats.
No horse have wasted me,
Nor foot, nor ships;
But a new and different host,
From eyes smiting me.

———

TO A DOVE

Lovely dove,
Whence, whence dost thou fly?
Whence, running on air,
Dost thou waft and diffuse
So many sweet ointments?
Who art? What thy errand? —
Anacreon sent me
To a boy, to Bathyllus,
Who lately is ruler and tyrant of all.
Cythere has sold me
For one little song,
And I'm doing this service
For Anacreon.
And now, as you see,
I bear letters from him.
And he says that directly
He'll make me free,
But though he release me,
His slave I will tarry with him.
For why should I fly
Over mountains and fields,
And perch upon trees,
Eating some wild thing?
Now indeed I eat bread,
Plucking it from the hands
Of Anacreon himself;
And he gives me to drink
The wine which he tastes,
And drinking, I dance,

And shadow my master's
Face with my wings;
And, going to rest,
On the lyre itself I sleep.
That is all; get thee gone.
Thou hast made me more talkative,
Man, than a crow.

ON LOVE

Love walking swiftly,
With hyacinthine staff,
Bade me to take a run with him;
And hastening through swift torrents,
And woody places, and over precipices,
A water-snake stung me.
And my heart leaped up to
My mouth, and I should have fainted;
But Love fanning my brows
With his soft wings, said,
Surely, thou art not able to love.

ON WOMEN

Nature has given horns
To bulls, and hoofs to horses,
Swiftness to hares,
To lions yawning teeth,
To fishes swimming,
To birds flight,
To men wisdom.
For woman she had nothing beside;
What then does she give? Beauty, —
Instead of all shields,
Instead of all spears;
And she conquers even iron
And fire, who is beautiful.

ON LOVERS

Horses have the mark
Of fire on their sides,
And some have distinguished
The Parthian men by their crests;
So I, seeing lovers,
Know them at once,
For they have a certain slight
Brand on their hearts.

TO A SWALLOW

What dost thou wish me to do to thee —
What, thou loquacious swallow?
Dost thou wish me taking thee
Thy light pinions to clip?
Or rather to pluck out
Thy tongue from within,
As that Tereus did?
Why with thy notes in the dawn
Hast thou plundered Bathyllus
From my beautiful dreams?

TO A COLT

Thracian colt, why at me
Looking aslant with thy eyes,
Dost thou cruelly flee,
And think that I know nothing wise?
Know I could well
Put the bridle on thee,
And holding the reins, turn
Round the bounds of the course.
But now thou browsest the meads,
And gambolling lightly dost play,
For thou hast no skillful horseman
Mounted upon thy back.

CUPID WOUNDED

Love once among roses
Saw not,
A sleeping bee, but was stung;
And being wounded in the finger
Of his hand, cried for pain.
Running as well as flying
To the beautiful Venus,
I am killed, mother, said he,
I am killed, and I die.
A little serpent has stung me,
Winged, which they call
A bee — the husbandmen.
And she said, If the sting
Of a bee afflicts you,
How, think you, are they afflicted,
Love, whom you smite?

Late in the afternoon, for we had lingered
long on the island, we raised our sail for the first
time, and for a short hour the south-west wind
was our ally; but it did not please Heaven to
abet us long. With one sail raised we swept
slowly up the eastern side of the stream, steering clear of the rocks, while from the top of a
hill which formed the opposite bank, some lumberers were rolling down timber to be rafted
down the stream. We could see their axes and
levers gleaming in the sun, and the logs came
down with a dust and a rumbling sound, which
was reverberated through the woods beyond
us on our side, like the roar of artillery. But
Zephyr soon took us out of sight and hearing of

this commerce. Having passed Read's Ferry,
and another island called McGaw's Island, we
reached some rapids called Moore's Falls, and
entered on "that section of the river, nine miles
in extent, converted, by law, into the Union
Canal, comprehending in that space six distinct
falls; at each of which, and at several interme-
diate places, work has been done." After passing Moore's Falls by means of locks, we again
had recourse to our oars, and went merrily on
our way, driving the small sand-piper from rock
to rock before us, and sometimes rowing near
enough to a cottage on the bank, though they
were few and far between, to see the sun-flowers,
and the seed vessels of the poppy, like small
goblets filled with the water of Lethe, before
the door, but without disturbing the sluggish
household behind. Thus we held on, sailing
or dipping our way along with the paddle up this
broad river, — smooth and placid, flowing over
concealed rocks, where we could see the pickerel
lying low in the transparent water, — eager to
double some distant cape, to make some great
bend as in the life of man, and see what new
perspective would open; looking far into a new
country, broad and serene, the cottages of settlers seen afar for the first time, yet with the moss
of a century on their roofs, and the third or
fourth generation in their shadow. Strange was
it to consider how the sun and the summer, the

Moore's Falls

buds of spring and the seared leaves of autumn, were related to these cabins along the shore; how all the rays which paint the landscape radiate from them, and the flight of the crow and the gyrations of the hawk have reference to their roofs. Still the ever rich and fertile shores accompanied us, fringed with vines and alive with small birds and frisking squirrels, the edge of some farmer's field or widow's wood-lot; or wilder, perchance, where the musk-rat, the little medicine of the river, drags it-self along stealthily over the alder leaves and mussel shells, and man and the memory of man are banished far.

At length the unwearied, never sinking shore, still holding on without break, with its cool copses and serene pasture grounds, tempted us to disembark; and we adventurously landed on this remote coast, to survey it, unknown to any human inhabitant probably to this day. But we still remember the gnarled and hospit-able oaks which grew even there for our enter-tainment, and were no strangers to us, the lonely horse in his pasture, and the patient cows, whose path to the river, so judiciously chosen to over-come the difficulties of the way, we followed, and disturbed their ruminations in the shade; and, above all, the cool free aspect of the wild apple trees, generously proffering their fruit to us, though still green and crude, the hard, round, glossy fruit, which, if not ripe, still was not poison, but New English too, brought hither its ancestors by ours once. These gentler trees imparted a half-civilized and twilight aspect to the otherwise barbarian land. Still further on we scrambled up the rocky channel of a brook, which had long served nature for a sluice there, leaping like it from rock to rock through tangled woods, at the bottom of a ravine, which grew darker and darker, and more and more hoarse the murmurs of the stream, until we reached the ruins of a mill, where now the ivy grew, and the trout glanced through the crumbling flume; and there we imagined what had been the dreams and speculations of some early settler. But the waning day compelled us to embark once more, and redeem this wasted time with long and vigorous sweeps over the rippling stream.

It was still wild and solitary, except that at intervals of a mile or two the roof of a cottage might be seen over the bank. This region, as we read, was once famous for the manufacture of straw bonnets of the Leghorn kind, of which it claims the invention in these parts, and occasionally some industrious damsel tripped down to the water's edge, as it appeared, to put her straw a-soak, and stood awhile to watch the retreating voyageurs, and catch the fragment of a boat song which we had made wafted over the water.

Thus, perchance, the Indian hunter,
  Many a lagging year agone,
Gliding o'er thy rippling waters ,
  Lowly hummed a natural song.

Now the sun's behind the willows,
  Now he gleams along the waves,
Faintly o'er the wearied billows
  Come the spirits of the braves.

Just before sundown we reached some more
falls in the town of Bedford, where some stone-
masons were employed repairing the locks in a
solitary part of the river.   They were interested
in our adventures, especially one young man of
our own age, who inquired at first if we were
bound up to " Skeag," and when he had heard
our story, and examined our outfit, asked us
other questions, but temperately still, and always
turning to his work again, though as if it were
become his duty.   It was plain that he would
like to go with us, and as he looked up the river,
many a distant cape and wooded shore were
reflected in his eye, as well as in his thoughts.
When we were ready he left his work, and helped
us through the locks with a sort of quiet enthusiasm, telling us we were at Coos Falls, and we
could still distinguish the strokes of his chisel
for many sweeps after we had left him.
    We wished to camp this night on a large rock
in the middle of the stream, just above these
falls, but the want of fuel, and the difficulty of

fixing our tent firmly, prevented us; so we made our bed on the main land opposite, on the west bank, in the town of Bedford, in a retired place, as we supposed, there being no house in sight.

WEDNESDAY

"Man is man's foe and destiny."
— COTTON

EARLY this morning, as we were rolling up our buffaloes and loading our boat amid the dew, while our embers were still smoking, the masons who worked at the locks, and whom we had seen crossing the river in their boat the evening before while we were examining the rock, came upon us as they were going to their work, and we found that we had pitched our tent directly in their path to their boat. This was the only time that we were observed on our camping ground. Thus, far from the beaten highways and the dust and din of travel, we beheld the country privately, yet freely, and at our leisure. Other roads do some violence to Nature, and bring the traveller to stare at her, but the river steals into the scenery it traverses without intrusion, silently creating and adoring it, and is as free to come and go as the zephyr.

As we shoved away from this rocky coast, before sunrise, the smaller bittern, the genius of the shore, was moping along its edge, or stood probing the mud for its food, with ever an eye on us, though so demurely at work, or else he ran along over the wet stones like a wrecker in his storm coat, looking out for wrecks of snails and cockles. Now away he goes, with a limping flight, uncertain where he will alight, until a rod of clear sand amid the alders invites his feet; and now our steady approach compels him to seek a new retreat. It is a bird of the oldest Thalesian school, and no doubt believes in the priority of water to the other elements; the relic of a twilight ante-diluvian age which yet inhabits these bright American rivers with us Yankees. There is something venerable in this melancholy and contemplative race of birds, which may have trodden the earth while it was yet in a slimy and imperfect state. Perchance their tracks too are still visible on the stones. It still lingers into our glaring summers, bravely supporting its fate without sympathy from man, as if it looked forward to some second advent of which *he* has no assurance. One wonders if, by its patient study by rocks and sandy capes, it has wrested the whole of her secret from Nature yet. What a rich experience it must have gained, standing on one leg and looking out from its dull eye so long on sunshine and rain, moon and stars! What could it tell of stagnant pools and reeds and dank night-fogs? It would be worth the while to look closely into the eye which has been

open and seeing at such hours, and in such
solitudes, its dull, yellowish, greenish eye.   Methinks my own soul must be a bright invisible
green.   I have seen these birds stand by the
half dozen together in the shallower water along
the shore, with their bills thrust into the mud at
the bottom, probing for food, the whole head
being concealed, while the neck and body formed
an arch above the water.

Cohass Brook, the outlet of Massabesic Pond,
— which last is five or six miles distant, and contains fifteen hundred acres, being the largest
body of fresh water in Rockingham county, —
comes in near here from the east.   Rowing between Manchester and Bedford, we passed, at
an early hour, a ferry and some falls, called
Goff's Falls, the Indian Cohasset, where there
is a small village, and a handsome green islet
in the middle of the stream.   From Bedford
and Merrimac have been boated the bricks of
which Lowell is made.   About twenty years
before, as they told us, one Moore, of Bedford,
having clay on his farm, contracted to furnish
eight millions of bricks to the founders of that
city within two years.   He fulfilled his contract
in one year, and since then bricks have been
the principal export from these towns.   The
farmers found thus a market for their wood, and
when they had brought a load to the kilns, they
could cart a load of bricks to the shore, and so

make a profitable day's work of it. Thus all parties were benefited. It was worth the while to see the place where Lowell was "dug out." So likewise Manchester is being built of bricks made still higher up the river at Hooksett.

There might be seen here on the bank of the Merrimack, near Goff's Falls, in what is now the town of Bedford, famous "for hops and for its fine domestic manufactures," some graves of the aborigines. The land still bears this scar here, and time is slowly crumbling the bones of a race. Yet without fail every spring since they first fished and hunted here, the brown thrasher has heralded the morning from a birch or alder spray, and the undying race of reed-birds still rustles through the withering grass. But these bones rustle not. These mouldering elements are slowly preparing for another metamorphosis, to serve new masters, and what was the Indian's will ere long be the white man's sinew.

We learned that Bedford was not so famous for hops as formerly, since the price is fluctuating, and poles are now scarce. Yet if the traveller goes back a few miles from the river, the hop kilns will still excite his curiosity.

There were few incidents in our voyage this forenoon, though the river was now more rocky and the falls more frequent than before. It was a pleasant change, after rowing incessantly for many hours, to lock ourselves through in some

retired place, — for commonly there was no lock-
man at hand, — one sitting in the boat, while
the other, sometimes with no little labor and
heave-yoing, opened and shut the gates, waiting
patiently to see the locks fill. We did not once
use the wheels which we had provided. Taking
advantage of the eddy, we were sometimes
floated up to the locks almost in the face of the
falls; and, by the same cause, any floating timber
was carried round in a circle and repeatedly
drawn into the rapids before it finally went
down the stream. These old gray structures,
with their quiet arms stretched over the river
in the sun, appeared like natural objects in the
scenery, and the king-fisher and sand-piper
alighted on them as readily as on stakes or rocks.

We rowed leisurely up the stream for several
hours, until the sun had got high in the sky, our
thoughts monotonously beating time to our oars.
For outward variety there was only the river
and the receding shores, a vista continually
opening behind and closing before us, as we sat
with our backs up stream, and for inward such
thoughts as the muses grudgingly lent us. We
were always passing some low inviting shore or
some overhanging bank, on which, however, we
never landed. —

> Such near aspects had we
> Of our life's scenery.

It might be seen by what tenure men held the earth.　The smallest stream is *mediterranean* sea, a smaller ocean creek within the land, where men may steer by their farm bounds and cottage lights.　For my own part, but for the geographers, I should hardly have known how large a portion of our globe is water, my life has chiefly passed within so deep a cove.　Yet I have sometimes ventured as far as to the mouth of my Snug Harbor.　From an old ruined fort on Staten Island, I have loved to watch all day some vessel whose name I had read in the morning through the telegraph glass, when she first came upon the coast, and her hull heaved up and glistened in the sun, from the moment when the pilot and most adventurous news-boats met her, past the Hook, and up the narrow channel of the wide outer bay, till she was boarded by the health officer, and took her station at Quarantine, or held on her unquestioned course to the wharves of New York.　It was interesting, too, to watch the less adventurous news-man, who made his assault as the vessel swept through the Narrows, defying plague and quarantine law, and fastening his little cock boat to her huge side, clambered up and disappeared in the cabin. And then I could imagine what momentous news was being imparted by the captain, which no American ear had ever heard, that Asia, Africa, Europe — were all sunk; for which at length he pays the price, and is seen descending the ship's side with his bundle of newspapers, but not where he first got up, for these arrivers do not stand still to gossip, — and he hastes away with steady sweeps to dispose of his wares to the highest bidder, and we shall erelong read something startling, — "By the latest arrival," — " by the good ship ———." — On Sunday I beheld from some interior hill the long procession of vessels getting to sea, reaching from the city wharves through the Narrows, and past the Hook, quite to the ocean-stream, far as the eye could reach, with stately march and silken sails, all counting on lucky voyages, but each time some of the number, no doubt, destined to go to Davy's locker, and never come on this coast again. — And again, in the evening of a pleasant day, it was my amusement to count the sails in sight. But as the setting sun continually brought more and more to light, still further in the horizon, the last count always had the advantage, till by the time the last rays streamed over the sea, I had doubled and trebled my first number; though I could no longer class them all under the several heads of ships, barques, brigs, schooners, and sloops, but most were faint generic *vessels* only. And then the temperate twilight light, perchance, revealed the floating home of some sailor whose thoughts were already alienated from this American coast, and directed towards the Europe of our dreams. — I have stood upon the same hill-top when a thunder shower rolling down from the Catskills and Highlands passed over the island, deluging the land, and when it had suddenly left us in sunshine, have seen it overtake successively with its huge shadow and dark descending wall of rain the vessels in the bay. Their bright sails were suddenly drooping and dark like the sides of barns, and they seemed to shrink before the storm; while still far beyond them on the sea, through this dark veil, gleamed the sunny sails of those vessels which the storm had not yet reached. — And at midnight, when all around and overhead was darkness, I have seen a field of trembling silvery light far out on the sea, the reflection of the moonlight from the ocean, as if beyond the precincts of our night, where the moon traversed a cloudless heaven, — and sometimes a dark speck in its midst, where some fortunate vessel was pursuing its happy voyage by night.

But to us river sailors the sun never rose out of ocean waves, but from some green coppice, and went down behind some dark mountain line. We, too, were but dwellers on the shore, like the bittern of the morning, and our pursuit the wrecks of snails and cockles. Nevertheless, we were contented to know the better one fair particular shore.

My life is like a stroll upon the beach,
    As near the ocean's edge as I can go,
My tardy steps its waves sometimes o'crreach,
    Sometimes I stay to let them overflow.

My sole employment 'tis, and scrupulous care,
    To place my gains beyond the reach of tides,
Each smoother pebble, and each shell more rare,
    Which ocean kindly to my hand confides.

I have but few companions on the shore,
    They scorn the strand who sail upon the sea,
Yet oft I think the ocean they've sailed o'er
    Is deeper known upon the strand to me.

The middle sea contains no crimson dulse,
    Its deeper waves cast up no pearls to view,
Along the shore my hand is on its pulse,
    And I converse with many a shipwrecked crew.

The small houses which were scattered along the river 'at intervals of a mile or more, were commonly out of sight to us, but sometimes when we rowed near the shore, we heard the peevish note of a hen, or some slight domestic sound, which betrayed them. The lock-men's houses were particularly well placed, retired, and high, always at falls or rapids, and commanding the pleasantest reaches of the river, — for it is generally wider and more lake-like just above a fall, — and there they wait for boats. These humble dwellings, homely and sincere, in which a hearth was still the essential part, were more pleasing to our eyes than palaces or castles would have been. In the noon of

these days, as we have said, we occasionally
climbed the banks and approached these houses,
to get a glass of water and make acquaintance
with their inhabitants. High in the leafy
bank, surrounded commonly by a small patch
of corn and beans, squashes and melons, with
sometimes a graceful hop-yard on one side, and
some running vine over the windows, they appeared like bee-hives set to gather honey for
a summer. I have not read of any Arcadian
life which surpasses the actual luxury and serenity of these New England dwellings. For the
outward gilding, at least, the age is golden enough.
As you approach the sunny door-way, awakening the echoes by your steps, still no sound from
these barracks of repose, and you fear that the
gentlest knock may seem rude to the oriental
dreamers. The door is opened, perchance, by
some Yankee-Hindoo woman, whose small-
voiced but sincere hospitality, out of the bottomless depths of a quiet nature, has travelled quite
round to the opposite side, and fears only to
obtrude its kindness. You step over the white-
scoured floor to the bright "dresser," lightly,
as if afraid to disturb the devotions of the household, — for oriental dynasties appear to have
passed away since the dinner table was last
spread here, — and thence to the frequented
curb, where you see your long-forgotten, un-
shaven face at the bottom, in juxtaposition

with new-made butter and the trout in the well. "Perhaps you would like some molasses and ginger," suggests the faint noon voice. Sometimes there sits the brother who follows the sea, their representative man; who knows only how far it is to the nearest port, no more distances, all the rest is sea and distant capes, — patting the dog, or dandling the kitten in arms that were stretched by the cable and the oar, pulling against Boreas or the trade-winds. He looks up at the stranger, half pleased, half astonished, with a mariner's eye, as if he were a dolphin within cast. If men will believe it, *sua si bona nôrint* there are no more quiet Tempes, nor more poetic and Arcadian lives, than may be lived in these New England dwellings. We thought that the employment of their inhabitants by day would be to tend the flowers and herds, and at night, like the shepherds of old, to cluster and give names to the stars from the river banks.

We passed a large and densely wooded island this forenoon, between Short's and Griffith's Falls, the fairest which we had met with, with a handsome grove of elms at its head. If it had been evening we should have been glad to camp there. Not long after one or two more occurred. The boatmen told us that the current had recently made important changes here. An island always pleases my imagination, even

the smallest, as a small continent and integral
portion of the globe. I have a fancy for building my hut on one. Even a bare grassy isle
which I can see entirely over at a glance, has
some undefined and mysterious charm for me.
It is commonly the offspring of the junction of
two rivers, whose currents bring down and deposit their respective sands in the eddy at their
confluence, as it were the womb of a continent.
By what a delicate and far-fetched contribution
every island is made! What an enterprise of
Nature thus to lay the foundations of and to
build up the future continent, of golden and
silver sands and the ruins of forests, with ant-
like industry! Pindar gives the following account of the origin of Thera, whence, in after
times, Libyan Cyrene was settled by Battus.
Triton, in the form of Eurypylus, presents a
clod to Euphemus, one of the Argonauts, as
they are about to return home. —

> " He knew of our haste,
> And immediately seizing a clod
> With his right hand, strove to give it
> As a chance stranger's gift.
> Nor did the hero disregard him, but leaping on the shore,
> Stretching hand to hand,
> Received the mystic clod.
> But I hear it sinking from the deck,
> Go with the sea brine
> At evening, accompanying the watery sea.
> Often indeed I urged the careless

Menials to guard it, but their minds forgot.
And now in this island the imperishable seed of spacious Libya
Is spilled before its hour."

It is a beautiful fable, also related by Pindar, how Helius, or the Sun, looked down into the sea one day, — when perchance his rays were first reflected from some increasing glittering sand-bar, — and saw the fair and fruitful island of Rhodes

" Springing up from the bottom,
Capable of feeding many men and suitable for flocks; "

and at the nod of Zeus,

——"The island sprang from the watery
Sea; and the Genial Father of penetrating beams,
Ruler of fire-breathing horses, has it."

The shifting islands! who would not be willing that his house should be undermined by such a foe! The inhabitants of an island can tell what currents formed the land which he cultivates; and his earth is still being created or destroyed. There before his door, perchance, still empties the stream which brought down the material of his farm ages before, and is still bringing it down or washing it away, — the graceful, gentle robber!

Not long after this we saw the Piscataquoag, or Sparkling Water, emptying in on our left, and heard the Falls of Amoskeag above. Large quantities of lumber, as we read in the gazetteer,

were still annually floated down the Piscata-
quoag to the Merrimack, and there are many
fine mill privileges on it.   Just about the mouth
of this river we passed the artificial falls where
the canals of the Manchester Manufacturing
Company discharge themselves into the Merrimack.   They are striking enough to have a
name, and, with the scenery of a Bashpish,
would be visited from far and near.   The water
falls thirty or forty feet over seven or eight steep
and narrow terraces of stone, probably to break
its force, and is converted into one mass of foam.
This canal water did not seem to be the worse
for the wear, but foamed and fumed as purely,
and boomed as savagely and impressively, as
a mountain torrent, and though it came from
under a factory, we saw a rainbow here.   These
are now the Amoskeag Falls, removed a mile
down stream.   But we did not tarry to examine
them minutely, making haste to get past the
village here collected, and out of hearing of
the hammer which was laying the foundation
of another Lowell on the banks.   At the time
of our voyage Manchester was a village of about
two thousand inhabitants, where we landed for
a moment to get some cool water, and where an
inhabitant told us that he was accustomed to
go across the river into Goffstown for his water.
But now, after nine years, as I have been told
and indeed have witnessed, it contains sixteen

thousand inhabitants. From a hill on the road between Goffstown and Hooksett, four miles distant, I have since seen a thunder shower pass over, and the sun break out and shine on a city there, where I had landed nine years before in the fields to get a draught of water; and there was waving the flag of its museum, — where " the only perfect skeleton of a Greenland or river whale in the United States " was to be seen, and I also read in its directory of a " Manchester Athenæum and Gallery of the Fine Arts."

According to the gazetteer, the descent of Amoskeag Falls, which are the most considerable in the Merrimack, is fifty-four feet in half a mile. We locked ourselves through here with much ado, surmounting the successive watery steps of this river's stair-case in the midst of a crowd of villagers, jumping into the canal, to their amusement, to save our boat from upsetting, and consuming much river water in our service. Amoskeag, or Namaskeak, is said to mean " great fishing place." It was hereabouts that the Sachem Wannalancet resided. Tradition says that his tribe, when at war with the Mohawks, concealed their provisions in the cavities of the rocks in the upper part of these falls. The Indians who hid their provisions in these holes, and affirmed " that God had cut them out for that purpose," understood their origin and use better than the Royal

Society, who in their Transactions, in the last century, speaking of these very holes, declare that "they seem plainly to be artificial." Similar "pot-holes" may be seen at the Stone Flume on this river, on the Ottaway, at Bellows' Falls on the Connecticut, and in the limestone rock at Shelburne Falls on Deerfield river in Massachusetts, and more or less generally about all falls. Perhaps the most remarkable curiosity of this kind in New England is the well-known Basin on the Pemigewasset, one of the head-waters of this river, twenty by thirty feet in extent and proportionably deep, with a smooth and rounded brim, and filled with a cold, pellucid and greenish water. At Amoskeag the river is divided into many separate torrents and trickling rills by the rocks, and its volume is so much reduced by the drain of the canals that it does not fill its bed. There are many pot-holes here on a rocky island which the river washes over in high freshets. As at Shelburne Falls, where I first observed them, they are from one foot to four or five in diameter, and as many in depth, perfectly round and regular, with smooth and gracefully curved brims, like goblets. Their origin is apparent to the most careless observer. A stone which the current has washed down, meeting with obstacles, revolves as on a pivot where it lies, gradually sinking in the course of centuries deeper and deeper into the rock, and in new freshets receiving the aid of fresh stones which are drawn into this trap and doomed to revolve there for an indefinite period, doing Sisyphus-like penance for stony sins, until they either wear out, or wear through the bottom of their prison, or else are released by some revolution of nature. There lie the stones of various sizes, from a pebble to a foot or two in diameter, some of which have rested from their labor only since the spring, and some higher up which have lain still and dry for ages, — we notice some here at least sixteen feet above the present level of the water, — while others are still revolving, and enjoy no respite at any season. In one instance, at Shelburne Falls, they have worn quite through the rock, so that a portion of the river leaks through in anticipation of the fall. Some of these pot-holes at Amoskeag, in a very hard brown stone, had an oblong cylindrical stone of the same material loosely fitting them. One, as much as fifteen feet deep and seven or eight in diameter, which was worn quite through to the water, had a huge rock of the same material, smooth but of irregular form, lodged in it. Everywhere there were the rudiments or the wrecks of a dimple in the rock; the rocky shells of whirlpools. As if, by force of example and sympathy after so many lessons, the rocks, the hardest material, had been endeavoring to whirl or flow into the forms of the most fluid. The finest workers in stone are not copper or steel tools, but the gentle touches of air and water working at their leisure with a liberal allowance of time.

Not only have some of these basins been forming for countless ages, but others exist which must have been completed in a former geological period. There are some, we are told, in the town of Canaan in this State, with the stones still in them, on the height of land between the Merrimack and Connecticut, and nearly a thousand feet above these rivers, proving that the mountains and the rivers have changed places. There lie the stones which completed their revolutions perhaps before thoughts began to revolve in the brain of man. The periods of Hindoo and Chinese history, though they reach back to the time when the race of mortals is confounded with the race of gods, are as nothing compared with the periods which these stones have inscribed. That which commenced a rock when time was young, shall conclude a pebble in the unequal contest. With such expense of time and natural forces are our very paving stones produced. They teach us lessons, these dumb workers; verily there are "sermons in stones and books in the running streams." In these very holes the Indians hid their provisions; but now there is no bread, but only its old neighbor stones at the bottom. Who knows how many races they have served thus? By as simple a law, some accidental by-law, per-chance, our system itself was made ready for its inhabitants.

These, and such as these, must be our antiqui-ties, for lack of human vestiges. The monu-ments of heroes and the temples of the gods which may once have stood on the banks of this river, are now, at any rate, returned to dust and primitive soil. The murmur of unchroni-cled nations has died away along these shores, and once more Lowell and Manchester are on the trail of the Indian.

The fact that Romans once inhabited her reflects no little dignity on Nature herself; that from some particular hill the Roman once looked out on the sea. She need not be ashamed of the vestiges of her children. How gladly the antiquary informs us that their vessels penetrated into this frith, or up that river of some remote isle! Their military monuments still remain on the hills and under the sod of the valleys. The oft-repeated Roman story is writ-ten in still legible characters in every quarter of the old world, and but to-day, perchance, a new coin is dug up whose inscription repeats and confirms their fame. Some "*Judœa Capta*," with a woman mourning under a palm tree, with silent argument and demonstration con-firms the pages of history.

"Rome living was the world's sole ornament;
And dead is now the world's sole monument."

*   *   *   *   *

"With her own weight down pressed now she lies,
And by her heaps her hugeness testifies."

If one doubts whether Grecian valor and patriotism are not a fiction of the poets, he may go to Athens and see still upon the walls of the temple of Minerva the circular marks made by the shields taken from the enemy in the Persian war, which were suspended there. We have not far to seek for living and unquestionable evidence. The very dust takes shape and confirms some story which we had read. As Fuller said, commenting on the zeal of Camden, "A broken urn is a whole evidence; or an old gate still surviving out of which the city is run out." When Solon endeavored to prove that Salamis had formerly belonged to the Athenians, and not to the Megareans, he caused the tombs to be opened, and showed that the inhabitants of Salamis turned the faces of their dead to the same side with the Athenians, but the Megareans to the opposite side. There they were to be interrogated.

Some minds are as little logical or argumentative as nature; they can offer no reason or "guess," but they exhibit the solemn and incontrovertible fact. If a historical question arises, they cause the tombs to be opened. Their

silent and practical logic convinces the reason
and the understanding at the same time. Of
such sort is always the only pertinent question
and the only unanswerable reply.

Our own country furnishes antiquities as
ancient and durable, and as useful, as any;
rocks at least as well covered with moss, and a
soil which, if it is virgin, is but virgin mould,
the very dust of nature. What if we cannot
read Rome, or Greece, Etruria, or Carthage,
or Egypt, or Babylon, on these; are our cliffs
bare? The lichen on the rocks is a rude and
simple shield which beginning and imperfect
Nature suspended there. Still hangs her wrin-
kled trophy. And here too the poet's eye may
still detect the brazen nails which fastened
Time's inscriptions, and if he has the gift,
decipher them by this clue. The walls that
fence our fields, as well as modern Rome, and
not less the Parthenon itself, are all built of
ruins. Here may be heard the din of rivers, and
ancient winds which have long since lost their
names sought through our woods; — the first
faint sounds of spring, older than the summer
of Athenian glory, the titmouse lisping in the
wood, the jay's scream and blue-bird's warble,
and the hum of

> "bees that fly
> About the laughing blossoms of sallowy."

Here is the gray dawn for antiquity, and our
to-morrow's future should be at least paulo-
post to theirs which we have put behind us.
There are the red-maple and birchen leaves, old
runes which are not yet deciphered; catkins,
pine-cones, vines, oak-leaves, and acorns; the
very things themselves, and not their forms in
stone,— so much the more ancient and venerable.
And even to the current summer there has come
down tradition of a hoary-headed master of all
art, who once filled every field and grove with
statues and god-like architecture, of every
design which Greece has lately copied; whose
ruins are now mingled with the dust, and not
one block remains upon another.   The century
sun and unwearied rain have wasted them, till
not one fragment from that quarry now exists;
and poets perchance will feign that gods sent
down the material from heaven.

What though the traveller tell us of the ruins
of Egypt, are we so sick or idle, that we must
sacrifice our America and to-day to some man's
ill-remembered and indolent story?   Carnac and
Luxor are but names, or if their skeletons remain, still more desert sand, and at length a
wave of the Mediterranean sea, are needed to
wash away the filth that attaches to their
grandeur. Carnac! Carnac! here is Carnac
for me. I behold the columns of a larger and
purer temple.

This is my Carnac, whose unmeasured dome
Shelters the measuring art and measurer's home.
Behold these flowers, let us be up with time,
Not dreaming of three thousand years ago,
Erect ourselves and let those columns lie,
Not stoop to raise a foil against the sky.
Where is the spirit of that time but in
This present day, perchance this present line?
Three thousand years ago are not agone,
They are still lingering in this summer morn,
And Memnon's Mother sprightly greets us now,
Wearing her youthful radiance on her brow.
If Carnac's columns still stand on the plain,
To enjoy our opportunities they remain.

In these parts dwelt the famous Sachem
Passaconaway, who was seen by Gookin "at
Pawtucket, when he was about one hundred and
twenty years old." He was reputed a wise
man and a powwow, and restrained his people
from going to war with the English. They believed "that he could make water burn, rocks
move, and trees dance, and metamorphose himself into a flaming man; that in winter he could
raise a green leaf out of the ashes of a dry one,
and produced a living snake from the skin of
a dead one." In 1660, according to Gookin,
at a great feast and dance, he made his farewell
speech to his people, in which he said, that as
he was not likely to see them met together again,
he would leave them this word of advice, to
take heed how they quarrelled with their English neighbors, for though they might do them

much mischief at first, it would prove the means
of their own destruction. He himself, he said,
had been as much an enemy to the English at
their first coming as any, and had used all his
arts to destroy them, or at least to prevent their
settlement, but could by no means effect it.
Gookin thought that he "possibly might have
such a kind of spirit upon him as was upon Ballam
who in xxiii. Numbers, 23, said 'Surely there
is no enchantment against Jacob, neither is
there any divination against Israel.'" His son
Wannalancet carefully followed his advice, and
when Philip's war broke out, he withdrew his
followers to Penacook, now Concord in New
Hampshire, from the scene of the war. On his
return afterwards he visited the minister of
Chelmsford, and, as is stated in the history
of that town, "wished to know whether Chelmsford had suffered much during the war; and being informed that it had not, and that God
should be thanked for it, Wannalancet replied,
'Me next.'"

Manchester was the residence of John Stark,
a hero of two wars, and survivor of a third, and
at his death the last but one of the American
generals of the Revolution. He was born in
the adjoining town of Londonderry, then Nur-
field, in 1728. As early as 1752, he was taken
prisoner by the Indians while hunting in the
wilderness near Baker's river; he performed

The Stark monument in Manchester

notable service as a captain of rangers in the
French war; commanded a regiment of the New
Hampshire militia at the battle of Bunker Hill;
and fought and won the battle of Bennington
in 1777.   He was past service in the last war,
and died here in 1822, at the age of 94.   His
monument stands upon the second bank of the
river, about a mile and a half above the falls,
and commands a prospect several miles up and
down the Merrimack.   It suggested how much
more impressive in the landscape is the tomb
of a hero than the dwellings of the inglorious
living.   Who is most dead, — a hero by whose
monument you stand, or his descendants of
whom you have never heard?

The graves of Passaconaway and Wannalancet are marked by no monument on the bank
of their native river.

Every town which we passed, if we may believe the gazetteer, had been the residence of
some great man.   But though we knocked at
many doors, and even made particular inquiries, we could not find that there were any now
living.   Under the head of Litchfield we read, —

"The Hon. Wyseman Clagett closed his life
in this town."   According to another, "He
was a classical scholar, a good lawyer, a wit, and
a poet."   We saw his old gray house just below Great Nesenkeag Brook. — Under the head

318 A WEEK ON THE CONCORD

of Merrimac, — " Hon. Matthew Thornton, one
of the signers of the Declaration of American
Independence, resided many years in this town."
His house too we saw from the river. — " Dr.
Jonathan Gove, a man distinguished for his
urbanity, his talents and professional skill,
resided in this town [Goffstown.] He was one
of the oldest practitioners of medicine in the
county. He was many years an active member
of the legislature." — " Hon. Robert Means, who
died Jan. 24, 1823, at the age of 80, was for a
long period a resident in Amherst. He was a
native of Ireland. In 1764 he came to this
country, where by his industry and application
to business, he acquired a large property, and
great respect." — " William Stinson, [one of the
first settlers of Dunbarton,] born in Ireland,
came to Londonderry with his father. He
was much respected and was a useful man.
James Rogers was from Ireland, and father to
Major Robert Rogers. He was shot in the woods,
being mistaken for a bear." — "Rev. Matthew
Clark, second minister of Londonderry, was a
native of Ireland, who had in early life been an
officer in the army, and distinguished himself
in the defence of the city of Londonderry, when
beseiged by the army of King James II., A.D.
1688-9. He afterwards relinquished a military
life for the clerical profession. He possessed a
strong mind, marked by a considerable degree

of eccentricity. He died Jan. 25, 1735, and was borne to the grave, at his particular request, by his former companions in arms, of whom there were a considerable number among the early settlers of this town; several of whom had been made free from taxes throughout the British dominions by King William, for their bravery in that memorable seige." — Col. George Reid and Capt. David M'Clary, also citizens of Londonderry, were " distinguished and brave" officers. — "Major Andrew M'Clary, a native of this town [Epsom], fell at the battle of Breed's Hill." — Many of these heroes, like the illustrious Roman, were plowing when the news of the massacre at Lexington arrived, and straightway left their plows in the furrow, and repaired to the scene of action. Some miles from where we now were, there once stood a guide-board which said, "3 miles to Squire MacGaw's." —

But generally speaking, the land is now, at any rate, very barren of men, and we doubt if there are as many hundreds as we read of. It may be that we stood too near.

Uncannunuc Mountain in Goffstown was visible from Amoskeag, five or six miles westward. Its name is said to mean "The Two Breasts," there being two eminences some distance apart. The highest, which is about fourteen hundred feet above the sea, probably affords a more extensive view of the Merrimack valley and the adjacent country than any other hill, though it is somewhat obstructed by woods. Only a few short reaches of the river are visible, but you can trace its course far down stream by the sandy tracts on its banks.

A little south of Uncannunuc, about sixty years ago, as the story goes, an old woman who went out to gather pennyroyal, tript her foot in the bail of a small brass kettle in the dead grass and bushes. Some say that flints and charcoal and some traces of a camp were also found. This kettle, holding about four quarts, is still preserved and used to dye thread in. It is supposed to have belonged to some old French or Indian hunter, who was killed in one of his hunting or scouting excursions, and so never returned to look after his kettle.

But we were most interested to hear of the pennyroyal, it is so soothing to be reminded that wild nature produces anything ready for the use of man. Men know that *something* is good. One says that it is yellow-dock, another that it is bitter-sweet, another that it is slippery-elm bark, burdock, catnip, calamint, elicampane, thoroughwort, or pennyroyal. A man may esteem himself happy when that which is his food is also his medicine. There is no kind of herb that grows, but somebody or other says that it is good. I am very glad to hear it. It reminds me of the first chapter of Genesis. But how should they know that it is good? That is the mystery to me. I am always agreeably disappointed; it is incredible that they should have found it out. Since all things are good, men fail at last to distinguish which is the bane, and which the antidote. There are sure to be two prescriptions diametrically opposite. Stuff a cold and starve a cold are but two ways. They are the two practices both always in full blast. Yet you must take advice of the one school as if there was no other. In respect to religion and the healing art, all nations are still in a state of barbarism. In the most civilized countries the priest is still but a Powwow, and the physician a Great Medicine. Consider the deference which is everywhere paid to a doctor's opinion. Nothing more strikingly betrays the credulity of mankind than medicine. Quackery is a thing universal, and universally successful. In this case it becomes literally true that no imposition is too great for the credulity of men. Priests and physicians should never look one another in the face. They have no common ground, nor is there any to mediate between them. When the one comes, the other goes. They could not come together without laughter, or a significant silence, for the one's profession is a satire on the other's, and either's success would be the other's failure.

It is wonderful that the physician should ever die, and that the priest should ever live. Why is it that the priest is never called to consult with the physician? It is because men believe practically that matter is independent of spirit. But what is quackery? It is commonly an attempt to cure the diseases of a man by addressing his body alone. There is need of a physician who shall minister to both soul and body at once, that is, to man. Now he falls between two stools.

After passing through the locks, we had poled ourselves through the canal here, about half a mile in length, to the boatable part of the river. Above Amoskeag the river spreads out into a lake reaching a mile or two without a bend. There were many canal boats here bound up to Hooksett, about eight miles, and as they were going up empty with a fair wind, one boatman offered to take us in tow if we would wait. But when we came alongside, we found that they meant to take us on board, since otherwise we should clog their motions too much; but as our boat was too heavy to be lifted aboard, we pursued our way up the stream, as before, while the boatmen were at their dinner, and came to anchor at length under some alders on the opposite shore, where we could take our lunch. Though far on one side, every sound was wafted over to us from the opposite bank,

Lake-like expanse north of Amoskeag

and from the harbor of the canal, and we could see everything that passed. By and by came several canal boats, at intervals of a quarter of a mile, standing up to Hooksett with a light breeze, and one by one disappeared round a point above. With their broad sails set, they moved slowly up the stream in the sluggish and fitful breeze, like one-winged antediluvian birds, and as if impelled by some mysterious counter current. It was a grand motion, so slow and stately, this "standing out," as the phrase is, expressing the gradual and steady progress of a vessel, as if it were by mere rectitude and disposition, without shuffling. Their sails, which stood so still, were like chips cast into the current of the air to show which way it set. At length the boat which we had spoken came along, keeping the middle of the stream, and when within speaking distance the steersmen called out ironically to say, that if we would come alongside now he would take us in tow; but not heeding his taunt, we still loitered in the shade till we had finished our lunch, and when the last boat had disappeared round the point with flapping sail, for the breeze had now sunk to a zephyr, with our own sails set, and plying our oars, we shot rapidly up the stream in pursuit, and as we glided close alongside, while they were vainly invoking Æolus to their aid, we returned their compliment by proposing, if they would throw us a rope, to "take them in tow," to which these Merrimack sailors had no suitable answer ready. Thus we gradually overtook each boat in succession until we had the river to ourselves again.

Our course this afternoon was between Manchester and Goffstown.

While we float here, far from that tributary stream on whose banks our friends and kindred dwell, our thoughts, like the stars, come out of their horizon still; for there circulates a finer blood than Lavoisier has discovered the laws of, — the blood, not of kindred merely, but of kindness, whose pulse still beats at any distance and forever. After years of vain familiarity, some distant gesture or unconscious behavior, which we remember, speaks to us with more emphasis than the wisest or kindest words. We are sometimes made aware of a kindness long passed, and realize that there have been times when our friends' thoughts of us were of so pure and lofty a character that they passed over us like the winds of heaven unnoticed; when they treated us not as what we were, but as what we aspired to be. There has just reached us, it may be, the nobleness of some such silent behavior, not to be forgotten, not to be remembered, and we shudder to think how it fell on us cold, though in some true but tardy hour we endeavor to wipe off these scores.

In my experience, persons, when they are made the subject of conversation, though with a friend, are commonly the most prosaic and trivial of facts. The universe seems bankrupt as soon as we begin to discuss the character of individuals. Our discourse all runs to slander, and our limits grow narrower as we advance. How is it that we are impelled to treat our old friends so ill when we obtain new ones? The housekeeper says, I never had any new crockery in my life but I began to break the old. I say, let us speak of mushrooms and forest trees rather. Yet we can sometimes afford to remember them in private. —

Lately, alas, I knew a gentle boy,
  Whose features all were cast in Virtues' mould,
As one she had designed for Beauty's toy,
  But after manned him for her own stronghold.

On every side he open was as day,
  That you might see no lack of strength within,
For walls and ports do only serve alway
  For a pretence to feebleness and sin.

Say not that Cæsar was victorious,
  With toil and strife who stormed the House of Fame,
In other sense this youth was glorious,
  Himself a kingdom wheresoe'er he came.

No strength went out to get him victory,
  When all was income of its own accord;
For where he went none other was to see,
  But all were parcel of their noble lord.

He forayed like the subtil haze of summer,
  That stilly shows fresh landscapes to our eyes,
And revolutions works without a murmur,
  Or rustling of a leaf beneath the skies.

So was I taken unawares by this,
  I quite forgot my homage to confess;
Yet now am forced to know, though hard it is,
  I might have loved him had I loved him less.

Each moment as we nearer drew to each,
  A stern respect withheld us further yet,
So that we seemed beyond each other's reach,
  And less acquainted than when first we met.

We two were one while we did sympathize,
  So could we not the simplest bargain drive;
And what avails it now that we are wise,
  If absence doth this doubleness contrive?

Eternity may not the chance repeat,
  But I must tread my single way alone,
In sad remembrance that we once did meet,
  And know that bliss irrevocably gone.

The spheres henceforth my elegy shall sing,
  For elegy has other subject none;
Each strain of music in my ears shall ring
  Knell of departure from that other one.

Make haste and celebrate my tragedy;
  With fitting strain resound ye woods and fields;
Sorrow is dearer in such case to me
  Than all the joys other occasion yields.

Is't then too late the damage to repair?
  Distance, forsooth, from my weak grasp hath reft
The empty husk, and clutched the useless tare,
  But in my hands the wheat and kernel left.

If I but love that virtue which he is,
  Though it be scented in the morning air,
Still shall we be truest acquaintances,
  Nor mortals know a sympathy more rare.

Friendship is evanescent in every man's experience, and remembered like heat lightning in past summers. Fair and flitting like a summer cloud; — there is always some vapor in the air, no matter how long the drought; there are even April showers. Surely from time to time, for its vestiges never depart, it floats through our atmosphere. It takes place, like vegetation in so many materials, because there is such a law, but always without permanent form, though ancient and familiar as the sun and moon, and as sure to come again. The heart is forever inexperienced. They silently gather as by magic, these never failing, never quite deceiving visions, like the bright and fleecy clouds in the calmest and clearest days. The Friend is some fair floating isle of palms eluding the mariner in Pacific seas. Many are the dangers to be encountered, equinoctial gales and coral reefs, ere he may sail before the constant trades. But who would not sail through mutiny and storm even over Atlantic waves, to reach the fabulous retreating shores of some continent man? The imagination still clings to the faintest tradition of

THE ATLANTIDES

The smothered streams of love, which flow
More bright than Phlegethon, more low,
Island us ever, like the sea,
In an Atlantic mystery.
Our fabled shores none ever reach,
No mariner has found our beach,
Only our mirage now is seen,
And neighboring waves with floating green,
Yet still the oldest charts contain
Some dotted outline of our main;
In ancient times midsummer days
Unto the western islands' gaze,
To Teneriffe and the Azores,
Have shown our faint and cloud-like shores.

But sink not yet, ye desolate isles,
Anon your coast with commerce smiles,
And richer freights ye'll furnish far
Than Africa or Malabar.
Be fair, be fertile evermore,
Ye rumored but untrodden shore,
Princes and monarchs will contend
Who first unto your land shall send,
And pawn the jewels of the crown
To call your distant soil their own.

Columbus has sailed westward of these isles
by the mariner's compass, but neither he nor
his successors have found them. We are no
nearer than Plato was. The earnest seeker
and hopeful discoverer of this New World always
haunts the outskirts of his time, and walks
through the densest crowd uninterrupted, and
as it were in a straight line. —

Sea and land are but his neighbors,
And companions in his labors,
Who on the ocean's verge and firm land's end
Doth long and truly seek his Friend.
Many men dwell far inland,
But he alone sits on the strand.
Whether he ponders men or books,
Always still he seaward looks,
Marine news he ever reads,
And the slightest glances heeds,
Feels the sea breeze on his cheek
At each word the landsmen speak,
In every companion's eye
A sailing vessel doth descry;
In the ocean's sullen roar
From some distant port he hears,
Of wrecks upon a distant shore,
And the ventures of past years.

Who does not walk on the plain as amid the columns of Tadmore of the desert? There is on the earth no institution which Friendship has established; it is not taught by any religion; no scripture contains its maxims. It has no temple, nor even a solitary column. There goes a rumor that the earth is inhabited, but the shipwrecked mariner has not seen a footprint on the shore. The hunter has found only fragments of pottery and the monuments of inhabitants.

However, our fates at least are social. Our courses do not diverge; but as the web of destiny is woven it is fulled, and we are cast more and more into the centre. Men naturally,

though feebly, seek this alliance, and their
actions faintly foretell it. We are inclined to
lay the chief stress on likeness and not on difference, and in foreign bodies we admit that
there are many degrees of warmth below blood
heat, but none of cold above it.

One or two persons come to my house from
time to time, there being proposed to them the
faint possibility of intercourse. They are as
full as they are silent, and wait for my plectrum
to stir the strings of their lyre. If they could
ever come to the length of a sentence, or hear
one, on that ground they are dreaming of! They
speak faintly, and do not obtrude themselves.
They have heard some news, which none, not
even they themselves, can impart. It is a
wealth they bear about them which can be ex-
pended in various ways. What came they out
to seek?

No word is oftener on the lips of men than
Friendship, and indeed no thought is more
familiar to their aspirations. All men are dreaming of it, and its drama, which is always a tragedy,
is enacted daily. It is the secret of the universe.
You may tread the town, you may wander the
country, and none shall ever speak of it, yet
thought is everywhere busy about it, and the
idea of what is possible in this respect affects
our behavior toward all new men and women,

and a great many old ones. Nevertheless, I can remember only two or three essays on this subject in all literature. No wonder that the Mythology, and Arabian Nights, and Shakespeare, and Scott's novels entertain us, — we are poets and fablers and dramatists and novelists ourselves. We are continually acting a part in a more interesting drama than any written. We are dreaming that our Friends are our *Friends*, and that we are our Friends' *Friends*. Our actual Friends are but distant relations of those to whom we are pledged. We never exchange more than three words with a Friend in our lives on that level to which our thoughts and feelings almost habitually rise. One goes forth prepared to say "Sweet Friends!" and the salutation is "Damn your eyes!" But never mind; faint heart never won true Friend. O my Friend, may it come to pass, once, that when you are my Friend I may be yours.

Of what use the friendliest disposition even, if there are no hours given to Friendship, if it is forever postponed to unimportant duties and relations? Friendship is first, Friendship last. But it is equally impossible to forget our Friends, and to make them answer to our ideal. When they say farewell, then indeed we begin to keep them company. How often we find ourselves turning our backs on our actual Friends, that we may go and meet their ideal cousins. I would that I were worthy to be any man's Friend.

What is commonly honored with the name of Friendship is no very profound or powerful instinct. Men do not, after all, *love* their Friends greatly. I do not often see the farmers made seers and wise to the verge of insanity by their Friendship for one another. They are not often transfigured and translated by love in each other's presence. I do not observe them purified, refined, and elevated by the love of a man. If one abates a little the price of his wood, or gives a neighbor his vote at town-meeting, or a barrel of apples, or lends him his wagon frequently, it is esteemed a rare instance of Friendship. Nor do the farmers' wives lead lives consecrated to Friendship. I do not see the pair of farmer friends of either sex pre-pared to stand against the world. There are only two or three couples in history. To say that a man is your Friend, means commonly no more than this, that he is not your enemy. Most contemplate only what would be the accidental and trifling advantages of Friendship, as that the Friend can assist in time of need, by his substance, or his influence, or his counsel; but he who foresees such advantages in this relation proves himself blind to its real advantage, or indeed wholly inexperienced in the relation it-self. Such services are particular and menial,

compared with the perpetual and all-embracing
service which it is.   Even the utmost good-will
and harmony and practical kindness are not
sufficient for Friendship, for Friends do not live
in harmony merely, as some say, but in melody.
We do not wish for Friends to feed and clothe
our bodies,—neighbors are kind enough for that,
— but to do the like office to our spirits.   For
this few are rich enough, however well disposed
they may be.

Think of the importance of Friendship in the
education of men.   It will make a man honest;
it will make him a hero; it will make him a
saint.   It is the state of the just dealing with the
just, the magnanimous with the magnanimous,
the sincere with the sincere, man with man. —

> "Why love among the virtues is not known,
> Is that love is them all contract in one."

All the abuses which are the object of reform
with the philanthropist, the statesman, and the
housekeeper, are unconsciously amended in the
intercourse of Friends.   A Friend is one who
incessantly pays us the compliment of expecting
from us all the virtues, and who can appreciate
them in us.   It takes two to speak the truth, —
one to speak, and another to hear.   How can
one treat with magnanimity mere wood and
stone?   If we dealt only with the false and dishonest, we should at last forget how to speak

truth. In our daily intercourse with men, our nobler faculties are dormant and suffered to rust. None will pay us the compliment to expect nobleness from us. We ask our neighbor to suffer himself to be dealt with truly, sincerely, nobly; but he answers no by his deafness. He does not even hear this prayer. He says practically, — I will be content if you treat me as no better than I should be, as deceitful, mean, dishonest, and selfish. For the most part, we are contented so to deal and to be dealt with, and we do not think that for the mass of men there is any truer and nobler relation possible. A man may have *good* neighbors, so called, and acquaintances, and even companions, wife, parents, brothers, sisters, children, who meet himself and one another on this ground only. The State does not demand justice of its members, but thinks that it succeeds very well with the least degree of it, hardly more than rogues practice; and so do the family and the neighborhood. What is commonly called Friendship even is only a little more honor among rogues.

But sometimes we are said to *love* another, that is to stand in a true relation to him, so that we give the best to, and receive the best from, him. Between whom there is hearty truth there is love; and in proportion to our truthfulness and confidence in one another, our lives are divine and miraculous, and answer to our ideal. There are passages of affection in our intercourse with mortal men and women, such as no prophecy had taught us to expect, which transcend our earthly life, and anticipate heaven for us. What is this Love that may come right into the middle of a prosaic Goffstown day, equal to any of the gods? that discovers a new world, fair and fresh and eternal, occupying the place of this old one, when to the common eye a dust has settled on the universe? which world cannot else be reached, and does not exist. What other words, we may almost ask, are memorable and worthy to be repeated than those which love has inspired? It is wonderful that they were ever uttered. They are few and rare, indeed, but, like a strain of music, they are incessantly repeated and modulated by the memory. All other words crumble off with the stucco which overlies the heart. We should not dare to repeat them now aloud. We are not competent to hear them at all times.

The books for young people say a great deal about the *selection* of Friends; it is because they really have nothing to say about *Friends*. They mean associates and confidants merely. "Know that the contrariety of foe and Friend proceeds from God." Friendship takes place between those who have an affinity for one another, and is a perfectly natural and inevitable result. No professions nor advances will avail. Even

speech, at first, necessarily has nothing to do
with it; but it follows after silence, as the buds
in the graft do not put forth into leaves till
long after the graft has taken. It is a drama
in which the parties have no part to act. We
are all Mussulmans and fatalists in this respect.
Impatient and uncertain lovers think that they
must say or do something kind whenever they
meet; they must never be cold. But they who
are Friends do not do what they *think* they
must, but what they *must*. Even their Friendship is in one sense but a sublime phenomenon
to them.

The true and not despairing Friend will
address his Friend in some such terms as these.

"I never asked thy leave to let me love thee, —
I have a right. I love thee not as something
private and personal, which is *your own*, but
as something universal and worthy of love,
which I have found. O how I think of you!
You are purely good, — you are infinitely good.
I can trust you forever. I did not think that
humanity was so rich. Give me an opportunity
to live."

"You are the fact in a fiction, — you are the
truth more strange and admirable than fiction.
Consent only to be what you are. I alone will
never stand in your way."

"This is what I would like, — to be as intimate

with you as our spirits are intimate, — respecting
you as I respect my ideal. Never to profane
one another by word or action, even by a thought.
Between us, if necessary, let there be no acquaintance."

"I have discovered you; how can you be
concealed from me?"

The Friend asks no return but that his Friend
will religiously accept and wear and not dis-
grace his apotheosis of him. They cherish each
other's hopes. They are kind to each other's
dreams.

Though the poet says, "'T is the preëmi-
nence of Friendship to impute excellence," yet
we can never praise our Friend, nor esteem him
praiseworthy, nor let him think that he can
please us by any *behavior*, or ever *treat* us well
enough. That kindness which has so good a
reputation elsewhere can least of all consist
with this relation, and no such affront can be
offered to a Friend, as a conscious good-will,
a friendliness which is not a necessity of the
Friend's nature.

The sexes are naturally most strongly attracted
to one another, by constant constitutional differences, and are most commonly and surely the
complements of one another. How natural
and easy it is for man to secure the attention
of woman to what interests himself. Men and

women of equal culture, thrown together, are sure to be of a certain value to one another, more than men to men. There exists already a natural disinterestedness and liberality in such society, and I think that any man will more confidently carry his favorite books to read to some circle of intelligent women, than to one of his own sex. The visit of man to man is wont to be an interruption, but the sexes naturally expect one another. Yet Friendship is no respecter of sex; and perhaps it is more rare between the sexes, than between two of the same sex.

Friendship is, at any rate, a relation of perfect equality. It cannot well spare any outward sign of equal obligation and advantage. The nobleman can never have a Friend among his retainers, nor the king among his subjects. Not that the parties to it are in all respects equal, but they are equal in all that respects or affects their Friendship. The one's love is exactly balanced and represented by the other's. Persons are only the vessels which contain the nectar, and the hydrostatic paradox is the symbol of love's law. It finds its level and rises to its fountain-head in all breasts, and its slenderest column balances the ocean. —

> Love equals swift and slow,
>   And high and low,
> Racer and lame,
>   The hunter and his game.

The one sex is not, in this respect, more tender than the other. A hero's love is as delicate as a maiden's.

Confucius said, "Never contract Friendship with a man that is not better than thyself." It is the merit and preservation of Friendship, that it takes place on a level higher than the actual characters of the parties would seem to warrant. The rays of light come to us in such a curve that every man whom we meet appears to be taller than he actually is. Such foundation has civility. My Friend is that one whom I can associate with my choicest thought. I always assign to him a nobler employment in my absence than I ever find him engaged in; and I imagine that the hours which he devotes to me were snatched from a higher society. The sorest insult which I ever received from a Friend was, when he behaved with the license which only long and cheap acquaintance allows to one's faults, in my presence, without shame, and still addressed me in friendly accents. Beware, lest thy Friend learn at last to tolerate one frailty of thine, and so an obstacle be raised to the progress of thy love.

Friendship is never established as an understood relation. Do you demand that I be less your Friend that you may know it? Yet what right have I to think that another cherishes so rare a sentiment for me? It is a miracle which

requires constant proofs. It is an exercise of
the purest imagination and the rarest faith.
It says by a silent but eloquent behavior, — " I
will be so related to thee as thou canst imagine;
even so thou mayest believe. I will spend truth,
— all my wealth on thee," — and the Friend
responds silently through his nature and life,
and treats his Friend with the same divine
courtesy. He knows us literally through thick
and thin. He never asks for a sign of love, but
can distinguish it by the features which it naturally wears. We never need to stand upon
ceremony with him with regard to his visits.
Wait not till I invite thee, but observe that I
am glad to see thee when thou comest. It
would be paying too dear for thy visit to ask
for it. Where my Friend lives there are all
riches and every attraction, and no slight
obstacle can keep me from him. Let me
never have to tell thee what I have not to tell.
Let our intercourse be wholly above ourselves,
and draw us up to it. The language of
Friendship is not words but meanings. It is
an intelligence above language. One imagines
endless conversations with his Friend, in which
the tongue shall be loosed, and thoughts be
spoken without hesitancy, or end; but the experience is commonly far otherwise. Acquaintances
may come and go, and have a word ready for
every occasion; but what puny word shall he

utter whose very breath is thought and meaning? Suppose you go to bid farewell to your Friend who is setting out on a journey; what other outward sign do you know of than to shake his hand? Have you any palaver ready for him then? any box of salve to commit to his pocket? any particular message to send by him? any statement which you had forgotten to make? — as if you could forget anything. — No, it is much that you take his hand and say Farewell; that you could easily omit; so far custom has prevailed. It is even painful, if he is to go, that he should linger so long. If he must go, let him go quickly. Have you any *last* words? Alas, it is only the word of words, which you have so long sought and found not; *you* have not a *first* word yet. There are few even whom I should venture to call earnestly by their most proper names. A name pronounced is the recognition of the individual to whom it belongs. He who can pronounce my name aright, he can call me, and is entitled to my love and service.

The violence of love is as much to be dreaded as that of hate. When it is durable it is serene and equable. Even its famous pains begin only with the ebb of love, for few are indeed lovers, though all would fain be. It is one proof of a man's fitness for Friendship that he is able to do without that which is cheap and passionate. A true Friendship is as wise as it is tender. The

parties to it yield implicitly to the guidance of
their love, and know no other law nor kindness.
It is not extravagant and insane, but what it
says is something established henceforth, and
will bear to be stereotyped. It is a truer truth,
it is better and fairer news, and no time will
ever shame it, or prove it false. This is a plant
which thrives best in a temperate zone, where
summer and winter alternate with one another.
The Friend is a *necessarius*, and meets his
Friend on homely ground; not on carpets and
cushions, but on the ground and on rocks they
will sit, obeying the natural and primitive laws.
They will meet without any outcry, and part
without loud sorrow. Their relation implies
such qualities as the warrior prizes; for it takes
a valor to open the hearts of men as well as the
gates of cities.

The Friendship which Wawatam testified
for Henry the fur-trader, as described in the
latter's "Adventures," so almost bare and
leafless, yet not blossomless nor fruitless, is
remembered with satisfaction and security. The
stern imperturbable warrior, after fasting, solitude, and mortification of body, comes to the
white man's lodge, and affirms that he is the
white brother whom he saw in his dream, and
adopts him henceforth. He buries the hatchet
as it regards his friend, and they hunt and feast
and make maple-sugar together. "Metals unite

from fluxility; birds and beasts from motives of convenience; fools from fear and stupidity; and just men at sight." If Wawatam would taste the "white man's milk" with his tribe, or take his bowl of human broth made of the trader's fellow-countrymen, he first finds a place of safety for his Friend, whom he has rescued from a similar fate. At length, after a long winter of undisturbed and happy intercourse in the family of the chieftain in the wilderness, hunting and fishing, they return in the spring to Michilimackinac to dispose of their furs; and it becomes necessary for Wawatam to take leave of his Friend at the Isle aux Outardes, when the latter, to avoid his enemies, proceeded to the Sault de Sainte Marie, supposing that they were to be separated for a short time only. "We now exchanged farewells," says Henry, "with an emotion entirely reciprocal. I did not quit the lodge without the most grateful sense of the many acts of goodness which I had experienced in it, nor without the sincerest re- spect for the virtues which I had witnessed among its members. All the family accompanied me to the beach; and the canoe had no sooner put off than Wawatam commenced an address to the Kichi Manito, beseeching him to take care of me, his brother, till we should next meet. — We had proceeded to too great a distance to allow of our hearing his voice, before Wawatam

had ceased to offer up his prayers." We
never hear of him again.

Friendship is not so kind as is imagined; it
has not much human blood in it, but consists
with a certain disregard for men and their
erections, the Christian duties and humanities,
while it purifies the air like electricity. There
may be the sternest tragedy in the relation of
two more than usually innocent and true to their
highest instincts. We may call it an essentially
heathenish intercourse, free and irresponsible
in its nature, and practising all the virtues gra-
tuitously. It is not the highest sympathy merely,
but a pure and lofty society, a fragmentary and
godlike intercourse of ancient date, still kept up
at intervals, which, remembering itself, does not
hesitate to disregard the humbler rights and
duties of humanity. It requires immaculate
and godlike qualities full-grown, and exists at
all only by condescension and anticipation of
the remotest future. We love nothing which is
merely good and not fair, if such a thing is
possible. Nature puts some kind of blossom
before every fruit, not simply a calyx behind it.
When the Friend comes out of his heathenism
and superstition, and breaks his idols, being
converted by the precepts of a newer testament;
when he forgets his mythology, and treats his
Friend like a Christian, or as he can afford; then
Friendship ceases to be Friendship, and becomes

charity; that principle which established the
almshouse is now beginning with its charity at
home, and establishing an almshouse and pauper
relations there.

As for the number which this society admits,
it is at any rate to be begun with one, the noblest
and greatest that we know, and whether the
world will ever carry it further, whether, as
Chaucer affirms,

"There be mo sterres in the skie than a pair,"

remains to be proved; —

"And certaine he is well begone
Among a thousand that findeth one."

We shall not surrender ourselves heartily to any
while we are conscious that another is more
deserving of our love. Yet Friendship does not
stand for numbers; the Friend does not count
his Friends on his fingers; they are not numer-
able. The more there are included by this
bond, if they are indeed included, the rarer
and diviner the quality of the love that binds
them. I am ready to believe that as private
and intimate a relation may exist by which
three are embraced, as between two. Indeed
we cannot have too many friends; the virtue
which we appreciate we to some extent appropriate, so that thus we are made at last more

fit for every relation of life. A base Friendship is of a narrowing and exclusive tendency, but a noble one is not exclusive; its very superfluity and dispersed love is the humanity which sweetens society, and sympathizes with foreign nations; for though its foundations are private, it is in effect, a public affair and a public advantage, and the Friend, more than the father of a family, deserves well of the state.

The only danger in Friendship is that it will end. It is a delicate plant though a native. The least unworthiness, even if it be unknown to one's self, vitiates it. Let the Friend know that those faults which he observes in his Friend his own faults attract. There is no rule more invariable than that we are paid for our suspicions by finding what we suspected. By our narrowness and prejudices we say, I will have so much and such of you, my Friend, no more. Perhaps there are none charitable, none disinterested, none wise, noble, and heroic enough, for a true and lasting Friendship.

I sometimes hear my Friends complain finely that I do not appreciate their fineness. I shall not tell them whether I do or not. As if they expected a vote of thanks for every fine thing which they uttered or did. Who knows but it was finely appreciated. It may be that your silence was the finest thing of the two. There

By the waterside

are some things which a man never speaks of, which are much finer kept silent about. To the highest communications we only lend a silent ear. Our finest relations are not simply kept silent about, but buried under a positive depth of silence, never to be revealed. It may be that we are not even yet acquainted. In human intercourse the tragedy begins, not when there is misunderstanding about words, but when silence is not understood. Then there can never be an explanation. What avails it that another loves you, if he does not understand you? Such love is a curse. What sort of companions are they who are presuming always that their silence is more expressive than yours? How foolish, and inconsiderate, and unjust, to conduct as if you were the only party aggrieved! Has not your Friend always equal ground of complaint? No doubt my Friends sometimes speak to me in vain, but they do not know what things I hear which they are not aware that they have spoken. I know that I have frequently disappointed them by not giving them words when they expected them, or such as they expected. Whenever I see my Friend I speak to him, but the expector, the man with the ears, is not he. They will complain too that you are hard. O ye that would have the cocoanut wrong side outwards, when next I weep I will let you know. They ask for words and deeds, when a true relation is word and deed. If they know not of these things, how can they be informed? We often forbear to confess our feelings, not from pride, but for fear that we could not continue to love the one who required us to give such proof of our affection.

I know a woman who possesses a restless and intelligent mind, interested in her own culture, and earnest to enjoy the highest possible advantages, and I meet her with pleasure as a natural person who not a little provokes me, and I suppose is stimulated in turn by myself. Yet our acquaintance plainly does not attain to that degree of confidence and sentiment which women, which all, in fact, covet. I am glad to help her, as I am helped by her; I like very well to know her with a sort of stranger's privilege, and hesitate to visit her often, like her other Friends. My nature pauses here, I do not well know why. Perhaps she does not make the highest demand on me, a religious demand. Some, with whose prejudices or peculiar bias I have no sympathy, yet inspire me with confidence, and I trust that they confide in me also as a religious heathen at least, — a good Greek. I too have principles as well founded as their own. If this person could conceive that, without wilfulness, I associate with her as far as our destinies are coincident, as far as our Good Geniuses permit, and still value such intercourse, it would be a grateful assurance to me. I feel as if I appeared careless, indifferent, and without principle to her, not expecting more, and yet not content with less. If she could know that I make an infinite demand on myself, as well as on all others, she would see that this true though incomplete intercourse, is infinitely better than a more unreserved but falsely grounded one, without the principle of growth in it. For a companion, I require one who will make an equal demand on me with my own genius. Such a one will always be rightly tolerant. It is suicide and corrupts good manners to welcome any less than this. I value and trust those who love and praise my aspiration rather than my performance. If you would not stop to look at me, but look whither I am looking and further, then my education could not dispense with your company.

My love must be as free
  As is the eagle's wing,
Hovering o'er land and sea
  And everything.

I must not dim my eye
  In thy saloon,
I must not leave my sky
  And nightly moon.

Be not the fowler's net
  Which stays my flight,
And craftily is set
  T' allure the sight.

But be the favoring gale
   That bears me on.
And still doth fill my sail
   When thou art gone.

I cannot leave my sky
   For thy caprice,
True love would soar as high
   As heaven is.

The eagle would not brook
   Her mate thus won,
Who trained his eye to look
   Beneath the sun.

Nothing is so difficult as to help a Friend in matters which do not require the aid of Friendship, but only a cheap and trivial service, if your Friendship wants the basis of a thorough practical acquaintance. I stand in the friendliest relation, on social and spiritual grounds, to one who does not perceive what practical skill I have, but when he seeks my assistance in such matters, is wholly ignorant of that one whom he deals with; does not use my skill, which in such matters is much greater than his, but only my hands. I know another, who, on the contrary, is remarkable for his discrimination in this respect; who knows how to make use of the talents of others when he does not possess the same; knows when not to look after or oversee, and stops short at his man. It is a rare pleasure to serve him, which all laborers know. I am not a little pained by the other kind of treatment. It is as if, after the friendliest and most ennobling intercourse, your Friend should use you as a hammer and drive a nail with your head, all in good faith; notwithstanding that you are a tolerable carpenter, as well as his good Friend, and would use a hammer cheerfully in his service. This want of perception is a defect which all the virtues of the heart cannot supply. —

> The Good how can we trust?
> Only the Wise are just.
> The Good we use,
> The Wise we cannot choose.
> These there are none above;
> The Good they know and love,
> But are not known again
> By those of lesser ken.
> They do not charm us with their eyes,
> But they transfix with their advice;
> No partial sympathy they feel
> With private woe or private weal,
> But with the universe joy and sigh,
> Whose knowledge is their sympathy.

Confucius said, "To contract ties of Friendship with any one, is to contract Friendship with his virtue. There ought not to be any other motive in Friendship." But men wish us to contract Friendship with their vice also. I have a Friend who wishes me to see that to be right which I know to be wrong. But if Friendship is to rob me of my eyes, if it is to darken the day, I will have none of it. It should be expansive and inconceivably liberalizing in its effects. True Friendship can afford true knowledge. It does not depend on darkness and ignorance. A want of discernment cannot be an ingredient in it. If I can see my Friend's virtues more distinctly than another's, his faults too are made more conspicuous by contrast. We have not so good a right to hate any as our Friend. Faults are not the less faults because they are invariably balanced by corresponding virtues, and for a fault there is no excuse, though it may appear greater than it is in many ways. I have never known one who could bear criticism, who could not be flattered, who would not bribe his judge, or was content that the truth should be loved always better than himself.

If two travellers would go their way harmoniously together, the one must take as true and just a view of things as the other, else their path will not be strewn with roses. Yet you can travel profitably and pleasantly even with a blind man, if he practises common courtesy, and when you converse about the scenery will remember that he is blind but that you can see; and you will not forget that his sense of hearing is probably quickened by his want of sight. Otherwise you will not long keep company. A blind man, and a man in whose eyes there was no defect, were walking together, when they came to the edge of a precipice, — "Take care! my friend," said the latter, "here is a steep precipice; go no further this way." — "I know better," said the other, and stepped off.

It is impossible to say all that we think, even to our truest Friend. We may bid him farewell forever sooner than complain, for our complaint is too well grounded to be uttered. There is not so good an understanding between any two, but the exposure by the one of a serious fault will produce a misunderstanding in proportion to its heinousness. The constitutional differences which always exist, and are obstacles to a perfect Friendship, are forever a forbidden theme to the lips of Friends. They advise by their whole behavior. Nothing can reconcile them but love. They are fatally late when they undertake to explain and treat with one another like foes. Who will take an apology for a Friend? They must apologize like dew and frost, which are off again with the sun, and which all men know in their hearts to be beneficent. The necessity itself for explanation, — what explanation will atone for that? True love does not quarrel for slight reasons, such mistakes as mutual acquaintances can explain away, but alas, however slight the apparent cause, only for adequate and fatal and everlasting reasons, which can never be set aside. Its quarrel, if there is any, is ever recurring, notwithstanding

the beams of affection which invariably come
to gild its tears; as the rainbow, however beautiful and unerring a sign, does not promise fair
weather forever, but only for a season. I have
known two or three persons pretty well, and yet
I have never known advice to be of use but in
trivial and transient matters. One may know
what another does not, but the utmost kindness
cannot impart what is requisite to make the
advice useful. We must accept or refuse one
another as we are. I could tame a hyena more
easily than my Friend. He is a material which
no tool of mine will work. A naked savage will
fell an oak with a fire-brand, and wear a hatchet
out of the rock by friction, but I cannot hew
the smallest chip out of the character of my
Friend, either to beautify or deform it.

The lover learns at last that there is no person
quite transparent and trustworthy, but every
one has a devil in him that is capable of any
crime in the long run. Yet, as an oriental philosopher has said, "Although Friendship between good men is interrupted, their principles
remain unaltered. The stalk of the lotus may
be broken, and the fibres remain connected."

Ignorance and bungling with love are better
than wisdom and skill without. There may be
courtesy, there may be even temper, and wit,
and talent, and sparkling conversation, there

may be good-will even, — and yet the humanest and divinest faculties pine for exercise. Our life without love is like coke and ashes. Men may be pure as alabaster and Parian marble, elegant as a Tuscan villa, sublime as Niagara, and yet if there is no milk mingled with the wine at their entertainments, better is the hospitality of Goths and Vandals. My Friend is not of some other race or family of men, but flesh of my flesh, bone of my bone. He is my real brother. I see his nature groping yonder so like mine. We do not live far apart. Have not the fates associated us in many ways? Is it of no significance that we have so long partaken of the same loaf, drank at the same fountain, breathed the same air, summer and winter, felt the same heat and cold; that the same fruits have been pleased to refresh us both, and we have never had a thought of different fibre the one from the other!

> Nature doth have her dawn each day,
>   But mine are far between;
> Content, I cry, for sooth to say,
>   Mine brightest are I ween.
>
> For when my sun doth deign to rise,
>   Though it be her noontide,
> Her fairest field in shadow lies,
>   Nor can my light abide.
>
> Sometimes I bask me in her day,
>   Conversing with my mate,
> But if we interchange one ray,
>   Forthwith her heats abate.

Through his discourse I climb and see,
  As from some eastern hill,
A brighter morrow rise to me
  Than lieth in her skill.

As 't were two summer days in one,
  Two Sundays come together,
Our rays united make one sun,
  With fairest summer weather.

As surely as the sunset in my latest November shall translate me to the ethereal world, and remind me of the ruddy morning of youth; as surely as the last strain of music which falls on my decaying ear shall make age to be forgotten, or, in short, the manifold influences of nature survive during the term of our natural life, so surely my Friend shall forever be my Friend, and reflect a ray of God to me, and time shall foster and adorn and consecrate our Friendship, no less than the ruins of temples. As I love nature, as I love singing birds, and gleaming stubble, and flowing rivers, and morning and evening, and summer and winter, I love thee, my Friend.

But all that can be said of Friendship, is like botany to flowers. How can the understanding take account of its friendliness?

Even the death of Friends will inspire us as much as their lives. They will leave consolation to the mourners, as the rich leave money to defray the expenses of their funerals, and their

memories will be incrusted over with sublime
and pleasing thoughts, as their monuments are
overgrown with moss.

This to our cis-Alpine and cis-Alantic Friends.

Also this other word of entreaty and advice to
the large and respectable nation of Acquaintances, beyond the mountains; — Greeting.

My most serene and irresponsible neighbors,
let us see that we have the whole advantage of
each other; we will be useful, at least, if not
admirable, to one another. I know that the
mountains which separate us are high, and
covered with perpetual snow, but despair not.
Improve the serene winter weather to scale
them. If need be, soften the rocks with vinegar.
For here lie the verdant plains of Italy ready to
receive you. Nor shall I be slow on my side to
penetrate to your Provence. Strike then boldly
at head or heart or any vital part. Depend
upon it the timber is well seasoned and tough,
and will bear rough usage; and if it should
crack, there is plenty more where it came from.
I am no piece of crockery that cannot be jostled
against my neighbor without danger of being
broken by the collision, and must needs ring
false and jarringly to the end of my days, when
once I am cracked; but rather one of the old
fashioned wooden trenchers, which one while
stands at the head of the table, and at another

is a milking-stool, and at another a seat for children, and finally goes down to its grave not unadorned with honorable scars, and does not die till it is worn out. Nothing can shock a brave man but dulness. Think how many rebuffs every man has experienced in his day; perhaps has fallen into a horse-pond, eaten fresh-water clams, or worn one shirt for a week without washing. Indeed, you cannot receive a shock unless you have an electric affinity for that which shocks you. Use me, then, for I am useful in my way, and stand as one of many petitioners, from toadstool and henbane up to dahlia and violet, supplicating to be put to my use, if by any means ye may find me serviceable; whether for a medicated drink or bath, as balm and lavender; or for fragrance, as verbena and geranium; or for sight, as cactus; or for thoughts, as pansy. — These humbler, at least, if not those higher uses.

Ah my dear Strangers and Enemies, I would not forget you. I can well afford to welcome you. Let me subscribe myself Yours ever and truly — your much obliged servant. We have nothing to fear from our foes; God keeps a standing army for that service; but we have no ally against our Friends, those ruthless Vandals.

Once more to one and all,
"Friends, Romans, Countrymen, and Lovers."

Let such pure hate still underprop
Our love, that we may be
Each other's conscience,
And have our sympathy
Mainly from thence.

We'll one another treat like gods,
And all the faith we have
In virtue and in truth, bestow
On either, and suspicion leave
To gods below.

Two solitary stars —
Unmeasured systems far
Between us roll,
But by our conscious light we are
Determined to one pole.

What need confound the sphere —
Love can afford to wait,
For it no hour 's too late
That witnesseth one duty's end,
Or to another doth beginning lend.

It will subserve no use,
More than the tints of flowers,
Only the independent guest
Frequents its bowers,
Inherits its bequest.

No speech though kind has it,
But kinder silence doles
Unto its mates,
By night consoles,
By day congratulates.

What saith the tongue to tongue?
What heareth ear of ear?
By the decrees of fate
From year to year,
Does it communicate.

Pathless the gulf of feeling yawns —
No trivial bridge of words,
Or arch of boldest span,
Can leap the moat that girds
The sincere man.

No show of bolts and bars
Can keep the foeman out,
Or 'scape his secret mine
Who entered with the doubt
That drew the line.

No warder at the gate
Can let the friendly in,
But, like the sun, o'er all
He will the castle win,
And shine along the wall.

There's nothing in the world I know
That can escape from love,
For every depth it goes below,
And every height above.

It waits as waits the sky,
Until the clouds go by,
Yet shines serenely on
With an eternal day,
Alike when they are gone,
And when they stay.

Implacable is Love, —
Foes may be bought or teazed
From their hostile intent,
But he goes unappeased
Who is on kindness bent.

Having rowed five or six miles above Amoskeag before sunset, and reached a pleasant part
of the river, one of us landed to look for a farm-
house, where we might replenish our stores,
while the other remained cruising about the
stream, and exploring the opposite shores to
find a suitable harbor for the night. In the
meanwhile the canal boats began to come round
a point in our rear, poling their way along close
to the shore, the breeze having quite died away.
This time there was no offer of assistance, but
one of the boatmen only called out to say, as
the truest revenge for having been the losers
in the race, that he had seen a wood-duck, which
we had scared up, sitting on a tall white-pine,
half a mile down stream; and he repeated the
assertion several times, and seemed really cha-
grined at the apparent suspicion with which this
information was received. But there sat the
summer duck still undisturbed by us.

By and by the other voyageur returned from
his inland expedition, bringing one of the natives
with him, a little flaxen-headed boy, with some
tradition, or small edition, of Robinson Crusoe
in his head, who had been charmed by the account of our adventures, and asked his father's
leave to join us. He examined, at first from the
top of the bank, our boat and furniture, with
sparkling eyes, and wished himself already his
own man. He was a lively and interesting boy,

and we should have been glad to ship him; but
Nathan was still his father's boy, and had not
come to years of discretion.

We had got a loaf of home-made bread, and
musk and water-melons for dessert. For this
farmer, a clever and well-disposed man, cultivated a large patch of melons for the Hooksett
and Concord markets. He hospitably entertained us the next day, exhibiting his hop-fields
and kiln and melon patch, warning us to step
over the tight rope which surrounded the latter
at a foot from the ground, while he pointed to
a little bower at the corner, where it connected
with the lock of a gun ranging with the line, and
where, as he informed us, he sometimes sat in
pleasant nights to defend his premises against
thieves. We stepped high over the line, and
sympathized with our host's, on the whole quite
human, if not humane, interest in the success
of his experiment. That night especially thieves
were to be expected, from rumors in the atmosphere, and the priming was not wet. He was
a Methodist man, who had his dwelling between
the river and Uncannunuc Mountain; who there
belonged, and stayed at home there, and by the
encouragement of distant political organiza-
tions, and by his own tenacity, held a property
in his melons, and continued to plant. We
suggested melon seeds of new varieties and fruit
of foreign flavor to be added to his stock. We

had come away up here among the hills to learn
the impartial and unbribable beneficence of
Nature. Strawberries and melons grow as well
in one man's garden as another's, and the sun
lodges as kindly under his hill-side, — when we
had imagined that she inclined rather to some
few earnest and faithful souls whom we know.

We found a convenient harbor for our boat
on the opposite or east shore, still in Hooksett,
at the mouth of a small brook which emptied into
the Merrimack, where it would be out of the
way of any passing boat in the night, — for they
commonly hug the shore if bound up stream,
either to avoid the current, or touch the bottom
with their poles, — and where it would be accessible without stepping on the clayey shore.
We set one of our largest melons to cool in the
still water among the alders at the mouth of this
creek, but when our tent was pitched and ready,
and we went to get it, it had floated out into the
stream and was nowhere to be seen. So taking
the boat in the twilight, we went in pursuit of
this property, and at length, after long straining
of the eyes, its green disk was discovered far
down the river, gently floating seaward with
many twigs and leaves from the mountains that
evening, and so perfectly balanced that it had
not keeled at all, and no water had run in at
the tap which had been taken out to hasten its
cooling.

As we sat on the bank eating our supper, the clear light of the western sky fell on the eastern trees and was reflected in the water, and we enjoyed so serene an evening as left nothing to describe. For the most part we think that there are few degrees of sublimity, and that the highest is but little higher than that which we now behold; but we are always deceived. Sublimer visions appear, and the former pale and fade away. We are grateful when we are reminded by interior evidence, of the permanence of universal laws; for our faith is but faintly remembered, indeed, is not a remembered assurance, but a use and enjoyment of knowledge. It is when we do not have to believe, but come into actual contact with Truth, and are related to her in the most direct and intimate way. Waves of serener life pass over us from time to time, like flakes of sunlight over the fields in cloudy weather. In some happier moment, when more sap flows in the withered stalk of our life, Syria and India stretch away from our present as they do in history. All the events which make the annals of the nations are but the shadows of our private experiences. Suddenly and silently the eras which we call history awake and glimmer in us, and *there* is room for Alexander and Hannibal to march and conquer. In other words, the history which we read is only a fainter memory of events which have happened in our

Straight reach of river below Hooksett

own experience. Tradition is a more interrupted and feebler memory.

This world is but canvass to our imaginations. I see men with infinite pains endeavoring to realize to their bodies, what I, with at least equal pains, would realize to my imagination, — its capacities; for certainly there is a life of the mind above the wants of the body and independent of it. Often the body is warmed, but the imagination is torpid; the body is fat, but the imagination is lean and shrunk. But what avails all other wealth if this is wanting? "Imagination is the air of mind," in which it lives and breathes. All things are as I am. Where is the House of Change? The past is only so heroic as we see it. It is the canvass on which our idea of heroism is painted, and so, in one sense, the dim prospectus of our future field. Our circumstances answer to our expectations and the demand of our natures. I have noticed that if a man thinks that he needs a thousand dollars, and cannot be convinced that he does not, he will commonly be found to have them, if he lives and thinks a thousand dollars will be forthcoming, though it be to buy shoe strings with. A thousand mills will be just as slow to come to one who finds it equally hard to convince himself that he needs *them*.

> Men are by birth equal in this, that given
> Themselves and their condition, they are even.

I am astonished at the singular pertinacity
and endurance of our lives. The miracle is, that
what is *is*, when it is so difficult, if not impossible,
for anything else to be; that we walk on in our
particular paths so far, before we fall on death
and fate, merely because we must walk in some
path; that every man can get a living, and so
few can do any more. So much only can I
accomplish ere health and strength are gone, and
yet this suffices. The bird now sits just out of
gunshot. I am never rich in money, and I am
never meanly poor. If debts are incurred, why,
debts are in the course of events cancelled, as
it were by the same law by which they were
incurred. I heard that an engagement was
entered into between a certain youth and a
maiden, and then I heard that it was broken off,
but I did not know the reason in either case.
We are hedged about, we think, by accident
and circumstance, now we creep as in a dream,
and now again we run, as if there were a fate in
it and all things thwarted or assisted. I cannot change my clothes but when I do, and yet
I do change them, and soil the new ones. It is
wonderful that this gets done, when some admirable deeds which I could mention do not
get done. Our particular lives seem of such
fortune and confident strength and durability
as piers of solid rock thrown forward into the
tide of circumstance. When every other path

would fail, with singular and unerring confidence
we advance on our particular course. What
risks we run! famine and fire and pestilence, and
the thousand forms of a cruel fate, — and yet
every man lives till he — dies. How did he
manage that? Is there no immediate danger?
We wonder superfluously when we hear of a
somnambulist walking a plank securely, — we
have walked a plank all our lives up to this particular string-piece where we are. My life will
wait for nobody, but is being matured still
without delay, while I go about the streets and
chaffer with this man and that to secure a
living. It is as indifferent and easy meanwhile
as a poor man's dog, and making acquaintance
with its kind. It will cut its own channel like
a mountain stream, and by the longest ridge is
not kept from the sea at last. I have found all
things thus far, persons and inanimate matter,
elements and seasons, strangely adapted to my
resources. No matter what imprudent haste
in my career; I am permitted to be rash. Gulfs
are bridged in a twinkling, as if some unseen bag-
gage train carried pontoons for my convenience,
and while from the heights I scan the tempting
but unexplored Pacific Ocean of Futurity, the
ship is being carried over the mountains piece-
meal on the backs of mules and llamas, whose
keel shall plow its waves and bear me to the
Indies. Day would not dawn if it were not for

THE INWARD MORNING

Packed in my mind lie all the clothes
  Which outward nature wears,
And in its fashion's hourly change
  It all things else repairs.

In vain I look for change abroad,
  And can no difference find,
Till some new ray of peace uncalled
  Illumes my inmost mind.

What is it gilds the trees and clouds,
  And paints the heavens so gay,
But yonder fast abiding light
  With its unchanging ray?

Lo, when the sun streams through the wood,
  Upon a winter's morn,
Where'er his silent beams intrude
  The murky night is gone.

How could the patient pine have known
  The morning breeze would come,
Or humble flowers anticipate
  The insect's noonday hum, —

Till the new light with morning cheer
  From far streamed through the aisles,
And nimbly told the forest trees
  For many stretching miles?

I've heard within my inmost soul
  Such cheerful morning news,
In the horizon of my mind
  Have seen such orient hues,

As in the twilight of the dawn,
  When the first birds awake,
Are heard within some silent wood,
  Where they the small twigs break,

Or in the eastern skies are seen,
  Before the sun appears,
The harbingers of summer heats
  Which from afar he bears.

Whole weeks and months of my summer life
slide away in thin volumes like mist and smoke,
till at length, some warm morning, perchance, I
see a sheet of mist blown down the brook to the
swamp, and I float as high above the fields with
it. I can recall to mind the stillest summer
hours, in which the grasshopper sings over the
mulleins, and there is a valor in that time the
bare memory of which is armor that can laugh
at any blow of fortune. For our lifetime the
strains of a harp are heard to swell and die
alternately, and death is but "the pause when
the blast is recollecting itself."

We lay awake a long while, listening to the
murmurs of the brook, in the angle formed by
whose bank with the river our tent was pitched,
and there was a sort of human interest in its
story, which ceases not in freshet or in drought
the livelong summer, and the profounder lapse
of the river was quite drowned by its din. But
the rill, whose

"Silver sands and pebbles sing
Eternal ditties with the spring,"

is silenced by the first frosts of winter, while mightier streams, on whose bottom the sun never shines, clogged with sunken rocks and the ruins of forests, from whose surface comes up no murmur, are strangers to the icy fetters which bind fast a thousand contributary rills.

I dreamed this night of an event which had occurred long before. It was a difference with a Friend, which had not ceased to give me pain, though I had no cause to blame myself. But in my dream ideal justice was at length done me for his suspicions, and I received that compensation which I had never obtained in my waking hours. I was unspeakably soothed and rejoiced, even after I awoke, because in dreams we never deceive ourselves, nor are deceived, and this seemed to have the authority of a final judgment.

We bless and curse ourselves. Some dreams are divine, as well as some waking thoughts. Donne sings of one

"Who dreamt devoutlier than most use to pray."

Dreams are the touchstones of our characters. We are scarcely less afflicted when we remember some unworthiness in our conduct in a dream, than if it had been actual, and the intensity of our grief, which is our atonement, measures inversely the degree by which this is separated

from an actual unworthiness. For in dreams
we but act a part which must have been learned
and rehearsed in our waking hours, and no doubt
could discover some waking consent thereto.
If this meanness has not its foundation in us,
why are we grieved at it? In dreams we see
ourselves naked and acting out our real characters, even more clearly than we see others
awake. But an unwavering and commanding
virtue would compel even its most fantastic
and faintest dreams to respect its ever wakeful
authority; as we are accustomed to say care-
lessly, we should never have *dreamed* of such a
thing. Our truest life is when we are in dreams
awake.

> "And, more to lull him in his slumber soft,
>   A trickling streame from high rock tumbling downe,
>   And ever-drizzling raine upon the loft,
>   Mixt with a murmuring winde, much like the sowne
>   Of swarming bees, did cast him in a swowne.
>   No other noyse, nor people's troublous cryes,
>   As still are wont t' annoy the walled towne,
>   Might there be heard; but careless Quiet lyes
> Wrapt in eternall silence farre from enemyes."

THURSDAY

"He trode the unplanted forest floor, whereon
The all-seeing sun for ages hath not shone,
Where feeds the moose, and walks the surly bear,
And up the tall mast runs the woodpecker.

   *   *   *   *   *

Where darkness found him he lay glad at night;
There the red morning touched him with its light.

   *   *   *   *   *

Go where he will, the wise man is at home,
His hearth the earth, — his hall the azure dome;
Where his clear spirit leads him, there's his road,
By God's own light illumined and foreshowed."

— EMERSON.

WHEN we awoke this morning, we heard the faint deliberate and ominous sound of rain drops on our cotton roof. The rain had pattered all night, and now the whole country wept, the drops falling in the river, and on the alders, and in the pastures, and instead of any bow in the heavens, there was the trill of the tree-sparrow all the morning. The cheery faith of this little bird atoned for the silence of the whole woodland quire besides. When we first stepped abroad, a flock of sheep, led by their rams, came rushing down a ravine in our rear, with heedless haste and unreserved frisk-

ing, as if unobserved by man, from some higher
pasture where they had spent the night, to
taste the herbage by the river-side; but when
their leaders caught sight of our white tent
through the mist, struck with sudden astonishment, with their fore feet braced, they sustained
the rushing torrent in their rear, and the whole
flock stood still, endeavoring to solve the mystery in their sheepish brains. At length, con-
cluding that it boded no mischief to them, they
spread themselves out quietly over the field.
We learned afterward that we had pitched our
tent on the very spot which a few summers
before had been occupied by a party of Penob-
scots. We could see rising before us through the
mist a dark conical eminence called Hooksett
Pinnacle, a landmark to boatmen, and also
Uncannunuc Mountain, broad off on the west
side of the river.

This was the limit of our voyage, for a few
hours more in the rain would have taken us
to the last of the locks, and our boat was too
heavy to be dragged around the long and numerous rapids which would occur. On foot, however, we continued up along the bank, feeling
our way with a stick through the showery and
foggy day, and climbing over the slippery logs
in our path with as much pleasure and buoyancy
as in brightest sunshine; scenting the fragrance
of the pines and the wet clay under our feet,

and cheered by the tones of invisible waterfalls; with visions of toadstools, and wandering frogs, and festoons of moss hanging from the spruce trees, and thrushes flitting silent under the leaves; our road still holding together through that wettest of weather, like faith, while we confidently followed its lead. We managed to keep our thoughts dry, however, and only our clothes were wet. It was altogether a cloudy and drizzling day, with occasional brightenings in the mist, when the trill of the tree-sparrow seemed to be ushering in sunny hours.

"Nothing that naturally happens to man, can *hurt* him, earthquakes and thunder storms not excepted," said a man of genius, who at this time lived a few miles further on our road. When compelled by a shower to take shelter under a tree, we may improve that opportunity for a more minute inspection of some of Nature's works. I have stood under a tree in the woods half a day at a time, during a heavy rain in the summer, and yet employed myself happily and profitably there prying with miscroscopic eye into the crevices of the bark or the leaves or the fungi at my feet. "Riches are the attendants of the miser: and the heavens rain plenteously upon the mountains." I can fancy that it would be a luxury to stand up to one's chin in some retired swamp a whole summer day, scenting the wild honeysuckle and bilberry blows, and lulled by the minstrelsy of gnats and mosquitoes! A day passed in the society of those Greek sages, such as described in the Banquet of Xenophon, would not be comparable with the dry wet of decayed cranberry vines, and the fresh Attic salt of the moss-beds. Say twelve hours of genial and familiar converse with the leopard frog; the sun to rise behind alder and dogwood, and climb buoyantly to his meridian of two hands' breadth, and finally sink to rest behind some bold western hummock. To hear the evening chant of the mosquito from a thousand green chapels, and the bittern begin to boom from some concealed fort like a sunset gun!— Surely one may as profitably be soaked in the juices of swamp for one day as pick his way dry-shod over sand. Cold and damp,—are they not as rich experience as warmth and dryness?

At present, the drops come trickling down the stubble while we lie drenched on a bed of withered wild oats, by the side of a bushy hill, and the gathering in of the clouds, with the last rush and dying breath of the wind, and then the regular dripping of twigs and leaves the country over, enhance the sense of inward comfort and sociableness. The birds draw closer and are more familiar under the thick foliage, seemingly composing new strains upon their roosts against the sunshine. What were the amusements of

the drawing room and the library in comparison, if we had them here? We should still
sing as of old, —

My books I'd fain cast off, I cannot read,
'Twixt every page my thoughts go stray at large
Down in the meadow, where is richer feed,
And will not mind to hit their proper targe.

Plutarch was good, and so was Homer too,
Our Shakspeare's life was rich to live again,
What Plutarch read, that was not good nor true,
Nor Shakspeare's books, unless his books were men.

Here while I lie beneath this walnut bough,
What care I for the Greeks or for Troy town,
If juster battles are enacted now
Between the ants upon this hummock's crown?

Bid Homer wait till I the issue learn,
If red or black the gods will favor most,
Or yonder Ajax will the phalanx turn,
Struggling to heave some rock against the host.

Tell Shakspeare to attend some leisure hour,
For now I've business with this drop of dew,
And see you not, the clouds prepare a shower, —
I'll meet him shortly when the sky is blue.

This bed of herd's-grass and wild oats was spread
Last year with nicer skill than monarchs use,
A clover tuft is pillow for my head,
And violets quite overtop my shoes.

And now the cordial clouds have shut all in,
And gently swells the wind to say all's well,
The scattered drops are falling fast and thin,
Some in the pool, some in the flower-bell.

I am well drenched upon my bed of oats;
But see that globe come rolling down its stem,
Now like a lonely planet there it floats,
And now it sinks into my garment's hem.

Drip, drip the trees for all the country round,
And richness rare distills from every bough,
The wind alone it is makes every sound,
Shaking down crystals on the leaves below.

For shame the sun will never show himself,
Who could not with his beams e'er melt me so,
My dripping locks — they would become an elf,
Who in a beaded coat does gaily go.

The Pinnacle is a small wooded hill which rises very abruptly to the height of about two hundred feet, near the shore at Hooksett Falls. As Uncannunuc Mountain is perhaps the best point from which to view the valley of the Merrimack, so this hill affords the best view of the river itself. I have sat upon its summit, a precipitous rock only a few rods long, in fairer weather, when the sun was setting and filling the river valley with a flood of light. You can see up and down the Merrimack several miles each way. The broad and straight river, full of light and life, with its sparkling and foaming falls, the islet which divides the stream, the village of Hooksett on the shore almost directly under your feet, so near that you can converse with its inhabitants or throw a stone into its yards, the woodland lake at its western base, and the mountains in the north and north-east, make a scene of rare beauty and completeness, which the traveller should take pains to behold.

We were hospitably entertained in Concord in New Hampshire, which we persisted in calling *New* Concord, as we had been wont, to distinguish it from our native town, from which we had been told that it was named and in part originally settled. This would have been the proper place to conclude our voyage, uniting Concord with Concord by these meandering rivers, but our boat was moored some miles below its port.

The richness of the intervals at Penacook, now Concord in New Hampshire, had been observed by explorers, and, according to the historian of Haverhill, in the "year 1726, considerable progress was made in the settlement, and a road was cut through the wilderness from Haverhill to Penacook. In the fall of 1727, the first family, that of Capt. Ebenezer Eastman, moved into the place. His team was driven by Jacob Shute, who was by birth a Frenchman, and he is said to have been the first person who drove a team through the wilderness. Soon after, says tradition, one Ayer, a lad of 18, drove a team consisting of ten yoke of oxen to Penacook, swam the river, and plowed a portion of the interval. He is supposed to have been the first person who plowed land in that place.

The Pinnacle

After he had completed his work, he started on his return at sunrise, drowned a yoke of oxen while recrossing the river, and arrived at Haverhill about midnight. The crank of the first saw-mill was manufactured in Haverhill, and carried to Penacook on a horse."

But we found that the frontiers were not this way any longer. This generation has come into the world fatally late for some enterprises. Go where we will on the *surface* of things, men have been there before us. We cannot now have the pleasure of erecting the *last* house; that was long ago set up in the suburbs of Astoria city, and our boundaries have literally been run to the South Sea, according to the old patents. But the lives of men, though more extended laterally in their range, are still as shallow as ever. Undoubtedly, as a western orator said, "men generally live over about the same surface; some live long and narrow, and others live broad and short;" but it is all superficial living. A worm is as good a traveller as a grasshopper or a cricket, and a much wiser settler. With all their activity these do not hop away from drought nor forward to summer. We do not avoid evil by fleeing before it, but by rising above or diving below its plane; as the worm escapes drought and frost by boring a few inches deeper. The frontiers are not east or west, north or south, but wherever a man *fronts* a fact, though that fact be his neighbor, there is an unsettled wilderness between him and Canada, between him and the setting sun, or, further still, between him and *it*. Let him build himself a log-house with the bark on where he is, *fronting* IT, and wage there an Old French war for seven or seventy years, with Indians and Rangers, or whatever else may come between him and the reality, and save his scalp if he can.

We now no longer sailed or floated on the river, but trod the unyielding land like pilgrims. Sadi tells who may travel; among others, — "A common mechanic, who can earn a subsistence by the industry of his hand, and shall not have to stake his reputation for every morsel of bread, as philosophers have said." — He may travel who can subsist on the wild fruits and game of the most cultivated country. A man may travel fast enough and earn his living on the road. I have frequently been applied to to do work when on a journey; to do tinkering and repair clocks, when I had a knapsack on my back. A man once applied to me to go into a factory, stating conditions and wages, observing that I succeeded in shutting the window of a railroad car in which we were travelling, when the other passengers had failed. "Hast thou not heard of a Sufi, who was hammering some nails into the sole of his sandal; an officer of cavalry took him by the sleeve, saying, come along and shoe my horse." Farmers have asked me to assist them in haying, when I was passing their fields. A man once applied to me to mend his umbrella, taking me for an umbrella mender, because, being on a journey, I carried an umbrella in my hand while the sun shone. Another wished to buy a tin cup of me, observing that I had one strapped to my belt, and a sauce-pan on my back. The cheapest way to travel, and the way to travel the furthest in the shortest distance, is to go afoot, carrying a dipper, a spoon, and a fish-line, some Indian meal, some salt, and some sugar. When you come to a brook or pond, you can catch fish and cook them; or you can boil a hasty-pudding; or you can buy a loaf of bread at a farmer's house for fourpence, moisten it in the next brook that crosses the road, and dip into it your sugar, — this alone will last you a whole day; — or, if you are accustomed to heartier living, you can buy a quart of milk for two cents, crumb your bread or cold pudding into it, and eat it with your own spoon out of your own dish. Any one of these things I mean, not all together. I have travelled thus some hundreds of miles without taking any meal in a house, sleeping on the ground when convenient, and found it cheaper, and in many respects more profitable, than staying at home. So that some have inquired why it would not be best to travel always. But I never thought of travelling simply as a means of getting a livelihood. A simple woman down in Tyngsboro', at whose house I once stopped to get a draught of water, when I said, recognizing the bucket, that I had stopped there nine years before for the same purpose, asked if I was not a traveller, supposing that I had been travelling ever since, and had now come round again, that travelling was one of the professions, more or less productive, which her husband did not follow. But continued travelling is far from productive. It begins with wearing away the soles of the shoes, and making the feet sore, and ere long it will wear a man clean up, after making his heart sore into the bargain. I have observed that the after-life of those who have travelled much is very pathetic. True and sincere travelling is no pastime, but it is as serious as the grave, or any other part of the human journey, and it requires a long probation to be broken into it. I do not speak of those that travel sitting, the sedentary travellers whose legs hang dangling the while, mere idle symbols of the fact, any more than when we speak of setting hens we mean those that sit standing, but I mean those to whom travelling is life for the legs. The traveller must be born again on the road, and earn a passport from the elements, the principal powers that be for him. He shall experience at last that old threat of his mother fulfilled, that he shall be skinned alive. His sores shall gradually deepen themselves that they may heal inwardly, while he gives no rest to the sole of his foot, and at night weariness must be his pillow, that so he may acquire experience against his rainy days. — So was it with us.

Sometimes we lodged at an inn in the woods, where trout-fishers from distant cities had arrived before us, and where, to our astonishment, the settlers dropped in at night-fall to have a chat and hear the news, though there was but one road, and no other house was visible, — as if they had come out of the earth. There we sometimes read old newspapers, who never before read new ones, and in the rustle of their leaves heard the dashing of the surf along the Atlantic shore, instead of the sough of the wind amongthe pines. But then walking had given us an appetite even for the least palatable and nutritious food.

Some hard and dry book in a dead language, which you have found it impossible to read at home, but for which you have still a lingering regard, is the best to carry with you on a journey. At a country inn, in the barren society of ostlers and travellers, I could undertake the writers of the silver or the brazen age with confidence. Almost the last regular service which I performed in the cause of literature was to read the works of

AULUS PERSIUS FLACCUS

If you have imagined what a divine work is spread out for the poet, and approach this author too, in the hope of finding the field at length fairly entered on, you will hardly dissent from the words of the prologue,

"Ipse semipaganus
Ad sacra Vatum carmen affero nostrum."

I half pagan
Bring my verses to the shrine of the poets.

Here is none of the interior dignity of Virgil, nor the elegance and vivacity of Horace, nor will any sybil be needed to remind you, that from those older Greek poets there is a sad descent to Persius. You can scarcely distinguish one harmonious sound amid this unmusical bickering with the follies of men.

One sees that music has its place in thought, but hardly as yet in language. When the Muse arrives, we wait for her to remould language, and impart to it her own rhythm. Hitherto the verse groans and labors with its load, and goes not forward blithely, singing by the way. The best ode may be parodied, indeed is itself a parody, and has a poor and trivial sound, like a man stepping on the rounds of a ladder. Homer, and Shakspeare, and Milton, and Mar-

vel, and Wordsworth, are but the rustling of
leaves and crackling of twigs in the forest, and
there is not yet the sound of any bird. The
Muse has never lifted up her voice to sing.
Most of all, satire will not be sung. A Juvenal
or Persius do not marry music to their verse,
but are measured fault-finders at best; stand
but just outside the faults they condemn, and
so are concerned rather about the monster
which they have escaped, than the fair prospect before them. Let them live on an age,
and they will have travelled out of his shadow
and reach, and found other objects to ponder.

As long as there is satire, the poet is, as it
were, *particeps criminis*. One sees not but he
had best let bad take care of itself, and have
to do only with what is beyond suspicion. If
you light on the least vestige of truth, and it is
the weight of the whole body still which stamps
the faintest trace, an eternity will not suffice to
extol it, while no evil is so huge, but you grudge
to bestow on it a moment of hate. Truth
never turns to rebuke falsehood; her own
straightforwardness is the severest correction.
Horace would not have written satire so well if
he had not been inspired by it, as by a passion,
and fondly cherished his vein. In his odes, the
love always exceeds the hate, so that the severest
satire still sings itself, and the poet is satisfied,
though the folly be not corrected.

A sort of necessary order in the development of Genius is, first, Complaint; second, Plaint; third, Love. Complaint, which is the condition of Persius, lies not in the province of poetry. Ere long the enjoyment of a superior good would have changed his disgust into regret. We can never have much sympathy with the complainer; for after searching nature through, we conclude that he must be both plaintiff and defendant too, and so had best come to a settlement without a hearing. He who receives an injury is to some extent an accomplice of the wrong doer.

Perhaps it would be truer to say, that the highest strain of the muse is essentially plaintive. The saint's are still *tears* of joy. Who has ever heard the *Innocent* sing?

But the divinest poem, or the life of a great man, is the severest satire; as impersonal as Nature herself, and like the sighs of her winds in the woods, which convey ever a slight reproof to the hearer. The greater the genius, the keener the edge of the satire.

Hence we have to do only with the rare and fragmentary traits, which least belong to Persius, or shall we say, are the properest utterances of his muse; since that which he says best at any time is what he can best say at all times. The Spectators and Ramblers have not failed to cull some quotable sentences from this garden too, so pleasant is it to meet even the most familiar truth in a new dress, when, if our neighbor had said it, we should have passed it by as hackneyed. Out of these six satires, you may perhaps select some twenty lines, which fit so well as many thoughts, that they will recur to the scholar almost as readily as a natural image; though when translated into familiar language, they lose that insular emphasis, which fitted them for quotation. Such lines as the following, translation cannot render common-place. Contrasting the man of true religion with those who, with jealous privacy, would fain carry on a secret commerce with the gods, he says, —

"Haud cuivis promptum est, murmurque humilesque susurros,
Tollere de templis; et aperto vivere voto."

    It is not easy for every one to take murmurs and low
    Whispers out of the temples, and live with open vow.

To the virtuous man, the universe is the only *sanctum sanctorum*, and the penetralia of the temple are the broad noon of his existence. Why should he betake himself to a subterranean crypt, as if it were the only holy ground in all the world which he had left unprofaned? The obedient soul would only the more discover and familiarize things, and escape more and more into light and air, as having henceforth done with secrecy, so that the universe shall not seem open enough for it. At length, it is neglectful even of that silence which is consistent with true modesty, but by its independence of all confidence in its disclosures, makes that which it imparts so private to the hearer, that it becomes the care of the whole world that modesty be not infringed.

To the man who cherishes a secret in his breast, there is a still greater secret unexplored. Our most indifferent acts may be matter for secrecy, but whatever we do with the utmost truthfulness and integrity, by virtue of its pureness, must be transparent as light.

In the third satire, he asks,

"Est aliquid quò tendis, et in quod dirigis arcum?
An passim sequeris corvos, testâve, lutove,
Securus quò pes ferat, atque ex tempore vivis?"

Is there anything to which thou tendest, and against which
    thou directest thy bow?
Or dost thou pursue crows, at random, with pottery or clay,
Careless whither thy feet bear thee, and live *ex tempore?*

The bad sense is always a secondary one. Language does not appear to have justice done it, but is obviously cramped and narrowed in its significance, when any meanness is described. The truest construction is not put upon it. What may readily be fashioned into a rule of wisdom, is here thrown in the teeth of the sluggard, and constitutes the front of his offence. Universally, the innocent man will come forth from the sharpest inquisition and lecturing, the combined din of reproof and commendation, with a faint sound of eulogy in his ears. Our vices always lie in the direction of our virtues, and in their best estate are but plausible imitations of the latter. Falsehood never attains to the dignity of entire falseness, but is only an inferior sort of truth; if it were more thoroughly false, it would incur danger of becoming true.

"Securus quo pes ferat, atque ex tempore *vivit*,"

is then the motto of a wise man. For first, as the subtle discernment of the language would have taught us, with all his negligence he is still secure; but the sluggard, notwithstanding his heedlessness, is insecure.

The life of a wise man is most of all extemporaneous, for he lives out of an eternity which includes all time. The cunning mind travels farther back than Zoroaster each instant, and comes quite down to the present with its revelation. The utmost thrift and industry of thinking give no man any stock in life; his credit with the inner world is no better, his capital no larger. He must try his fortune again to-day as yesterday. All questions rely on the present for their solution. Time measures nothing but itself. The word that is written may be postponed, but not that on the lip. If this is what the occasion says, let the occasion say it. All the world is forward to prompt him who gets up to live without his creed in his pocket.

In the fifth satire, which is the best, I find, —

> "Stat contrà ratio, et secretam garrit in aurem,
>   Ne liceat facere id, quod quis vitiabit agendo."

> Reason opposes, and whispers in the secret ear,
> That it is not lawful to do that which one will spoil by doing.

Only they who do not see how anything might be better done, are forward to try their hand on it.   Even the master workman must be encouraged by the reflection, that his awkwardness will be incompetent to do that thing harm, to which his skill may fail to do justice.   Here is no apology for neglecting to do many things from a sense of our incapacity, — for what deed does not fall maimed and imperfect from our hands? — but only a warning to bungle less.

The satires of Persius are the farthest possible from inspired; evidently a chosen, not imposed subject.   Perhaps I have given him credit for more earnestness than is apparent; but it is certain, that that which alone we can call Persius, which is forever independent and consistent, *was* in earnest, and so sanctions the sober consideration of all.   The artist and his work are not to be separated.   The most wilfully foolish man cannot stand aloof from his folly, but the deed and the doer together make ever one sober fact.   There is but one stage for the peasant and the actor. The buffoon cannot bribe you to laugh always at his grimaces; they shall sculpture themselves in Egyptian granite, to stand heavy as the pyramids on the ground of his character.

Suns rose and set and found us still on the dank forest path which meanders up the Pemigewasset, now more like an otter's or a marten's trail, or where a beaver had dragged his trap, than where the wheels of travel raise a dust; where towns begin to serve as gores, only to hold the earth together. The wild pigeon sat secure above our heads, high on the dead limbs of naval pines, reduced to a robin's size. The very yards of our hostelries inclined upon the skirts of mountains, and, as we passed, we looked up at a steep angle at the stems of maples waving in the clouds.

Far up in the country, — for we would be faithful to our experience, — in Thornton, perhaps, we met a soldier lad in the woods, going to muster in full regimentals, and holding the middle of the road; deep in the forest with shouldered musket and military step, and thoughts of war and glory all to himself. It was a sore trial to the youth, tougher than many a battle, to get by us creditably and with soldier-like bearing. Poor man! He actually shivered like a reed in his thin military pants, and by the

time we had got up with him, all the sternness
that becomes the soldier had forsaken his face,
and he skulked past as if he were driving his
father's sheep under a sword-proof helmet.   It
was too much for him to carry any extra armor
then, who could not easily dispose of his natural
arms.   And for his legs, they were like heavy
artillery in boggy places; better to cut the
traces and forsake them.   His greaves chafed
and wrestled one with another for want of other
foes.   But he did get by and get off with all his
munitions, and lived to fight another day; and
I do not record this as casting any suspicion
on his honor and real bravery in the field.

Wandering on through notches which the
streams had made, by the side and over the
brows of hoar hills and mountains, across the
stumpy, rocky, forested and bepastured country, we at length crossed on prostrate trees over
the Amonoosuck, and breathed the free air of
Unappropriated Land.   Thus, in fair days as
well as foul, we had traced up the river to which
our native stream is a tributary, until from
Merrimack it became the Pemigewasset that
leaped by our side, and when we had passed its
fountainhead, the Wild Amonoosuck, whose
puny channel was crossed at a stride, guiding us
toward its distant source among the mountains,
and at length, without its guidance, we were
enabled to reach the summit of AGIOCOCHOOK.

"Sweet days, so cool, so calm, so bright,
  The bridal of the earth and sky,
Sweet dews shall weep thy fall to-night,
  For thou must die."

— Herbert.

When we returned to Hooksett, a week afterward, the melon man, in whose corn-barn we
had hung our tent and buffaloes and other
things to dry, was already picking his hops,
with many women and children to help him.
We bought one watermelon, the largest in his
patch, to carry with us for ballast. It was
Nathan's, which he might sell if he pleased,
having been conveyed to him in the green
state, and owned daily by his eyes. After due
consultation with "Father," the bargain was
concluded, — we to buy it at a venture on the
vine, green or ripe, our risk, and pay "what
the gentlemen pleased." It proved to be ripe;
for we had had honest experience in selecting
this fruit.

Finding our boat safe in its harbor, under
Uncannunuc Mountain, with a fair wind and
the current in our favor, we commenced our voyage at noon, sitting at our ease and conversing,
or in silence watching for the last trace of each
reach in the river as a bend concealed it from
our view. As the season was further advanced,
the wind now blew steadily from the north, and
with our sail set we could occasionally lie on

our oars without loss of time. The lumbermen throwing down wood from the top of the high bank, thirty or forty feet above the water, that it might be sent down stream, paused in their work to watch our retreating sail. By this time, indeed, we were well known to the boatmen, and were hailed as the Revenue Cutter of the stream. As we sailed rapidly down the river, shut in between two mounds of earth, the sound of this timber rolled down the bank enhanced the silence and vastness of the noon, and we fancied that only the primeval echoes were awakened. The vision of a distant scow just heaving in sight round a headland, also increased by contrast the solitude.

Through the din and desultoriness of noon, even in the most oriental city, is seen the fresh and primitive and savage nature, in which Scythians, and Ethiopians, and Indians dwell. What is echo, what are light and shade, day and night, ocean and stars, earthquake and eclipse, there? The works of man are everywhere swallowed up in the immensity of Nature. The Ægean Sea is but Lake Huron still to the Indian. Also there is all the refinement of civilized life in the woods under a sylvan garb. The wildest scenes have an air of domesticity and homeliness even to the citizen, and when the flicker's cackle is heard in the clearing, he is reminded that civilization has wrought but

Hooksett Falls

little change there. Science is welcome to the
deepest recesses of the forest, for there too
nature obeys the same old civil laws. The little
red bug on the stump of a pine, for it the wind
shifts and the sun breaks through the clouds.
In the wildest nature, there is not only the
material of the most cultivated life, and a sort
of anticipation of the last result, but a greater
refinement already than is ever attained by
man. There is papyrus by the river-side, and
rushes for light, and the goose only flies overhead, ages before the studious are born or letters
invented, and that literature which the former
suggest, and even from the first have rudely
served, it may be man does not yet use them
to express. Nature is prepared to welcome into
her scenery the finest work of human art, for
she is herself an art so cunning that the artist
never appears in his work.

Art is not tame, and Nature is not wild, in the
ordinary sense. A perfect work of man's art
would also be wild or natural in a good sense.
Man tames Nature only that he may at last
make her more free even than he found her,
though he may never yet have succeeded.

With this propitious breeze, and the help of
our oars, we soon reached the Falls of Amoskeag,
and the mouth of the Piscataquoag, and recognized, as we swept rapidly by, many a fair bank

and islet on which our eyes had rested in the upward passage. Our boat was like that which Chaucer describes in his Dream, in which the knight took his departure from the island,

> "To journey for his marriage,
> And return with such an host,
> That wedded might be least and most. * *
> Which barge was as a man's thought,
> After his pleasure to him brought,
> The queene herself accustomed aye
> In the same barge to play,
> It needed neither mast ne rother,
> I have not heard of such another,
> No master for the goverance,
> Hie sayled by thought and pleasaunce
> Without labor east and west,
> All was one, calme or tempest."

So we sailed this afternoon, thinking of the saying of Pythagoras, though we had no peculiar right to remember it, — "It is beautiful when prosperity is present with intellect, and when sailing as it were with a prosperous wind, actions are performed looking to virtue; just as a pilot looks to the motions of the stars."   All the world reposes in beauty to him who preserves equipoise in his life, and moves serenely on his path without secret violence; as he who sails down a stream, he has only to steer, keeping his bark in the middle, and carry it round the falls.   The ripples curled away in our wake, like ringlets from the head of a child, while we steadily held on our course, and under the bows we watched

"The swaying soft,
Made by the delicate wave parted in front,
As through the gentle element we move
Like shadows gliding through untroubled dreams."

The forms of beauty fall naturally around the path of him who is in the performance of his proper work; as the curled shavings drop from the plane, and borings cluster round the auger. Undulation is the gentlest and most ideal of motions, produced by one fluid falling on another. Rippling is a more graceful flight. From a hilltop you may detect in it the wings of birds endlessly repeated. The two *waving* lines which represent the flight of birds appear to have been copied from the ripple.

The trees made an admirable fence to the landscape, skirting the horizon on every side. The single trees and the groves left standing on the interval, appeared naturally disposed, though the farmer had consulted only his convenience, for he too falls into the scheme of Nature. Art can never match the luxury and superfluity of Nature. In the former all is seen; it cannot afford concealed wealth, and is niggardly in comparison; but Nature, even when she is scant and thin outwardly, satisfies us still by the assurance of a certain generosity at the roots. In swamps, where there is only here and there an evergreen tree amid the quaking moss and cranberry beds, the bare-ness does not suggest poverty. The double-spruce, which I had hardly noticed in gardens, attracts me in such places, and now first I understand why men try to make them grow about their houses. But though there may be very perfect specimens in front-yard plots, their beauty is for the most part ineffectual there, for there is no such assurance of kindred wealth beneath and around them to make them show to advantage. As we have said, Nature is a greater and more perfect art, the art of God; though, referred to herself, she is genius, and there is a similarity between her operations and man's art even in the details and trifles. When the overhanging pine drops into the water, by the sun and water, and the wind rubbing it against the shore, its boughs are worn into fantastic shapes, and white and smooth, as if turned in a lathe. Man's art has wisely imitated those forms into which all matter is most inclined to run, as foliage and fruit. A hammock swung in a grove assumes the exact form of a canoe, broader or narrower, and higher or lower at the ends, as more or fewer persons are in it, and it rolls in the air with the motion of the body, like a canoe in the water. Our art leaves its shavings and its dust about; her art exhibits itself even in the shavings and the dust which we make. She has perfected herself by an eternity of practice. The world is well kept; no rubbish accumulates; the morning air is clear even at this day, and no dust has settled on the grass. Behold how the evening now steals over the fields, the shadows of the trees creeping further and further into the meadow, and ere long the stars will come to bathe in these retired waters. Her undertakings are secure and never fail. If I were awakened from a deep sleep, I should know which side of the meridian the sun might be by the aspect of nature, and by the chirp of the crickets, and yet no painter can paint this difference. The landscape contains a thousand dials which indicate the natural divisions of time, the shadows of a thousand styles point to the hour. —

"Not only o'er the dial's face,
    This silent phantom day by day,
With slow, unseen, unceasing pace,
    Steals moments, months, and years away;
From hoary rock and aged tree,
    From proud Palmyra's mouldering walls,
From Teneriffe, towering o'er the sea,
    From every blade of grass it falls."

It is almost the only game which the trees play at, this tit-for-tat, now this side in the sun, now that, the drama of the day. In deep ravines under the eastern sides of cliffs, Night forwardly plants her foot even at noonday, and as Day retreats she steps into his trenches, skulking from tree to tree, from fence to fence, until at

last she sits in his citadel and draws out her
forces into the plain. It may be that the forenoon is brighter than the afternoon, not only
because of the greater transparency of its atmosphere, but because we naturally look most into
the west, as forward into the day, and so in the
forenoon see the sunny side of things, but in the
afternoon the shadow of every tree.

The afternoon is now far advanced, and a fresh
and leisurely wind is blowing over the river,
making long reaches of bright ripples.   The
river has done its stint, and appears not to flow,
but lie at its length reflecting the light, and the
haze over the woods is like the inaudible panting,
or rather the gentle perspiration of resting nature,
rising from a myriad of pores into the attenuated
atmosphere.

On the thirty-first day of March, one hundred
and forty-two years before this, probably about
this time in the afternoon, there were hurriedly
paddling down this part of the river, between
the pine woods which then fringed these banks,
two white women and a boy, who had left an
island at the mouth of the Contoocook before
daybreak. They were slightly clad for the
season, in the English fashion, and handled
their paddles unskilfully, but with nervous
energy and determination, and at the bottom
of their canoe lay the still bleeding scalps of ten

of the aborigines.   They were Hannah Dustan,
and her nurse, Mary Neff, both of Haverhill,
eighteen miles from the mouth of this river, and
an English boy, named Samuel Lennardson,
escaping from captivity among the Indians.
On the 15th of March previous, Hannah Dustan
had been compelled to rise from childbed, and
half-dressed, with one foot bare, accompanied by
her nurse, commence an uncertain march, in
still inclement weather, through the snow and
the wilderness.   She had seen her seven elder
children flee with their father, but knew not of
their fate.   She had seen her infant's brains
dashed out against an apple tree, and had left
her own and her neighbors' dwellings in ashes.
When she reached the wigwam of her captor,
situated on an island in the Merrimack, more
than twenty miles above where we now are,
she had been told that she and her nurse were
soon to be taken to a distant Indian settlement,
and there made to run the gauntlet naked.
The family of this Indian consisted of two men,
three women, and seven children, beside an
English boy, whom she found a prisoner among
them.   Having determined to attempt her escape, she instructed the boy to inquire of one
of the men, how he should despatch an enemy
in the quickest manner, and take his scalp.
"Strike 'em there," said he, placing his finger
on his temple, and he also showed him how to

take off the scalp. On the morning of the 31st she arose before daybreak, and awoke her nurse and the boy, and taking the Indians' tomahawks, they killed them all in their sleep, excepting one favorite boy, and one squaw who fled wounded with him to the woods. The English boy struck the Indian who had given him the information on the temple, as he had been directed. They then collected all the provision they could find, and took their master's tomahawk and gun, and scuttling all the canoes but one, commenced their flight to Haverhill, distant about sixty miles by the river. But after having proceeded a short distance, fearing that her story would not be believed if she should escape to tell it, they returned to the silent wigwam, and taking off the scalps of the dead, put them into a bag as proofs of what they had done, and then retracing their steps to the shore in the twilight, recommenced their voyage.

Early this morning this deed was performed, and now, perchance, these tired women and this boy, their clothes stained with blood, and their minds racked with alternate resolution and fear, are making a hasty meal of parched corn and moose meat, while their canoe glides under these pine roots whose stumps are still standing on the bank. They are thinking of the dead whom they have left behind on that solitary isle far up the stream, and of the relentless living warriors who are in pursuit. Every withered leaf which the winter has left seems to know their story, and in its rustling to repeat it and betray them. An Indian lurks behind every rock and pine, and their nerves cannot bear the tapping of a woodpecker. Or they forget their own dangers and their deeds in conjecturing the fate of their kindred, and whether, if they escape the Indians, they shall find the former still alive. They do not stop to cook their meals upon the bank, nor land, except to carry their canoe about the falls. The stolen birch forgets its master and does them good service, and the swollen current bears them swiftly along with little need of the paddle, except to steer and keep them warm by exercise. For ice is floating in the river; the spring is opening; the muskrat and the beaver are driven out of their holes by the flood; deer gaze at them from the bank; a few faint-singing forest birds, perchance, fly across the river to the northernmost shore; the fish-hawk sails and screams overhead, and geese fly over with a startling clangor; but they do not observe these things, or they speedily forget them. They do not smile or chat all day. Sometimes they pass an Indian grave surrounded by its paling on the bank, or the frame of a wigwam, with a few coals left behind, or the withered stalks still rustling in the Indian's solitary corn-field on the interval. The birch stripped of its bark, or the charred stump where a tree has been burned down to be made into a canoe, these are the only traces of man, — a fabulous wild man to us. On either side, the primeval forest stretches away uninterrupted to Canada or to the "South Sea"; to the white man a drear and howling wilderness, but to the Indian a home, adapted to his nature, and cheerful as the smile of the Great Spirit.

While we loiter here this autumn evening, looking for a spot retired enough, where we shall quietly rest to-night, they thus, in that chilly March evening, one hundred and forty-two years before us, with wind and current favoring, have already glided out of sight, not to camp, as we shall, at night, but while two sleep one will manage the canoe, and the swift stream bear them onward to the settlements, it may be, even to old John Lovewell's house on Salmon Brook to-night.

According to the historian, they escaped as by a miracle all roving bands of Indians, and reached their homes in safety, with their trophies, for which the General Court paid them fifty pounds. The family of Hannah Dustan all assembled alive once more, except the infant whose brains were dashed out against the apple tree, and there have been many who in later times have lived to say that they had eaten of the fruit of that apple tree.

A glimpse of Litchfield

This seems a long while ago, and yet it happened since Milton wrote his Paradise Lost.
But its antiquity is not the less great for that, for
we do not regulate our historical time by the
English standard, nor did the English by the
Roman, nor the Roman by the Greek. "We
must look a long way back," says Raleigh, "to
find the Romans giving laws to nations, and
their consuls bringing kings and princes bound
in chains to Rome in triumph; to see men go
to Greece for wisdom, or Ophir for gold; when
now nothing remains but a poor paper remembrance of their former condition." — And yet,
in one sense, not so far back as to find the Penacooks and Pawtuckets using bows and arrows
and hatchets of stone, on the banks of the
Merrimack. From this September afternoon,
and from between these now cultivated shores,
those times seem more remote than the dark
ages. On beholding an old picture of Concord,
as it appeared but seventy-five years ago, with
a fair, open prospect and a light on trees and
river, as if it were broad noon, I find that I
had not thought the sun shone in those days, or
that men lived in broad daylight then. Still
less do we imagine the sun shining on hill and
valley during Philip's war, on the warpath of
Church or Philip, or later of Lovewell or Paugus,
with serene summer weather, but they must
have lived and fought in a dim twilight or night.

The age of the world is great enough for our imaginations, even according to the Mosaic account, without borrowing any years from the geologist. From Adam and Eve at one leap sheer down to the deluge, and then through the ancient monarchies, through Babylon and Thebes, Brahma and Abraham, to Greece and the Argonauts; whence we might start again with Orpheus and the Trojan war, the Pyramids and the Olympic games, and Homer and Athens, for our stages; and after a breathing space at the building of Rome, continue our journey down through Odin and Christ to — America. It is a wearisome while. — And yet the lives of but sixty old women, such as live under the hill, say of a century each, strung together, are sufficient to reach over the whole ground. Taking hold of hands they would span the interval from Eve to my own mother. A respectable tea-party merely, — whose gossip would be Universal History. The fourth old woman from myself suckled Columbus, — the ninth was nurse to the Norman Conqueror, — the nineteenth was the Virgin Mary, — the twenty-fourth the Cumæan Sibyl, — the thirtieth was at the Trojan war and Helen her name, — the thirty-eighth was Queen Semiramis, — the sixtieth was Eve the mother of mankind. So much for the

—"old woman that lives under the hill,
And if she 's not gone she lives there still."

It will not take a very great grand-daughter of hers to be in at the death of time.

We can never safely exceed the actual facts in our narratives. Of pure invention, such as some suppose, there is no instance. To write a true work of fiction even, is only to take leisure and liberty to describe some things more exactly as they are. A true account of the actual is the rarest poetry, for common sense always takes a hasty and superficial view. Though I am not much acquainted with the works of Goethe, I should say that it was one of his chief excellencies as a writer, that he is satisfied with giving an exact description of things as they appear to him, and their effect upon him. Most travellers have not self-respect enough to do this simply, and make objects and events stand around them as the centre, but still imagine more favorable positions and relations than the actual ones, and so we get no valuable report from them at all. In his Italian Travels Goethe jogs along at a snail's pace, but always mindful that the earth is beneath and the heavens are above him. His Italy is not merely the fatherland of lazzaroni and virtuosi, and scene of splendid ruins, but a solid turf-clad soil, daily shined on by the sun, and nightly by the moon. Even the few showers are faithfully recorded. He speaks as an unconcerned spectator, whose object is faithfully to describe what he sees, and that, for the most part, in the order in which he sees it. Even his reflections do not interfere with his descriptions. In one place he speaks of himself as giving so glowing and truthful a description of an old tower to the peasants who had gathered around him, that they who had been born and brought up in the neighborhood must needs look over their shoulders, "that," to use his own words, "they might behold with their eyes, what I had praised to their ears"— "and I added nothing, not even the ivy which for centuries had decorated the walls." It would thus be possible for inferior minds to produce invaluable books, if this very moderation were not the evidence of superiority; for the wise are not so much wiser than others as respecters of their own wisdom. Some, poor in spirit, record plaintively only what has happened to them; but others how they have happened to the universe, and the judgment which they have awarded to circumstances. Above all, he possessed a hearty good-will to all men, and never wrote a cross or even careless word. On one occasion the post-boy snivelling "Signor perdonate, quésta è la mia patria," he confesses that "to me poor northerner came something tear-like into the eyes."

Goethe's whole education and life were those of the artist. He lacks the unconsciousness of the poet. In his autobiography he describes accurately the life of the author of Wilhelm Meister. For as there is in that book, mingled with a rare and serene wisdom, a certain pettiness or exaggeration of trifles, wisdom applied to produce a constrained and partial and merely well-bred man, — a magnifying of the theatre till life itself is turned into a stage, for which it is our duty to study our parts well, and conduct with propriety and precision, — so in the autobiography, the fault of his education is, so to speak, its artistic completeness. Nature is hindered, though she prevails at last in making an unusually catholic impression on the boy. It is the life of a city boy, whose toys are pictures and works of art, whose wonders are the theatre and kingly processions and crownings. As the youth studied minutely the order and the degrees in the imperial procession, and suffered none of its effect to be lost on him; so the man aimed to secure a rank in society which would satisfy his notion of fitness and respectability. He was defrauded of much which the savage boy enjoys. Indeed he himself has occasion to say in this very autobiography, when at last he escapes into the woods without the gates, — "Thus much is certain, that only the undefinable, wide-expanding feelings of youth and of uncultivated nations are adapted to the sublime, which whenever it may be excited in us through external objects, since it is either formless, or else moulded into forms which are incomprehensible, must surround us with a grandeur which we find above our reach." He further says of himself, — "I had lived among painters from my childhood, and had accustomed myself to look at objects as they did, with reference to art." And this was his practice to the last. He was even too *well-bred* to be thoroughly bred. He says that he had had no intercourse with the lowest class of his towns-boys. The child should have the advantage of ignorance as well as of knowledge, and is fortunate if he gets his share of neglect and exposure. —

"The laws of Nature break the rules of Art."

The Man of Genius may at the same time be, indeed is commonly, an Artist, but the two are not to be confounded. The Man of Genius, referred to mankind, is an originator, an inspired or demonic man, who produces a perfect work in obedience to laws yet unexplored. The Artist is he who detects and applies the law from observation of the works of Genius, whether of man or nature. The Artisan is he who merely applies the rules which others have detected. There has been no man of pure Genius; as there has been none wholly destitute of Genius.

Poetry is the mysticism of mankind.

The expressions of the poet cannot be analyzed; his sentence is one word, whose syllables

are words.   There are indeed no *words* quite
worthy to be set to his music.   But what matter
if we do not hear the words always, if we hear
the music?

Much verse fails of being poetry because it
was not written exactly at the right crisis,
though it may have been inconceivably near to
it.   It is only by a miracle that poetry is written
at all.   It is not recoverable thought, but a
hue caught from a vaster receding thought.

A poem is one undivided unimpeded expression fallen ripe into literature, and it is undivid-
edly and unimpededly received by those for
whom it was matured.

If you can speak what you will never hear, —
if you can write what you will never read, you
have done rare things.

> The work we choose should be our own,
> God lets alone.

The unconsciousness of man is the conscious-
ness of God.

Deep are the foundations of sincerity.   Even
stone walls have their foundation below the
frost.

What is produced by a free stroke charms us,
like the forms of lichens and leaves.   There is
a certain perfection in accident which we never
consciously attain.   Draw a blunt quill filled
with ink over a sheet of paper, and fold the

paper before the ink is dry, transversely to this line, and a delicately shaded and regular figure will be produced, in some respects more pleasing than an elaborate drawing.

The talent of composition is very dangerous,— the striking out the heart of life at a blow, as the Indian takes off a scalp. I feel as if my life had grown more outward when I can express it.

On his journey from Brenner to Verona, Goethe writes, "The Tees flows now more gently, and makes in many places broad sands. On the land, near to the water, upon the hill-sides, everything is so closely planted one to another, that you think they must choke one another, — vineyards, maize, mulberry trees, apples, pears, quinces, and nuts. The dwarf elder throws itself vigorously over the walls. Ivy grows with strong stems up the rocks, and spreads itself wide over them, the lizard glides through the intervals, and everything that wanders to and fro reminds one of the loveliest pictures of art. The women's tufts of hair bound up, the men's bare breasts and light jackets, the excellent oxen which they drive home from market, the little asses with their loads, — everything forms a living, animated Heinrich Roos. And now that it is evening, in the mild air a few clouds rest upon the mountains, in the heavens more stand

still than move, and immediately after sunset
the chirping of crickets begins to grow more
loud; then one feels for once at home in the world,
and not as concealed or in exile. I am contented
as though I had been born and brought up here,
and were now returning from a Greenland or
whaling voyage. Even the dust of my Fatherland, which is often whirled about the wagon,
and which for so long a time I had not seen, is
greeted. The clock-and-bell jingling of the
crickets is altogether lovely, penetrating, and
agreeable. It sounds bravely when roguish
boys whistle in emulation of a field of such
songstresses. One fancies that they really enhance one another. Also the evening is perfectly mild as the day."

"If one who dwelt in the south and came
hither from the south should hear of my rapture
hereupon, he would deem me very childish.
Alas! what I here express I have long known
while I suffered under an unpropitious heaven,
and now may I joyful feel this joy as an exception, which we should enjoy everforth as an
eternal necessity of our nature."

Thus we "sayled by thought and pleasaunce,"
as Chaucer says, and all things seemed with us
to flow; the shore itself, and the distant cliffs,
were dissolved by the undiluted air. The
hardest material seemed to obey the same law

with the most fluid, and so indeed in the long
run it does.   Trees were but rivers of sap and
woody fibre, flowing from the atmosphere, and
emptying into the earth by their trunks, as
their roots flowed upward to the surface.   And
in the heavens there were rivers of stars, and
milky ways, already beginning to gleam and
ripple over our heads.   There were rivers of
rock on the surface of the earth, and rivers of
ore in its bowels, and our thoughts flowed and
circulated, and this portion of time was but the
current hour.   Let us wander where we will,
the universe is built round about us, and we are
central still.   If we look into the heavens they
are concave, and if we were to look into a gulf
as bottomless, it would be concave also.   The
sky is curved downward to the earth in the horizon, because we stand on the plain.   I draw down
its skirts.   The stars so low there seem loath
to depart, but by a circuitous path to be remembering me, and returning on their steps.

We had already passed by broad daylight
the scene of our encampment at Coos Falls,
and at length we pitched our camp on the west
bank, in the northern part of Merrimack,
nearly opposite to the large island on which
we had spent the noon in our way up the river.

There we went to bed that summer evening,
on a sloping shelf in the bank, a couple of rods
from our boat, which was drawn up on the sand,

and just behind a thin fringe of oaks which bordered the river; without having disturbed any inhabitants but the spiders in the grass, which came out by the light of our lamp and crawled over our buffaloes. When we looked out from under the tent, the trees were seen dimly through the mist, and a cool dew hung upon the grass, which seemed to rejoice in the night, and with the damp air we inhaled a solid fragrance. Having eaten our supper of hot cocoa and bread and watermelon, we soon grew weary of conversing and writing in our journals, and putting out the lantern which hung from the tent pole, fell asleep.

Unfortunately many things have been omitted which should have been recorded in our journal, for though we made it a rule to set down all our experiences therein, yet such a resolution is very hard to keep, for the important experience rarely allows us to remember such obligations, and so indifferent things get recorded, while that is frequently neglected. It is not easy to write in a journal what interests us at any time, because to write it is not what interests us.

Whenever we awoke in the night, still eking out our dreams with half-awakened thoughts, it was not till after an interval, when the wind breathed harder than usual, flapping the curtains of the tent, and causing its cords to vi-

brate, that we remembered that we lay on the
bank of the Merrimack, and not in our chamber
at home.   With our heads so low in the grass,
we heard the river whirling and sucking, and
lapsing downward, kissing the shore as it went,
sometimes rippling louder than usual, and again
its mighty current making only a slight limpid
trickling sound, as if our water-pail had sprung
a leak, and the water were flowing into the grass
by our side.   The wind, rustling the oaks and
hazels, impressed us like a wakeful and inconsiderate person up at midnight, moving about
and putting things to rights, occasionally stirring up whole drawers full of leaves at a puff.
There seemed to be a great haste and preparation throughout Nature, as for a distinguished
visitor; all her aisles had to be swept in the night,
by a thousand hand-maidens, and a thousand
pots to be boiled for the next day's feasting; —
such a whispering bustle, as if ten thousand
fairies made their fingers fly, silently sewing at
the new carpet with which the earth was to be
clothed, and the new drapery which was to
adorn the trees.   And then the wind would lull
and die away and we like it fell asleep again.

FRIDAY

"The Boteman strayt
Held on his course with stayed stedfastnesse,
Ne ever shroncke, ne ever sought to bayt
His tryed armes for toylesome wearinesse;
But with his oares did sweepe the watry wildernesse."
— SPENCER.

"Summer's robe grows
Dusky, and like an oft-dyed garment shows."
— DONNE.

AS we lay awake long before daybreak, listening to the rippling of the river and the rustling of the leaves, in suspense whether the wind blew up or down the stream, was favorable or unfavorable to our voyage, we already suspected that there was a change in the weather, from a freshness as of autumn in these sounds. The wind in the woods sounded like an incessant waterfall dashing and roaring amid rocks, and we even felt encouraged by the unusual activity of the elements. He who hears the rippling of rivers in these degenerate days will not utterly despair. That night was the turning point in the season. We had gone to bed in summer, and we awoke in autumn; for summer passes into autumn in some unimaginable point of time, like the turning of a leaf.

We found our boat in the dawn just as we had left it, and as if waiting for us, there on the shore, in autumn, all cool and dripping with dew, and our tracks still fresh in the wet sand around it, the fairies all gone or concealed. Before five o'clock we pushed it into the fog, and leaping in, at one shove were out of sight of the shores, and began to sweep downward with the rushing river, keeping a sharp look out for rocks. We could see only the yellow gurgling water, and a solid bank of fog on every side forming a small yard around us. We soon passed the mouth of the Souhegan and the village of Merrimack, and as the mist gradually rolled away, and we were relieved from the trouble of watching for rocks, we saw by the flitting clouds, by the first russet tinge on the hills, by the rushing river, the cottages on shore, and the shore itself, so coolly fresh and shining with dew, and later in the day, by the hue of the grape vine, the goldfinch on the willow, the flickers flying in flocks, and when we passed near enough to the shore, as we fancied, by the faces of men, that the Fall had commenced. The cottages looked more snug and comfortable, and their inhabitants were seen only for a moment, and then went quietly in and shut

Souhegan River

the door, retreating inward to the haunts of summer.

"And now the cold autumnal dews are seen
    To cobweb ev'ry green;
And by the low-shorn rowens doth appear
    The fast declining year."

We heard the sigh of the first autumnal wind, and even the water had acquired a grayer hue. The sumach, grape, and maple were already changed, and the milkweed had turned to a deep rich yellow. In all woods the leaves were fast ripening for their fall; for their full veins and lively gloss mark the ripe leaf, and not the sered one of the poets; and we knew that the maples, stripped of their leaves among the earliest, would soon stand like a wreath of smoke along the edge of the meadow. Already the cattle were heard to low wildly in the pastures and along the highways, restlessly running to and fro, as if in apprehension of the withering of the grass and of the approach of winter. Our thoughts too began to rustle.

As I pass along the streets of our village of Concord on the day of our annual Cattle Show, when it usually happens that the leaves of the elms and buttonwoods begin first to strew the ground under the breath of the October wind, the lively spirits in their sap seem to mount as high as any plow-boy's let loose that day; and they lead my thoughts away to the rustling woods, where the trees are preparing for their winter campaign. This autumnal festival, when men are gathered in crowds in the streets as regularly and by as natural a law as the leaves cluster and rustle by the wayside, is naturally associated in my mind with the fall of the year. The low of cattle in the streets sounds like a hoarse symphony or running base to the rustling of the leaves. The wind goes hurrying down the country, gleaning every loose straw that is left in the fields, while every farmer lad too appears to scud before it, — having donned his best pea-jacket and pepper-and-salt waistcoat, his un-bent trousers, outstanding rigging of duck, or kersymere, or corduroy, and his furry hat withal, — to country fairs and cattle shows, to that Rome among the villages where the treasures of the year are gathered. All the land over they go leaping the fences with their tough idle palms, which have never learned to hang by their sides, amid the low of calves and the bleating of sheep, — Amos, Abner, Elnathan, Elbridge, —

"From steep pine-bearing mountains to the plain."

I love these sons of earth, every mother's son of them, with their great hearty hearts rushing tu-multuously in herds from spectacle to spectacle, as if fearful lest there should not be time be-tween sun and sun to see them all, and the sun does not wait more than in haying time.

"Wise nature's darlings, they live in the world
Perplexing not themselves how it is hurled."

Running hither and thither with appetite for
the coarse pastimes of the day, now with boisterous speed at the heels of the inspired negro from
whose larynx the melodies of all Congo and
Guinea coast have broke loose into our streets;
now to see the procession of a hundred yoke
of oxen, all as august and grave as Osiris, or
the droves of neat cattle and milch cows as un-
spotted as Isis or Io.   Such as had no love for
Nature

"at all,
Came lovers home from this great festival."

They may bring their fattest cattle and richest
fruits to the fair, but they are all eclipsed by the
show of men.   These are stirring autumn days,
when men sweep by in crowds, amid the rustle
of leaves, like migrating finches, this is the true
harvest of the year, when the air is but the
breath of men, and the rustling of leaves is as the
trampling of the crowd.   We read now-a-days
of the ancient festivals, games, and processions
of the Greeks and Etruscans, with a little in-
credulity, or at least with little sympathy; but
how natural and irrepressible in every people
is some hearty and palpable greeting of Nature.
The Corybantes, the Bacchantes, the rude
primitive tragedians with their procession and
goat-song, and the whole paraphernalia of the

Panathenæa, which appear so antiquated and
peculiar, have their parallel now. The husbandman is always a better Greek than the scholar
is prepared to appreciate, and the old custom
still survives, while antiquarians and scholars
grow gray in commemorating it. The farmers
crowd to the fair to-day in obedience to the
same ancient law which Solon or Lycurgus did
not enact, as naturally as bees swarm and
follow their queen.

It is worth the while to see the country's
people, how they pour into the town, the sober
farmer folk, now all agog, their very shirt and
coat collars pointing forward, — collars so broad
as if they had put their shirts on wrong end
upward, for the fashions always tend to superfluity, — and with an unusual springiness in
their gait, jabbering earnestly to one another.
The more supple vagabond, too, is sure to appear
on the least rumor of such a gathering, and the
next day to disappear, and go into his hole like
the seventeen-year locust, in an ever shabby
coat, though finer than the farmer's best, yet
never dressed; come to see the sport, and have
a hand in what is going, — to know "what's the
row," if there is any; to be where some men are
drunk, some horses race, some cockerels fight;
anxious to be shaking props under a table, and
above all to see the "striped pig." He especially
is the creature of the occasion. He empties

both his pockets and his character into the stream, and swims in such a day. He dearly loves the social slush. There is no reserve of soberness in him.

I love to see the herd of men feeding heartily on coarse and succulent pleasures, as cattle on the husks and stalks of vegetables. Though there are many crooked and crabbed specimens of humanity among them, run all to thorn and rind, and crowded out of shape by adverse circumstances, like the third chestnut in the burr, so that you wonder to see some heads wear a whole hat, yet fear not that the race will fail or waiver in them; like the crabs which grow in hedges, they furnish the stocks of sweet and thrifty fruits still. Thus is nature recruited from age to age, while the fair and palatable varieties die out and have their period. This is that mankind. How cheap must be the material of which so many are made.

The wind blew steadily down the stream, so that we kept our sails set, and lost not a moment of the forenoon by delays, but from early morning until noon, were continually dropping downward. With our hands on the steering paddle, which was thrust deep into the river, or bending to the oar, which indeed we rarely relinquished, we felt each palpitation in the veins

of our steed, and each impulse of the wings
which drew us above. The current of our
thoughts made as sudden bends as the river,
which was continually opening new prospects to
the east or south, but we are aware that rivers
flow most rapidly and shallowest at these
points. The steadfast shores never once turned
aside for us, but still trended as they were made;
why then should we always turn aside for them?

A man cannot wheedle nor overawe his
Genius. It requires to be conciliated by nobler
conduct than the world demands or can appreciate. These winged thoughts are like birds, and
will not be handled; even hens will not let you
touch them like quadrupeds. Nothing was
ever so unfamiliar and startling to a man as his
own thoughts.

To the rarest genius it is the most expensive
to succumb and conform to the ways of the
world. Genius is the worst of lumber, if the
poet would float upon the breeze of popularity.
The bird of paradise is obliged constantly to fly
against the wind, lest its gay trappings, pressing
close to its body, may impede its free movements.

He is the best sailor who can steer within the
fewest points of the wind, and exact a motive
power out of the greatest obstacles. Most
begin to veer and tack as soon as the wind
changes from aft, and as within the tropics it
does not blow from all points of the compass,

there are some harbors which they can never reach.

The poet is no tender slip of fairy stock, who requires peculiar institutions and edicts for his defence, but the toughest son of earth and of Heaven, and by his greater strength and endurance his fainting companions will recognize the God in him. It is the worshippers of beauty, after all, who have done the real pioneer work of the world.

The poet will prevail to be popular in spite of his faults, and in spite of his beauties too. He will hit the nail on the head, and we shall not know the shape of his hammer. He makes us free of his hearth and heart, which is greater than to offer one the freedom of a city.

Great men, unknown to their generation, have their fame among the great who have preceded them, and all true worldly fame subsides from their high estimate beyond the stars.

Orpheus does not hear the strains which issue from his lyre, but only those which are breathed into it; for the original strain precedes the sound, by as much as the echo follows after; the rest is the perquisite of the rocks and trees and beasts.

When I stand in a library where is all the recorded wit of the world, but none of the recording, a mere accumulated, and not truly cumulative treasure, where immortal works stand side by side with anthologies which did not survive their moth, and cobweb and mildew have already spread from these to the binding of those; and happily I am reminded of what poetry is, I perceive that Shakspeare and Milton did not foresee into what company they were to fall. Alas! that so soon the work of a true poet should be swept into such a dust-hole!

The poet will write for his peers alone. He will remember only that he saw truth and beauty from his position, and expect the time when a vision as broad shall overlook the same field as freely.

We are often prompted to speak our thoughts to our neighbors, or the single travellers whom we meet on the road, but poetry is a communication from our home and solitude addressed to all Intelligence. It never whispers in a private ear. Knowing this, we may understand those sonnets said to be addressed to particular persons, or "to a Mistress' Eyebrow." Let none feel flattered by them. For poetry write love, and it will be equally true.

No doubt it is an important difference between men of genius or poets, and men not of genius, that the latter are unable to grasp and confront the thought which visits them. But it is because it is too faint for expression, or even conscious impression. What merely quickens or retards the blood in their veins and fills their afternoons with pleasure they know not whence, conveys a distinct assurance to the finer organization of the poet.

We talk of genius as if it were a mere knack, and the poet could only express what other men conceived. But in comparison with his task the poet is the least talented of any; the writer of prose has more skill. See what talent the smith has. His material is pliant in his hands. When the poet is most inspired, is stimulated by an *aura* which never even colors the afternoons of common men, then his talent is all gone, and he is no longer a poet. The gods do not grant him any skill more than another. They never put their gifts into his hands, but they encompass and sustain him with their breath.

To say that God has given a man many and great talents, frequently means, that he has brought his heavens down within reach of his hands.

When the poetic frenzy seizes us, we run and scratch with our pen, intent only on worms, calling our mates around us, like the cock, and delighting in the dust we make, but do not detect where the jewel lies, which, perhaps, we have in the meantime cast to a distance, or quite covered up again.

The poet's body even is not fed simply like

other men's, but he sometimes tastes the genuine nectar and ambrosia of the gods, and lives a divine life. By the healthful and invigorating thrills of inspiration his life is preserved to a serene old age.

Some poems are for holidays only. They are polished and sweet, but it is the sweetness of sugar, and not such as toil gives to sour bread. The breath with which the poet utters his verse must be that by which he lives.

Great prose, of equal elevation, commands our respect more than great verse, since it implies a more permanent and level height, a life more pervaded with the grandeur of the thought. The poet often only makes an irruption, like a Parthian, and is off again, shooting while he retreats; but the prose writer has conquered like a Roman, and settled colonies.

The true poem is not that which the public read. There is always a poem not printed on paper, coincident with the production of this, stereotyped in the poet's life. It is *what he has become through his work.* Not how is the idea expressed in stone, or on canvas or paper, is the question, but how far it has obtained form and expression in the life of the artist. His true work will not stand in any prince's gallery.

> My life has been the poem I would have writ,
> But I could not both live and utter it.

THE POET'S DELAY

In vain I see the morning rise,
  In vain observe the western blaze,
Who idly look to other skies,
  Expecting life by other ways.

Amidst such boundless wealth without,
  I only still am poor within,
The birds have sung their summer out,
  But still my spring does not begin.

Shall I then wait the autumn wind,
  Compelled to seek a milder day,
And leave no curious nest behind,
  No woods still echoing to my lay?

This raw and gusty day, and the creaking of the oaks and pines on shore, reminded us of more northern climes than Greece, and more wintry seas than the Ægean.

The genuine remains of Ossian, or those ancient poems which bear his name, though of less fame and extent, are, in many respects, of the same stamp with the Iliad itself. He asserts the dignity of the bard no less than Homer, and in his era we hear of no other priest than he. It will not avail to call him a heathen, because he personifies the sun and addresses it; and what if his heroes did "worship the ghosts of their fathers," their thin, airy, and unsubstantial forms? we but worship the ghosts of our fathers in more substantial forms. We cannot but respect the vigorous faith of those heathen, who sternly believed somewhat, and we are inclined

to say to the critics, who are offended by their
superstitious rites, — Don't interrupt these men's
prayers.   As if we knew more about human life
and a God, than the heathen and ancients.
Does English theology contain the recent
discoveries?

Ossian reminds us of the most refined and
rudest eras, of Homer, Pindar, Isaiah, and the
American Indian.   In his poetry, as in Homer's,
only the simplest and most enduring features of
humanity are seen, such essential parts of a
man as Stonehenge exhibits of a temple; we
see the circles of stone, and the upright shaft
alone.   The phenomena of life acquire almost
an unreal and gigantic size seen through his
mists.   Like all older and grander poetry, it is
distinguished by the few elements in the lives
of its heroes.   They stand on the heath, between
the stars and the earth, shrunk to the bones and
sinews.   The earth is a boundless plain for
their deeds.   They lead such a simple, dry, and
everlasting life, as hardly needs depart with the
flesh, but is transmitted entire from age to age.
There are but few objects to distract their sight,
and their life is as unincumbered as the course
of the stars they gaze at. —

> "The wrathful kings, on cairns apart,
>   Look forward from behind their shields,
>   And mark the wandering stars,
>   That brilliant westward move."

It does not cost much for these heroes to live; they do not want much furniture. They are such forms of men only as can be seen afar through the mist, and have no costume nor dialect, but for language there is the tongue itself, and for costume there are always the skins of beasts and the bark of trees to be had. They live out their years by the vigor of their constitutions. They survive storms and the spears of their foes, and perform a few heroic deeds, and then,

> "Mounds will answer questions of them,
> For many future years."

Blind and infirm, they spend the remnant of their days listening to the lays of the bards, and feeling the weapons which laid their enemies low, and when at length they die, by a convulsion of nature, the bard allows us a short and misty glance into futurity, yet as clear, perchance, as their lives had been. When MacRoine was slain,

> "His soul departed to his warlike sires,
> To follow misty forms of boars,
> In tempestuous islands bleak."

The hero's cairn is erected, and the bard sings a brief significant strain, which will suffice for epitaph and biography.

> "The weak will find his bow in the dwelling,
> The feeble will attempt to bend it."

Compared with this simple, fibrous life, our civilized history appears the chronicle of debility, of fashion, and the arts of luxury. But the civilized man misses no real refinement in the poetry of the rudest era. It reminds him that civilization does but dress men. It makes shoes, but it does not toughen the soles of the feet. It makes cloth of finer texture, but it does not touch the skin. Inside the civilized man stands the savage still in the place of honor. We are those blue-eyed, yellow-haired Saxons, those slender, dark-haired Normans.

The profession of the bard attracted more respect in those days from the importance attached to fame. It was his province to record the deeds of heroes. When Ossian hears the traditions of inferior bards, he exclaims, —

> "I straightway seize the unfutile tales,
> And send them down in faithful verse."

His philosophy of life is expressed in the opening of the third Duan of Ca-Lodin.

> "Whence have sprung the things that are?
> And whither roll the passing years?
> Where does Time conceal its two heads,
> In dense impenetrable gloom,
> Its surface marked with heroes' deeds alone?
> I view the generations gone;
> The past appears but dim;
> As objects by the moon's faint beams,
> Reflected from a distant lake.

> I see, indeed, the thunderbolts of war,
> But there the unmighty joyless dwell,
> All those who send not down their deeds
> To far, succeeding times."

The ignoble warriors die and are forgotten;

> "Strangers come to build a tower,
> And throw their ashes overhand;
> Some rusted swords appear in dust;
> One, bending forward, says,
> 'The arms belonged to heroes gone;
> We never heard their praise in song.'"

The grandeur of the similes is another feature which characterizes great poetry. Ossian seems to speak a gigantic and universal language. The images and pictures occupy even much space in the landscape, as if they could be seen only from the sides of mountains, and plains with a wide horizon, or across arms of the sea. The machinery is so massive that it cannot be less than natural. Oivana says to the spirit of her father, "Grey-haired Torkil of Torne," seen in the skies,

> "Thou glidest away like receding ships."

So when the hosts of Fingal and Starne approach to battle,

> "With murmurs loud, like rivers far,
> The race of Torne hither moved."

And when compelled to retire,

> ——"dragging his spear behind,
> Cudulin sank in the distant wood,
> Like a fire upblazing ere it dies."

Nor did Fingal want a proper audience when he spoke;

> "A thousand orators inclined
> To hear the lay of Fingal."

The threats too would have deterred a man. Vengeance and terror were real. Trenmore threatens the young warrior whom he meets on a foreign strand,

> "Thy mother shall find thee pale on the shore,
> While lessening on the waves she spies
> The sails of him who slew her son."

If Ossian's heroes weep, it is from excess of strength, and not from weakness, a sacrifice or libation of fertile natures, like the perspiration of stone in summer's heat. We hardly know that tears have been shed, and it seems as if weeping were proper only for babes and heroes. Their joy and their sorrow are made of one stuff, like rain and snow, the rainbow and the mist. When Fillan was worsted in fight, and ashamed in the presence of Fingal,

> "He strode away forthwith,
> And bent in grief above a stream,
> His cheeks bedewed with tears.
> From time to time the thistles gray
> He lopped with his inverted lance."

Crodar, blind and old, receives Ossian, son of
Fingal, who comes to aid him in war; —

> "'My eyes have failed,' says he, 'Crodar is blind,
> Is thy strength like that of thy fathers?
> Stretch, Ossian, thine arm to the hoary-haired.'
>   I gave my arm to the king.
> The aged hero seized my hand;
> He heaved a heavy sigh;
> Tears flowed incessant down his cheek.
> 'Strong art thou, son of the mighty,
> Though not so dreadful as Morven's prince. * * *
> Let my feast be spread in the hall,
> Let every sweet-voiced minstrel sing;
> Great is he who is within my wall,
> Sons of wave-echoing Croma.' "

Even Ossian himself, the hero-bard, pays
tribute to the superior strength of his father
Fingal.

> "How beauteous, mighty man, was thy mind,
> Why succeeded Ossian without its strength?"

While we sailed fleetly before the wind, with
the river gurgling under our stern, the thoughts
of autumn coursed as steadily through our
minds, and we observed less what was passing
on the shore, than the dateless associations and
impressions which the season awakened, anticipating in some measure the progress of the
year. —

I hearing get, who had but ears,
  And sight, who had but eyes before,
I moments live, who lived but years,
  And truth discern, who knew but learning's lore.

Sitting with our faces now up stream, we studied the landscape by degrees, as one unrolls a map, — rock, tree, house, hill, and meadow, assuming new and varying positions as wind and water shifted the scene, and there was variety enough for our entertainment in the metamorphoses of the simplest objects. Viewed from this side the scenery appeared new to us.

The most familiar sheet of water viewed from a new hill-top, yields a novel and unexpected pleasure. When we have travelled a few miles, we do not recognize the profiles even of the hills which overlook our native village, and perhaps no man is quite familiar with the horizon as seen from the hill nearest to his house, and can recall its outline distinctly when in the valley. We do not commonly know, beyond a short distance, which way the hills range which take in our houses and farms in their sweep. As if our birth had at first sundered things, and we had been thrust up through into nature like a wedge, and not till the wound heals and the scar disappears, do we begin to discover where we are, and that nature is one and continuous everywhere. It is an important epoch when a man who has always lived on the east side of a mountain and seen it in the west, travels round and sees it in the east. Yet the universe is a sphere whose centre is wherever there is intelligence. The sun is not so central as a man. Upon an isolated hill-top, in an open country, we seem to ourselves to be standing on the boss of an immense shield, the immediate landscape being apparently depressed below the more remote, and rising gradually to the horizon, which is the rim of the shield, villas, steeples, forests, mountains, one above another, till they are swallowed up in the heavens. The most distant mountains appear to rise directly from the shore of that lake in the woods by which we chance to be standing, while from the mountain top, not only this, but a thousand nearer and larger lakes, are equally unobserved.

Seen through this clear atmosphere, the works of the farmer, his plowing and reaping, had a beauty to our eyes which he never saw. How fortunate were we who did not own an acre of these shores, who had not renounced our title to the whole. One who knew how to appropriate the true value of this world would be the poorest man in it. The poor rich man! all he has is what he has bought. What I see is mine. I am a large owner in the Merrimack intervals. —

> Men dig and dive but cannot my wealth spend,
>   Who yet no partial store appropriate,
> Who no armed ship into the Indies send,
>   To rob me of my orient estate.

He is the rich man, and enjoys the fruits of riches, who summer and winter forever can find delight in his own thoughts. Buy a farm! What have I to pay for a farm which a farmer will take?

When I visit again some haunt of my youth, I am glad to find that nature wears so well. The landscape is indeed something real, and solid, and sincere, and I have not put my foot through it yet. There is a pleasant tract on the bank of the Concord, called Conantum, which I have in my mind; — the old deserted farm-house, the desolate pasture with its bleak cliff, the open wood, the river-reach, the green meadow in the midst, and the moss-grown wild-apple orchard, — places where one may have many thoughts and not decide anything. It is a scene which I can not only remember, as I might a vision, but when I will can bodily revisit, and find it even so, unaccountable, yet unpretending in its pleasant dreariness. When my thoughts are sensible of change, I love to see and sit on rocks which I *have* known, and pry into their moss, and see unchangeableness so established. I not yet gray on rocks forever gray, I no longer green under the evergreens. There is something even in the lapse of time by which time recovers itself.

As we have said, it proved a cool as well as breezy day, and by the time we reached Peni-

Near the mouth of Pennichook Brook

chook Brook, we were obliged to sit muffled in
our cloaks, while the wind and current carried
us along. We bounded swiftly over the rippling
surface, far by many cultivated lands and the
ends of fences which divided innumerable farms,
with hardly a thought for the various lives
which they separated; now by long rows of
alders or groves of pines or oaks, and now by
some homestead where the women and children
stood outside to gaze at us, till we had swept
out of their sight, and beyond the limit of their
longest Saturday ramble. We glided past the
mouth of the Nashua, and not long after, of
Salmon Brook, without more pause than the
wind. —

> Salmon Brook,
> Penichook,
> Ye sweet waters of my brain,
> When shall I look,
> Or cast the hook,
> In your waves again?

> Silver eels,
> Wooden creels,
> These the baits that still allure,
> And dragon-fly
> That floated by, —
> May they still endure?

The shadows chased one another swiftly over
wood and meadow, and their alternation harmo-
nized with our mood. We could distinguish the
clouds which cast each one, though never so

high in the heavens. When a shadow flits
across the landscape of the soul, where is the
substance? Probably, if we were wise enough,
we should see to what virtue we are indebted
for any happier moment we enjoy. No doubt
we have earned it at some time; for the gifts
of Heaven are never quite gratuitous. The
constant abrasion and decay of our lives makes
the soil of our future growth. The wood which
we now mature, when it becomes virgin mould,
determines the character of our second growth,
whether that be oaks or pines. Every man
casts a shadow; not his body only, but his
imperfectly mingled spirit; this is his grief;
let him turn which way he will, it falls opposite
to the sun; short at noon, long at eve. Did you
never see it? — But, referred to the sun, it is
widest at its base, which is no greater than his
own opacity. The divine light is diffused
almost entirely around us, and by means of the
reflection of light, or else by a certain self-
luminousness, or, as some will have it, transparency, if we preserve ourselves untarnished,
we are able to enlighten our shaded side. At
any rate, our darkest grief has that bronze
color of the moon eclipsed. There is no ill
which may not be dissipated, like the dark, if
you let in a stronger light upon it. Shadows,
referred to the source of light, are pyramids
whose bases are never greater than those of the

substances which cast them, but light is a spherical congeries of pyramids, whose very apexes are the sun itself, and hence the system shines with uninterrupted light. But if the light we use is but a paltry and narrow taper, most objects will cast a shadow wider than themselves.

The places where we had stopped or spent the night in our way up the river, had already acquired a slight historical interest for us; for many upward days' voyaging were unravelled in this rapid downward passage. When one landed to stretch his limbs by walking, he soon found himself falling behind his companion, and was obliged to take advantage of the curves, and ford the brooks and ravines in haste, to recover his ground. Already the banks and the distant meadows wore a sober and deepened tinge, for the September air had shorn them of their summer's pride. —

> "And what's a life? The flourishing array
> Of the proud summer meadow, which to-day
> Wears her green plush, and is to-morrow hay."

The air was really the "fine element" which the poets describe. It had a finer and sharper grain, seen against the russet pastures and meadows, than before, as if cleansed of the summer's impurities.

Having passed the New Hampshire line and reached the Horseshoe Interval in Tyngsboro', where there is a high and regular second bank,

we climbed up this in haste to get a nearer sight
of the autumnal flowers, asters, golden-rod, and
yarrow, and the *trichostema dichotoma*, humble
road-side blossoms, and, lingering still, the harebell and the *rhexia Virginica*. The last, growing
in patches of lively pink flowers on the edge of
the meadows, had almost too gay an appearance
for the rest of the landscape, like a pink ribbon
on the bonnet of a Puritan woman. Asters and
golden-rods were the livery which nature wore
at present. The latter alone expressed all the
ripeness of the season, and shed their mellow
lustre over the fields, as if the now declining
summer's sun had bequeathed its hues to them.
It is the floral solstice a little after mid-summer,
when the particles of golden light, the sun-dust,
have, as it were, fallen like seeds on the earth,
and produced these blossoms. On every hill-
side, and in every valley, stood countless asters,
coreopses, tansies, golden-rods, and the whole
race of yellow flowers, like Brahminical devotees,
turning steadily with their luminary from morning till night.

> "I see the golden-rod shine bright,
>   As sun-showers at the birth of day,
> A golden plume of yellow light,
>   That robs the Day-god's splendid ray.
>
> "The aster's violet rays divide
>   The bank with many stars for me,
> And yarrow in blanch tints is dyed,
>   As moonlight floats across the sea.

"I see the emerald woods prepare
    To shed their vestiture once more,
And distant elm-trees spot the air
    With yellow pictures softly o'er. * *

"No more the water-lily's pride
    In milk-white circles swims content,
No more the blue-weed's clusters ride
    And mock the heaven's element. * *

"Autumn, thy wreath and mine are blent
    With the same colors, for to me
A richer sky than all is lent,
    While fades my dream-like company.

"Our skies glow purple, but the wind
    Sobs chill through green trees and bright grass,
To-day shines fair, and lurk behind
    The times that into winter pass.

"So fair we seem, so cold we are,
    So fast we hasten to decay,
Yet through our night glows many a star,
    That still shall claim its sunny day."

So sang a Concord poet once.

There is a peculiar interest belonging to the still later flowers, which abide with us the approach of winter. There is something witch-like in the appearance of the witch-hazel, which blossoms late in October and in November, with its irregular and angular spray and petals like furies' hair, or small ribbon streamers. Its blossoming, too, at this irregular period, when other shrubs have lost their leaves, as well as

blossoms, looks like witches' craft. Certainly
it blooms in no garden of man's. There is
a whole fairy-land on the hill-side where it
grows.

Some have thought that the gales do not at
present waft to the voyager the natural and
original fragrance of the land, such as the early
navigators described, and that the loss of many
odoriferous native plants, sweet-scented grasses
and medicinal herbs, which formerly sweetened
the atmosphere, and rendered it salubrious, by
the grazing of cattle and the rooting of swine,
is the source of many diseases which now prevail; the earth, say they, having been long subjected to extremely artificial and luxurious
modes of cultivation, to gratify the appetite,
converted into a stye and hot-bed, where men
for profit increase the ordinary decay of nature.

According to the record of an old inhabitant
of Tyngsboro', now dead, whose farm we were
now gliding past, one of the greatest freshets on
this river took place in October, 1785, and its
height was marked by a nail driven into an
apple tree behind his house. One of his descendants has shown this to me, and I judged it to
be at least seventeen or eighteen feet above the
level of the river at the time. Before the Lowell
and Nashua railroad was built, the engineer
made inquiries of the inhabitants along the

banks as to how high they had known the river
to rise. When he came to this house he was
conducted to the apple tree, and as the nail was
not then visible, the lady of the house placed
her hand on the trunk where she said that she
remembered the nail to have been from her
childhood. In the meanwhile the old man put
his arm inside the tree, which was hollow, and
felt the point of the nail sticking through, and
it was exactly opposite to her hand. The spot
is now plainly marked by a notch in the bark.
But as no one else remembered the river to
have risen so high as this, the engineer disre-
garded this statement, and I learn that there has
since been a freshet which rose within nine
inches of the rails at Biscuit Brook, and such a
freshet as that of 1785 would have covered the
railroad two feet deep.

The revolutions of nature tell as fine tales,
and make as interesting revelations, on this
river's banks, as on the Euphrates or the Nile.
This apple tree, which stands within a few rods
of the river, is called "Elisha's apple tree,"
from a friendly Indian, who was anciently in
the service of Jonathan Tyng, and, with one
other man, was killed here by his own race in one
of the Indian wars, — the particulars of which
affair were told us on the spot. He was buried
close by, no one knew exactly where, but in the
flood of 1785, so great a weight of water stand-

ing over the grave, caused the earth to settle
where it had once been disturbed, and when the
flood went down, a sunken spot, exactly of the
form and size of the grave, revealed its locality,
but this was now lost again, and no future flood
can detect it; yet, no doubt, Nature will know
how to point it out in due time, if it be necessary,
by methods yet more searching and unexpected.
Thus there is not only the crisis when the spirit
ceases to inspire and expand the body, marked
by a fresh mound in the church-yard, but there
is also a crisis when the body ceases to take up
room as such in nature, marked by a fainter
depression in the earth.

We sat awhile to rest us here upon the brink
of the western bank, surrounded by the glossy
leaves of the red variety of the mountain laurel,
just above the head of Wicasuck Island, where
we could observe some scows which were loading with clay from the opposite shore, and also
overlook the grounds of the farmer, of whom I
have spoken, who once hospitably entertained
us for a night. He had on his pleasant farm,
besides an abundance of the beach plum, or
prunus littoralis, which grew wild, the Canada
plum under cultivation, fine Porter apples,
some peaches, and large patches of musk and
watermelons, which he cultivated for the Lowell
market. Elisha's apple tree, too, bore a native
fruit, which was prized by the family. He

raised the blood peach, which, as he showed us
with satisfaction, was more like the oak in the
color of its bark and in the setting of its branches,
and was less liable to break down under the
weight of the fruit, or the snow, than other
varieties. It was of slower growth, and its
branches strong and tough. There, also, was
his nursery of native apple trees, thickly set
upon the bank, which cost but little care, and
which he sold to the neighboring farmers when
they were five or six years old. To see a single
peach upon its stem makes an impression of
paradisaical fertility and luxury. This reminded us even of an old Roman farm, as described by Varro: "Cæsar Vopiscus Ædilicius,
when he pleaded before the Censors, said that
the grounds of Rosea were the garden (*sumen*
the tid-bit) of Italy, in which a pole being left
would not be visible the day after, on account of
the growth of the herbage." This soil may not
have been remarkably fertile, yet at this distance we thought that this anecdote might be
told of the Tyngsboro' farm.

When we passed Wicasuck Island, there was
a pleasure boat containing a youth and a maiden
on the island brook, which we were pleased to
see, since it proved that there were some hereabouts to whom our excursions would not be
wholly strange. Before this, a canal-boatman, of
whom we made some inquiries respecting Wica-

suck Island, and who told us that it was disputed property, supposed that we had a claim upon it, and though we assured him that all this was news to us, and explained, as well as we could, why we had come to see it, he believed not a word of it, and seriously offered us one hundred dollars for our title.   The only other small boats which we met with were used to pick up driftwood.   Some of the poorer class along the stream collect, in this way, all the fuel which they require.   While one of us landed not far from this island to forage for provisions among the farm-houses whose roofs we saw, for our supply was now exhausted, the other, sitting in the boat, which was moored to the shore, was left alone to his reflections.

If there is nothing new on the earth, still the traveller always has a resource in the skies. They are constantly turning a new page to view. The wind sets the types on this blue ground, and the inquiring may always read a new truth there.   There are things there written with such fine and subtil tinctures, paler than the juice of limes, that to the diurnal eye they leave no trace, and only the chemistry of night reveals them.   Every man's daylight firmament answers in his mind to the brightness of the vision in his starriest hour.

These continents and hemispheres are soon run over, but an always unexplored and infinite region makes off on every side from the mind, further than to sunset, and we can make no highway or beaten track into it, but the grass immediately springs up in the path, for we travel there chiefly with our wings.

Sometimes we see objects as through a thin haze, in their eternal relations, and they stand like Palenque and the Pyramids, and we wonder who set them up, and for what purpose. If we see the reality in things, of what moment is the superficial and apparent longer? What are the earth and all its interests beside the deep surmise which pierces and scatters them? While I sit here listening to the waves which ripple and break on this shore, I am absolved from all obligation to the past, and the council of nations may reconsider its votes. The grating of a pebble annuls them. Still occasionally in my dreams I remember that rippling water. —

> Oft, as I turn me on my pillow o'er,
> I hear the lapse of waves upon the shore,
> Distinct as if it were at broad noon-day,
> And I were drifting down from Nashua.

With a bending sail we glided rapidly by Tyngsboro' and Chelmsford, each holding in one hand half of a tart country apple-pie which we had purchased to celebrate our return, and in the other a fragment of the newspaper in which it was wrapped, devouring these with divided relish, and learning the news which had transpired

since we sailed. The river here opened into a
broad and straight reach of great length, which
we bounded merrily over before a smacking
breeze, with a devil-may-care look in our faces,
and our boat a white bone in its mouth, and a
speed which greatly astonished some scow
boatmen whom we met. The wind in the horizon
rolled like a flood over valley and plain, and
every tree bent to the blast, and the mountains
like school-boys turned their cheeks to it. They
were great and current motions, the flowing
sail, the running stream, the waving tree, the
roving wind. The north wind stepped readily
into the harness which we had provided, and
pulled us along with good will. Sometimes we
sailed as gently and steadily as the clouds overhead, watching the receding shores and the motions of our sail; the play of its pulse so like our
own lives, so thin and yet so full of life, so noise-
less when it labored hardest, so noisy and impatient when least effective; now bending to
some generous impulse of the breeze, and then
fluttering and flapping with a kind of human
suspense. It was the scale on which the varying
temperature of distant atmospheres was graduated, and it was some attraction for us that the
breeze it played with had been out of doors so
long. Thus we sailed, not being able to fly, but
as next best, making a long furrow in the fields
of the Merrimack toward our home, with our

wings spread, but never lifting our heel from the watery trench; gracefully plowing homeward with our brisk and willing team, wind and stream, pulling together, the former yet a wild steer, yoked to his more sedate fellow. It was very near flying, as when the duck rushes through the water with an impulse of her wings, throwing the spray about her, before she can rise. How we had stuck fast if drawn up but a few feet on the shore!

When we reached the great bend just above Middlesex, where the river runs east thirty-five miles to the sea, we at length lost the aid of this propitious wind, though we contrived to make one long and judicious tack carry us nearly to the locks of the canal. We were here locked through at noon by our old friend, the lover of the higher mathematics, who seemed glad to see us safe back again through so many locks; but we did not stop to consider any of his problems, though we could cheerfully have spent a whole autumn in this way another time, and never have asked what his religion was. It is so rare to meet with a man out-doors who cherishes a worthy thought in his mind, which is independent of the labor of his hands. Behind every man's busy-ness there should be a level of undisturbed serenity and industry, as within the reef encircling a coral isle there is always an expanse of still water, where the depositions are going on which will finally raise it above the surface.

The eye which can appreciate the naked and absolute beauty of a scientific truth is far more rare than that which is attracted by a moral one. Few detect the morality in the former, or the science in the latter. Aristotle defined art to be Λόγος τοῦ ἔργου ἄνευ ὕλης *the principle of the work without the wood;* but most men prefer to have some of the wood along with the principle; they demand that the truth be clothed in flesh and blood and the warm colors of life. They prefer the partial statement because it fits and measures them and their commodities best. But science still exists everywhere as the sealer of weights and measures at least.

We have heard much about the poetry of mathematics, but very little of it has yet been sung. The ancients had a juster notion of their poetic value than we. The most distinct and beautiful statement of any truth must take at last the mathematical form. We might so simplify the rules of moral philosophy, as well as of arithmetic, that one formula would express them both. All the moral laws are readily translated into natural philosophy, for often we have only to restore the primitive meaning of the words by which they are expressed, or to attend to their literal instead of their metaphorical sense. They are already *supernatural* philosophy. The whole

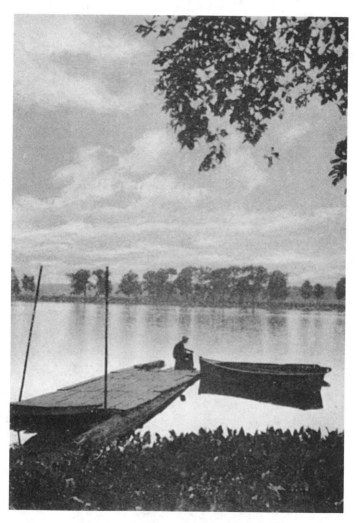

The Merrimack opposite the Middlesex Locks

body of what is now called moral or ethical truth existed in the golden age as abstract science. Or, if we prefer, we may say that the laws of Nature are the purest morality. The Tree of Knowledge is a Tree of Knowledge of good and evil. He is not a true man of science who does not bring some sympathy to his studies, and expect to learn something by behavior as well as by application. It is childish to rest in the discovery of mere coincidences, or of partial and extraneous laws. The study of geometry is a petty and idle exercise of the mind, if it is applied to no larger system than the starry one. Mathematics should be mixed not only with physics but with ethics, *that* is *mixed* mathematics. The fact which interests us most is the life of the naturalist. The purest science is still biographical. Nothing will dignify and elevate science while it is sundered so wholly from the moral life of its devotee, and he professes another religion than it teaches, and worships at a foreign shrine. Anciently the faith of a philosopher was identical with his system, or, in other words, his view of the universe.

My friends mistake when they communicate facts to me with so much pains. Their presence, even their exaggerations and loose statements, are equally good facts for me. I have no respect for facts even except when I would use them, and for the most part I am independent of those which I hear, and can afford to be inaccurate, or, in other words, to substitute more present and pressing facts in their place.

The poet uses the results of science and philosophy, and generalizes their widest deductions.

The process of discovery is very simple. An unwearied and systematic application of known laws to nature, causes the unknown to reveal themselves. Almost any *mode* of observation will be successful at last, for what is most wanted is method. Only let something be determined and fixed around which observation may rally. How many new relations a foot-rule alone will reveal, and to how many things still this has not been applied! What wonderful discoveries have been, and may still be, made, with a plumb-line, a level, a surveyor's compass, a thermometer, or a barometer! Where there is an observatory and a telescope, we expect that any eyes will see new worlds at once. I should say that the most prominent scientific men of our country, and perhaps of this age, are either serving the arts, and not pure science, or are performing faithful but quite subordinate labors in particular departments. They make no steady and systematic approaches to the central fact. A discovery is made, and at once the attention of all observers is distracted to that, and it draws many analogous discoveries in its train; as if their work were not already laid out for them, but they had been lying on their oars. There is wanting constant and accurate observation with enough of theory to direct and discipline it.

But above all, there is wanting genius. Our books of science, as they improve in accuracy, are in danger of losing the freshness and vigor and readiness to appreciate the real laws of Nature, which is a marked merit in the ofttimes false theories of the ancients. I am attracted by the slight pride and satisfaction, the emphatic and even exaggerated style in which some of the older naturalists speak of the operations of Nature, though they are better qualified to appreciate than to discriminate the facts. Their assertions are not without value when disproved. If they are not facts, they are suggestions for Nature herself to act upon. "The Greeks," says Gesner, "had a common proverb (Λαγὸς καθεύδων) a sleeping hare, for a dissembler or counterfeit; because the hare sees when she sleeps; for this is an admirable and rare work of Nature, that all the residue of her bodily parts take their rest, but the eye standeth continually sentinel."

Observation is so wide awake, and facts are being so rapidly added to the sum of human experience, that it appears as if the theorizer would always be in arrears, and were doomed forever to arrive at imperfect conclusions; but the power to perceive a law is equally rare in all ages of the world, and depends but little on the number of facts observed. The senses of the savage will furnish him with facts enough to set him up as a philosopher. The ancients can still speak to us with authority even on the themes of geology and chemistry, though these studies are thought to have had their birth in modern times. Much is said about the progress of science in these centuries. I should say that the useful results of science had accumulated, but that there had been no accumulation of knowledge, strictly speaking, for posterity; for knowledge is to be acquired only by a corresponding experience. How can we *know* what we are *told* merely? Each man can interpret another's experience only by his own. We read that Newton discovered the law of gravitation, but how many who have heard of his famous discovery have recognized the same truth that he did? It may be not one. The revelation which was then made to him has not been superseded by the revelation made to any successor. —

> We see the *planet* fall,
> And that is all.

In a review of Sir James Clark Ross' Antarctic Voyage of Discovery, there is a passage which shows how far a body of men are commonly impressed by an object of sublimity, and which is also a good instance of the step from the sublime to the ridiculous. After describing the discovery of the Antarctic Continent, at first seen a hundred miles distant over fields of ice, — stupendous ranges of mountains from seven and eight to twelve and fourteen thousand feet high, covered with eternal snow and ice, in solitary and inaccessible grandeur, at one time the weather being beautifully clear, and the sun shining on the icy landscape; a continent whose islands only are accessible, and these exhibited "not the smallest trace of vegetation," only in a few places the rocks protruding through their icy covering, to convince the beholder that land formed the nucleus, and that it was not an iceberg; — the practical British reviewer proceeds thus, sticking to his last, "On the 22d of January, afternoon, the Expedition made the latitude of 74° 20′, and by 7ʰ P. M., having ground to believe that they were then in a higher southern latitude than had been attained by that enterprising seaman, the late Captain James Weddel, and therefore higher than all their predecessors, an extra allowance of grog was issued to the crews as a reward for their perseverance."

Let not us sailors of late centuries take upon ourselves any airs on account of our Newtons and our Cuviers. We deserve an extra allowance of grog only.

We endeavored in vain to persuade the wind to blow through the long corridor of the canal, which is here cut straight through the woods, and were obliged to resort to our old expedient of drawing by a cord. When we reached the Concord, we were forced to row once more in good earnest, with neither wind nor current in our favor, but by this time the rawness of the day had disappeared, and we experienced the warmth of a summer afternoon. This change in the weather was favorable to our contemplative mood, and disposed us to dream yet deeper at our oars, while we floated in imagination further down the stream of time, as we had floated down the stream of the Merrimack, to poets of a milder period than had engaged us in the morning. Chelmsford and Billerica appeared like old English towns, compared with Merrimack and Nashua, and many generations of civil poets might have lived and sung here.

What a contrast between the stern and desolate poetry of Ossian, and that of Chaucer, and even of Shakspeare and Milton, much more of Dryden, and Pope, and Gray. Our summer of English poetry, like the Greek and Latin before it, seems well advanced toward its fall, and laden with the fruit and foliage of the season, with bright autumnal tints, but soon the winter will scatter its myriad clustering and shading leaves, and leave only a few desolate and fibrous boughs to sustain the snow and rime, and creak in the blasts of ages. We cannot escape the impression that the Muse has stooped a little in her flight, when we come to the literature of civilized eras. Now first we hear of various ages and styles of poetry; it is pastoral, and lyric, and narrative, and didactic; but the poetry of runic monuments is of one style, and for every age. The bard has in a great measure lost the dignity and sacredness of his office. Formerly he was called a *seer*, but now it is thought that one man sees as much as another. He has no longer the bardic rage, and only conceives the deed, which he formerly stood ready to perform. Hosts of warriors earnest for battle could not mistake nor dispense with the ancient bard. His lays were heard in the pauses of the fight. There was no danger of his being overlooked by his contemporaries. But now the hero and the bard are of different professions. When we come to the pleasant English verse, the storms have all cleared away, and it will never thunder and lighten more. The poet has come within doors, and exchanged the forest and crag for the fireside, the hut of the Gael, and Stonehenge with its circles of stones, for the house of the Englishman. No hero stands at the door prepared to break forth into song or heroic action, but a homely Englishman, who

cultivates the art of poetry. We see the comfortable fireside, and hear the crackling fagots
in all the verse.

Nothwithstanding the broad humanity of
Chaucer, and the many social and domestic
comforts which we meet with in his verse, we
have to narrow our vision somewhat to consider
him, as if he occupied less space in the landscape, and did not stretch over hill and valley
as Ossian does. Yet, seen from the side of
posterity, as the father of English poetry,
preceded by a long silence or confusion in
history, unenlivened by any strain of pure
melody, we easily come to reverence him. Passing over the earlier continental poets, since we
are bound to the pleasant archipelago of English
poetry, Chaucer's is the first name after that
misty weather in which Ossian lived, which can
detain us long. Indeed, though he represents
so different a culture and society, he may be
regarded as in many respects the Homer of the
English poets. Perhaps he is the youthfullest of
them all. We return to him as to the purest
well, the fountain furthest removed from the
highway of desultory life. He is so natural and
cheerful, compared with later poets, that we
might almost regard him as a personification
of spring. To the faithful reader his muse has
even given an aspect to his times, and when he
is fresh from perusing him, they seem related to

the golden age. It is still the poetry of youth and life, rather than of thought; and though the moral vein is obvious and constant, it has not yet banished the sun and daylight from his verse. The loftiest strains of the muse are, for the most part, sublimely plaintive, and not a carol as free as nature's. The content which the sun shines to celebrate from morning to evening, is unsung. The muse solaces herself, and is not ravished but consoled. There is a catastrophe implied, and a tragic element in all our verse, and less of the lark and morning dews, than of the nightingale and evening shades. But in Homer and Chaucer there is more of the innocence and serenity of youth, than in the more modern and moral poets. The Iliad is not Sabbath but morning reading, and men cling to this old song, because they still have moments of unbaptized and uncommitted life, which give them an appetite for more. To the innocent there are neither cherubim nor angels. At rare intervals we rise above the necessity of virtue into an unchangeable morning light, in which we have only to live right on and breathe the ambrosial air. The Iliad represents no creed nor opinion, and we read it with a rare sense of freedom and irresponsibility, as if we trod on native ground, and were autochthones of the soil.

Chaucer had eminently the habits of a literary

man and a scholar. There were never any times so stirring that there were not to be found some sedentary still. He was surrounded by the din of arms. The battles of Halidon Hill and Neville's Cross, and the still more memorable battles of Cressy and Poictiers, were fought in his youth; but these did not concern our poet much, Wickliffe and his reform much more. He regarded himself always as one privileged to sit and converse with books. He helped to establish the literary class. His character as one of the fathers of the English language, would alone make his works important, even those which have little poetical merit. He was as simple as Wordsworth in preferring his homely but vigorous Saxon tongue, when it was neglected by the court, and had not yet attained to the dignity of a literature, and rendered a similar service to his country to that which Dante rendered to Italy. If Greek sufficeth for Greek, and Arabic for Arabian, and Hebrew for Jew, and Latin for Latin, then English shall suffice for him, for any of these will serve to teach truth "right as divers pathes leaden divers folke the right waye to Rome." In the Testament of Love he writes, "Let then clerkes enditen in Latin, for they have the propertie of science, and the knowinge in that facultie, and lette Frenchmen in their Frenche also enditen their queinte termes, for it is kyndely to their mouthes,

and let us shewe our fantasies in soche wordes
as we lerneden of our dames tonge."

He will know how to appreciate Chaucer best,
who has come down to him the natural way,
through the meagre pastures of Saxon and ante-
Chaucerian poetry; and yet, so human and wise
he appears after such diet, that we are liable to
misjudge him still. In the Saxon poetry extant,
in the earliest English, and the contemporary
Scottish poetry, there is less to remind the
reader of the rudeness and vigor of youth, than
of the feebleness of a declining age. It is for
the most part translation or imitation merely,
with only an occasional and slight tinge of
poetry, oftentimes the falsehood and exaggeration of fable, without its imagination to redeem
it, and we look in vain to find antiquity restored,
humanized, and made blithe again by some
natural sympathy between it and the present.
But Chaucer is fresh and modern still, and no
dust settles on his true passages. It lightens
along the line, and we are reminded that flowers
have bloomed, and birds sung, and hearts
beaten, in England. Before the earnest gaze of
the reader, the rust and moss of time gradually
drop off, and the original green life is revealed.
He was a homely and domestic man, and did
breathe quite as modern men do.

There is no wisdom that can take place of
humanity, and we find *that* in Chaucer. We can

expand at last in his breath, and we think that
we could have been that man's acquaintance.
He was worthy to be a citizen of England, while
Petrarch and Boccaccio lived in Italy, and Tell
and Tamerlane in Switzerland and in Asia, and
Bruce in Scotland, and Wickliffe, and Gower,
and Edward the Third, and John of Gaunt, and
the Black Prince, were his own countrymen as
well as contemporaries; all stout and stirring
names. The fame of Roger Bacon came down
from the preceding century, and the name of
Dante still possessed the influence of a living
presence. On the whole, Chaucer impresses us
as greater than his reputation, and not a little
like Homer and Shakspeare, for he would have
held up his head in their company. Among
early English poets he is the landlord and host,
and has the authority of such. The affectionate
mention which succeeding early poets make of
him, coupling him with Homer and Virgil, is to
be taken into the account in estimating his
character and influence. King James and Dun-
bar of Scotland speak of him with more love and
reverence than any modern author of his predecessors of the last century. The same childlike
relation is without a parallel now. For the most
part we read him without criticism, for he does
not plead his own cause, but speaks for his
readers, and has that greatness of trust and
reliance which compels popularity. He confides

in the reader, and speaks privily with him, keeping nothing back. And in return the reader has great confidence in him, that he tells no lies, and reads his story with indulgence, as if it were the circumlocution of a child, but often discovers afterwards that he has spoken with more directness and economy of words than a sage. He is never heartless,

> "For first the thing is thought within the hart,
> Er any word out from the mouth astart."

And so new was all his theme in those days, that he did not have to invent, but only to tell.

We admire Chaucer for his sturdy English wit. The easy height he speaks from in his Prologue to the Canterbury Tales, as if he were equal to any of the company there assembled, is as good as any particular excellence in it. But though it is full of good sense and humanity, it is not transcendent poetry. For picturesque descriptions of persons it is, perhaps, without a parallel in English poetry; yet it is essentially humorous, as the loftiest genius never is. Humor, however broad and genial, takes a narrower view than enthusiasm. To his own finer vein he added all the common wit and wisdom of his time, and everywhere in his works his remarkable knowledge of the world and nice perception of character, his rare common sense and proverbial wisdom, are apparent. His genius does not soar like Milton's, but is genial and familiar. It shows great tenderness and delicacy, but not the heroic sentiment. It is only a greater portion of humanity with all its weakness. He is not heroic, as Raleigh, nor pious, as Herbert, nor philosophical, as Shakspeare, but he is the child of the English muse, that child which is the father of the man. The charm of his poetry consists often only in an exceeding naturalness, perfect sincerity, with the behavior of a child rather than of a man.

Gentleness and delicacy of character are everywhere apparent in his verse. The simplest and humblest words come readily to his lips. No one can read the Prioress' tale, understanding the spirit in which it was written, and in which the child sings *O alma redemptoris mater*, or the account of the departure of Constance with her child upon the sea, in the Man of Lawe's tale, without feeling the native innocence and refinement of the author. Nor can we be mistaken respecting the essential purity of his character, disregarding the apology of the manners of the age. A simple pathos and feminine gentleness, which Wordsworth only occasionally approaches, but does not equal, are peculiar to him. We are tempted to say that his genius was feminine, not masculine. It was such a feminineness, however, as is rarest to find in woman, though not the appreciation of it; perhaps it is not to be found at all in woman, but is only the feminine in man.

Sure pure, and genuine, and childlike love of Nature is hardly to be found in any poet.

Chaucer's remarkably trustful and affectionate character appears in his familiar, yet innocent and reverent, manner of speaking of his God. He comes into his thought without any false reverence, and with no more parade than the zephyr to his ear. If Nature is our mother, then God is our father. There is less love and simple practical trust in Shakspeare and Milton. How rarely in our English tongue do we find expressed any affection for God. Certainly, there is no sentiment so rare as the love of God. Herbert almost alone expresses it, "Ah, my dear God!" Our poet uses similar words with propriety, and whenever he sees a beautiful person, or other object, prides himself on the "maistry" of his God. He even recommends Dido to be his bride, —

> ——"if that God that heaven and yearth made,
> Would have a love for beauty and goodnesse,
> And womanhede, trouth, and semeliness."

But in justification of our praise, we must refer to his works themselves; to the Prologue to the Canterbury Tales, the account of Gentilesse, the Flower and the Leaf, the stories of Griselda, Virginia, Ariadne, and Blanche the Dutchesse, and much more of less distinguished

merit. There are many poets of more **taste** and
better manners, who knew how to leave out
their dulness, but such negative genius cannot
detain us long; we shall return to Chaucer still
with love. Some natures which are really rude
and ill developed, have yet a higher standard
of perfection than others which are refined and
well balanced. Even the clown has taste,
whose dictates, though he disregards them, are
higher and purer than those which the artist
obeys. If we have to wander through many
dull and prosaic passages in Chaucer, we have
at least the satisfaction of knowing that it is not
an artificial dulness, but too easily matched by
many passages in life. We confess that we feel
a disposition commonly to concentrate sweets,
and accumulate pleasures, but the poet may be
presumed always to speak as a traveller, who
leads us through a varied scenery, from one
eminence to another, and it is, perhaps, more
pleasing, after all, to meet with a fine thought
in its natural setting. Surely fate has enshrined
it in these circumstances for some end. Nature
strews her nuts and flowers broadcast, and never
collects them into heaps. This was the soil it
grew in, and this the hour it bloomed in; if sun,
wind, and rain came here to cherish and expand
the flower, shall not we come here to pluck it?

A true poem is distinguished not so much by a
felicitous expression, or any thought it suggests,

as by the atmosphere which surrounds it. Most
have beauty of outline merely, and are striking
as the form and bearing of a stranger, but true
verses come toward us indistinctly, as the very
breath of all friendliness, and envelop us in
their spirit and fragrance. Much of our poetry
has the very best manners, but no character.
It is only an unusual precision and elasticity
of speech, as if its author had taken, not an
intoxicating draught, but an electuary. It has
the distinct outline of sculpture, and chronicles
an early hour. Under the influence of passion
all men speak thus distinctly, but wrath is not
always divine.

There are two classes of men called poets.
The one cultivates life, the other art, — one
seeks food for nutriment, the other for flavor;
one satisfies hunger, the other gratifies the
palate. There are two kinds of writing, both
great and rare; one that of genius, or the inspired, the other of intellect and taste, in the
intervals of inspiration. The former is above
criticism, always correct, giving the law to
criticism. It vibrates and pulsates with life
forever. It is sacred, and to be read with reverence, as the works of nature are studied. There
are few instances of a sustained style of this
kind; perhaps every man has spoken words,
but the speaker is then careless of the record.
Such a style removes us out of personal relations

with its author, we do not take his words on our
lips, but his sense into our hearts.　It is the
stream of inspiration, which bubbles out, now
here, now there, now in this man, now in that.
It matters not through what ice-crystals it is
seen, now a fountain, now the ocean stream
running under ground.　It is in Shakspeare,
Alpheus, in Burns, Arethuse; but ever the
same. — The other is self-possessed and wise.
It is reverent of genius, and greedy of inspiration.　It is conscious in the highest and the
least degree.　It consists with the most perfect
command of the faculties.　It dwells in a repose
as of the desert, and objects are as distinct in
it as oases or palms in the horizon of sand.　The
train of thought moves with subdued and
measured step, like a caravan.　But the pen is
only an instrument in its hand, and not instinct
with life, like a longer arm.　It leaves a thin
varnish or glaze over all its work.　The works
of Goethe furnish remarkable instances of the
latter.

There is no just and serene criticism as yet.
Nothing is considered simply as it lies in the
lap of eternal beauty, but our thoughts, as well
as our bodies, must be dressed after the latest
fashions.　Our taste is too delicate and particular.
It says nay to the poet's work, but never yea
to his hope.　It invites him to adorn his de-
formities, and not to cast them off by expansion,

as the tree its bark. We are a people who live in a bright light, in houses of pearl and porcelain, and drink only light wines, whose teeth are easily set on edge by the least natural sour. If we had been consulted, the backbone of the earth would have been made, not of granite, but of Bristol spar. A modern author would have died in infancy in a ruder age. But the poet is something more than a scald, "a smoother and polisher of language;" he is a Cincinnatus in literature, and occupies no west end of the world. Like the sun, he will indifferently select his rhymes, and with a liberal taste weave into his verse the planet and the stubble.

In these old books the stucco has long since crumbled away, and we read what was sculptured in the granite. They are rude and massive in their proportions, rather than smooth and delicate in their finish. The workers in stone polish only their chimney ornaments, but their pyramids are roughly done. There is a soberness in a rough aspect, as of unhewn granite, which addresses a depth in us, but a polished surface hits only the ball of the eye. The true finish is the work of time and the use to which a thing is put. The elements are still polishing the pyramids. Art may varnish and gild, but it can do no more. A work of genius is rough-hewn from the first, because it anticipates the lapse of time, and has an ingrained polish, which still appears when fragments are broken off, an essential quality of its substance. Its beauty is at the same time its strength, and it breaks with a lustre.

The great poem must have the stamp of greatness as well as its essence. The reader easily goes within the shallowest contemporary poetry, and informs it with all the life and promise of the day, as the pilgrim goes within the temple, and hears the faintest strains of the worshippers; but it will have to speak to posterity, traversing these deserts, through the ruins of its outmost walls, by the grandeur and beauty of its proportions.

———

But here on the stream of the Concord, where we have all the while been bodily, Nature, who is superior to all styles and ages, is now, with pensive face, composing her poem Autumn, with which no work of man will bear to be compared.

In summer we live out of doors, and have only impulses and feelings, which are all for action, and must wait commonly for the stillness and longer nights of autumn and wholly new life, which no man has lived; that even this earth was made for more mysterious and nobler inhabitants than men and women. In the hues of October sunsets, we see the portals to other mansions than those which we occupy, not far off geographically. —

"There is a place beyond that flaming hill,
  From whence the stars their thin appearance shed,
A place beyond all place, where never ill,
  Nor impure thought was ever harbored."

Sometimes a mortal feels in himself Nature, not his Father but his Mother stirs within him, and he becomes immortal with her immortality. From time to time she claims kindredship with us, and some globule from her veins steals up into our own.

I am the autumnal sun,
With autumn gales my race is run;
When will the hazel put forth its flowers,
Or the grape ripen under my bowers?
When will the harvest or the hunter's moon,
Turn my mid-night into mid-noon?
   I am all sere and yellow,
   And to my core mellow.
The mast is dropping within my woods,
The winter is lurking within my moods,
And the rustling of the withered leaf
Is the constant music of my grief.

To an unskilful rhymer the Muse thus spoke in prose: —

The moon no longer reflects the day, but rises to her absolute rule, and the husbandman and hunter acknowledge her for their mistress. Asters and golden-rods reign along the way, and the life-ever-lasting withers not. The fields are reaped and shorn of their pride, but an inward verdure still crowns them. The thistle scatters its down on the pool, and yellow leaves clothe the vine, and naught disturbs the serious life of men. But behind the sheaves, and under the sod, there lurks a ripe fruit, which the reapers have not gathered, the true harvest of the year, which it bears for ever, annually watering and maturing it, and man never severs the stalk which bears this palatable fruit.

Men nowhere, east or west, live yet a *natural* life, round which the vine clings, and which the elm willingly shadows. Man would desecrate it by his touch, and so the beauty of the world remains veiled to him. He needs not only to be spiritualized, but *naturalized*, on the soil of earth. Who shall conceive what kind of roof the heavens might extend over him, what seasons minister to him, and what employment dignify his life! Only the convalescent raise the veil of nature. An immortality in his life would confer immortality on his abode. The winds should be his breath, the seasons his moods, and he should impart of his serenity to Nature herself. But such as we know him he is ephemeral like the scenery that surrounds him, and does not aspire to an enduring existence. When we come down into the distant village, visible from the mountain top, the nobler inhabitants with whom we peopled it have departed, and left only vermin in its desolate streets. It is the imagination of poets which puts those brave speeches into the mouths of their heroes. They may feign that Cato's last words were

> "The earth, the air, and seas I know, and all
> The joys and horrors of their peace and wars;
> And now will view the Gods' state and the stars,"

but such are not the thoughts nor the destiny of common men. What is this heaven which they expect, if it is no better than they expect? Are they prepared for a better than they can now imagine? Here or nowhere is our heaven. —

> "Although we see celestial bodies move
> Above the earth, the earth we till and love."

We can conceive of nothing more fair than something which we have experienced. "The remembrance of youth is a sigh." We linger in manhood to tell the dreams of our childhood, and they are half forgotten ere we have learned the language. We have need to be earth-born as well as heaven-born, γηγενεῖς, as was said of the Titans of old, or in a better sense than they. There have been heroes for whom this world seemed expressly prepared, as if creation had at last succeeded; whose daily life was the stuff of which our dreams are made, and whose pressence enhanced the beauty and ampleness of Nature herself. Where they walked,

> "Largior hic campos æther et lumine vestit
> Purpureo: Solemque suum, sua sidera nôrunt."

"Here a more copious air invests the fields, and clothes with purple light; and they know their own sun and their own stars." We love to hear some men speak, though we hear not what they say; the very air they breathe is rich and perfumed, and the sound of their voices falls on the ear like the rustling of leaves or the crackling of the fire. They stand many deep. They have the heavens for their abettors, as those who have never stood from under them, and they look at the stars with an answering ray. Their eyes are like glow-worms, and their motions graceful and flowing, as if a place were already found for them, like rivers flowing through valleys. The distinctions of morality, of right and wrong, sense and nonsense, are petty, and have lost their significance, beside these pure primeval natures. When I consider the clouds stretched in stupendous masses across the sky, frowning with darkness, or glowing with downy light, or gilded with the rays of the setting sun, like the battlements of a city in the heavens, their grandeur appears thrown away on the meanness of my employment; the drapery is altogether too rich for such poor acting. I am hardly worthy to be a suburban dweller outside those walls.

"Unless above himself he can
Erect himself, how poor a thing is man!"

With our music we would fain challenge transiently another and finer sort of intercourse than our daily toil permits. The strains come back to us amended in the echo, as when a friend reads our verse. Why have they so painted the fruits, and freighted them with such fragrance as to satisfy a more than animal appetite?

> "I asked the schoolman, his advice was free,
> But scored me out too intricate a way."

These things imply, perchance, that we live on the verge of another and purer realm, from which these odors and sounds are wafted over to us. The borders of our plot are set with flowers, whose seeds were blown from more Elysian fields adjacent. They are the pot-herbs of the gods. Some fairer fruits and sweeter fragrances wafted over to us, betray another realm's vicinity. There, too, does Echo dwell, and there is the abutment of the rainbow's arch.

> A finer race and finer fed
> Feast and revel o'er our head,
> And we titmen are only able
> To catch the fragments from their table.
> Theirs is the fragrance of the fruits,
> While we consume the pulp and roots.
> What are the moments that we stand
> Astonished on the Olympian land!

We need pray for no higher heaven than the pure senses can furnish, a *purely* sensuous life. Our present senses are but the rudiments of what they are destined to become. We are

comparatively deaf and dumb and blind, and
without smell or taste or feeling. Every generation makes the discovery, that its divine vigor
has been dissipated, and each sense and faculty
misapplied and debauched. The ears were
made, not for such trivial uses as men are wont
to suppose, but to hear celestial sounds. The
eyes were not made for such grovelling uses as
they are now put to and worn out by, but to
behold beauty now invisible. May we not *see*
God? Are we to be put off and amused in this
life, as it were with a mere allegory? Is not
Nature, rightly read, that of which she is commonly taken to be the symbol merely? When
the common man looks into the sky, which he
has not so much profaned, he thinks it less gross
than the earth, and with reverence speaks of
"the Heavens," but the seer will in the same
sense speak of "the Earths," and his Father who
is in them. "Did not he that made that which
is *within*, make that which is *without* also?"
What is it, then, to educate but to develop these
divine germs called the senses? for individuals
and states to deal magnanimously with the rising
generation, leading it not into temptation, —
not teach the eye to squint, nor attune the ear to
profanity? But where is the instructed teacher?
Where are the *normal* schools?

A Hindoo sage said, "As a dancer having
exhibited herself to the spectator, desists from

the dance, so does Nature desist, having manifested herself to soul. — Nothing, in my opinion, is more gentle than Nature; once aware of having been seen, she does not again expose herself to the gaze of soul."

It is easier to discover another such a new world as Columbus did, than to go within one fold of this which we appear to know so well; the land is lost sight of, the compass varies, and mankind mutiny; and still history accumulates like rubbish before the portals of nature. But there is only necessary a moment's sanity and sound senses, to teach us that there is a nature behind the ordinary, in which we have only some vague preëmption right and western reserve as yet. We live on the outskirts of that region. Carved wood, and floating boughs, and sunset skies, are all that we know of it. We are not to be imposed on by the longest spell of weather. Let us not, my friends, be wheedled and cheated into good behavior to earn the salt of our eternal porridge, whoever they are that attempt it. Let us wait a little, and not purchase any clearing here, trusting that richer bottoms will soon be put up. It is but thin soil where we stand; I have felt my roots in a richer ere this. I have seen a bunch of violets in a glass vase, tied loosely with a straw, which reminded me of myself. —

I am a parcel of vain strivings tied
  By a chance bond together,
    Dangling this way and that, their links
    Were made so loose and wide,
        Methinks,
      For milder weather.

A bunch of violets without their roots,
  And sorrel intermixed,
    Encircled by a wisp of straw
    Once coiled about their shoots,
        The law
      By which I'm fixed.

A nosegay which Time clutched from out
  Those fair Elysian fields,
    With weeds and broken stems, in haste,
    Doth make the rabble rout
        That waste
      The day he yields.

And here I bloom for a short hour unseen,
  Drinking my juices up,
    With no root in the land
    To keep my branches green,
        But stand
      In a bare cup.

Some tender buds were left upon my stem
  In mimicry of life,
    But ah! the children will not know,
    Till time has withered them,
        The wo
      With which they're rife.

But now I see I was not plucked for naught,
  And after in life's vase
    Of glass set while I might survive,
    But by a kind hand brought
        Alive
      To a strange place.

That stock thus thinned will soon redeem its hours,
And by another year,
Such as God knows, with freer air,
More fruits and fairer flowers
Will bear,
While I droop here.

This world has many rings, like Saturn, and we live now on the outmost of them all. None can say deliberately that he inhabits the same sphere, or is contemporary with, the flower which his hands have plucked, and though his feet may seem to crush it, inconceivable spaces and ages separate them, and perchance there is no danger that he will hurt it. What after all do the botanists know? Our lives should go between the lichen and the bark. The eye may see for the hand, but not for the mind. We are still being born, and have as yet but a dim vision of sea and land, sun, moon and stars, and shall not see clearly till after nine days at least. That is a pathetic inquiry among travellers and geographers after the site of ancient Troy. It is not near where they think it is. When a thing is decayed and gone, how indistinct must be the place it occupied!

The anecdotes of modern astronomy affect me in the same way as do those faint revelations of the Real which are vouchsafed to men from time to time, or rather from eternity to eternity. When I remember the history of that faint light in our firmament, which we call Venus, which

ancient men regarded, and which most modern
men still regard, as a bright spark attached to a
hollow sphere revolving about our earth, but
which we have discovered to be *another world* in
itself, — how Copernicus, reasoning long and
patiently about the matter, predicted confidently concerning it, before yet the telescope
had been invented, that if ever men came to
see it more clearly than they did then, they
would discover that it had phases like our moon,
and that within a century after his death the
telescope was invented, and that prediction veri-
fied, by Galileo, — I am not without hope that
we may, even here and now, obtain some accurate
information concerning that OTHER WORLD
which the instinct of mankind has so long
predicted. Indeed, all that we call science, as
well as all that we call poetry, is a particle of
such information, accurate as far as it goes,
though it be but to the confines of the truth. If
we can reason so accurately, and with such
wonderful confirmation of our reasoning, respecting so-called material objects and events
infinitely removed beyond the range of our
natural vision, so that the mind hesitates to
trust its calculations even when they are confirmed by observation, why may not our speculations penetrate as far into the immaterial
starry system, of which the former is but the
outward and visible type? Surely, we are

provided with senses as well fitted to penetrate the spaces of the real, the substantial, the eternal, as these outward are to penetrate the material universe. Veias, Menu, Zoroaster, Socrates, Christ, Shakspeare, Swedenborg, — these are some of our astronomers.

There are perturbations in our orbits produced by the influence of outlying spheres, and no astronomer has ever yet calculated the elements of that undiscovered world which produces them. I perceive in the common train of my thoughts a natural and uninterrupted sequence, each implying the next, or, if interruption occurs it is occasioned by a new object being presented to my *senses*. But a steep, and sudden, and by these means unaccountable transition, is that from a comparatively narrow and partial, what is called common sense view of things, to an infinitely expanded and liberating one, from seeing things as men describe them, to seeing them as men cannot describe them. This implies a sense which is not common, but rare in the wisest man's experience; which is sensible or sentient of more than common.

In what inclosures does the astronomer loiter! His skies are shoal; and imagination, like a thirsty traveller, pants to be through their desert. The roving mind impatiently bursts the fetters of astronomical orbits, like cobwebs in a corner of its universe, and launches itself to where distance fails to follow, and law, such as science has discovered, grows weak and weary. The mind knows a distance and a space of which all those sums combined do not make a unit of measure, — the interval between that which *appears* and that which *is*. I know that there are many stars, I know that they are far enough off, bright enough, steady enough in their orbits, — but what are they all worth? They are more waste land in the West, — star territory, — to be made slave States, perchance, if we colonize them. I have interest but for six feet of star, and that interest is transient. Then farewell to all ye bodies, such as I have known ye.

Every man, if he is wise, will stand on such bottom as will sustain him, and if one gravitates downward more strongly than another, he will not venture on those meads where the latter walks securely, but rather leave the cranberries which grow there unraked by himself. Perchance, some spring a higher freshet will float them within his reach, though they may be watery and frost-bitten by that time. Such shrivelled berries I have seen in many a poor man's garret, aye, in many a church bin and state coffer, and with a little water and heat they swell again to their original size and fairness, and added sugar enough, stead mankind for sauce to this world's dish.

What is called common sense is excellent in its department, and as invaluable as the virtue of conformity in the army and navy, — for there must be subordination, — but uncommon sense, that sense which is common only to the wisest, is as much more excellent as it is more rare. Some aspire to excellence in the subordinate department, and may God speed them. What Fuller says of masters of colleges is universally applicable, that "a little alloy of dulness in a master of a college makes him fitter to manage secular affairs."

"He that wants faith, and apprehends a grief
Because he wants it, hath a true belief;
And he that grieves because his grief 's so small,
Has a true grief, and the best Faith of all."

Or be encouraged by this other poet's strain.

"By them went Fido marshal of the field:
Weak was his mother when she gave him day;
And he at first a sick and weakly child,
As e'er with tears welcomed the sunny ray;
Yet when more years afford more growth and might,
A champion stout he was, and puissant knight,
As ever came in field, or shone in armor bright.

"Mountains he flings in seas with mighty hand;
Stops and turns back the sun's impetuous course;
Nature breaks Nature's laws at his command;
No force of Hell or Heaven withstands his force;
Events to come yet many ages hence,
He present makes, by wondrous prescience;
Proving the senses blind by being blind to sense."

"Yesterday, at dawn," says Hafiz, "God delivered me from all worldly affliction; and amidst the gloom of night presented me with the water of immortality."

In the life of Sadi by Dowlat Shah, occurs this sentence. "The eagle of the immaterial soul of Shaikh Sadi shook from his plumage the dust of his body."

Thus thoughtfully we were rowing homeward to find some autumnal work to do, and help on the revolution of the seasons. Perhaps Nature would condescend to make use of us even without our knowledge, as when we help to scatter her seeds in our walks, and carry burrs and cockles on our clothes from field to field.

> All things are current found
> On earthly ground,
> Spirits and elements
> Have their descents.
>
> Night and day, year on year,
> High and low, far and near,
> These are our own aspects,
> These are our own regrets.
>
> Ye gods of the shore,
> Who abide evermore,
> I see your far headland,
> Stretching on either hand;
>
> I hear the sweet evening sounds
> From your undecaying grounds;
> Cheat me no more with time,
> Take me to your clime.

Rowing Homeward

As it grew later in the afternoon, and we rowed leisurely up the gentle stream, shut in between fragrant and blooming banks, where we had first pitched our tent, and drew nearer to the fields where our lives had passed, we seemed to detect the hues of our native sky in the south-west horizon. The sun was just setting behind the edge of a wooded hill, so rich a sunset as would never have ended but for some reason unknown to men, and to be marked with brighter colors than ordinary in the scroll of time. Though the shadows of the hills were beginning to steal over the stream, the whole river valley undulated with mild light, purer and more memorable than the noon. For so day bids farewell even to solitary vales uninhabited by man. Two blue-herons, *ardea herodias*, with their long and slender limbs relieved against the sky, were seen travelling high over our heads, — their lofty and silent flight, as they were wending their way at evening, surely not to alight in any marsh on the earth's surface, but, perchance, on the other side of our atmosphere, a symbol for the ages to study, whether impressed upon the sky, or sculptured amid the hieroglyphics of Egypt. Bound to some northern meadow, they held on their stately, stationary flight, like the storks in the picture, and disappeared at length behind the clouds. Dense flocks of blackbirds were winging their way

along the river's course, as if on a short evening
pilgrimage to some shrine of theirs, or to celebrate so fair a sunset.

> "Therefore, as doth the pilgrim, whom the night
>   Hastes darkly to imprison on his way,
> Think on thy home, my soul, and think aright
>   Of what's yet left thee of life's wasting day:
>   Thy sun posts westward, passed is thy morn,
>   And twice it is not given thee to be born."

The sun-setting presumed all men at leisure
and in a contemplative mood; but the farmer's
boy only whistled the more thoughtfully as he
drove his cows home from pasture, and the
teamster refrained from cracking his whip, and
guided his team with a subdued voice. The last
vestiges of daylight at length disappeared, and
as we rowed silently along with our backs toward
home through the darkness, only a few stars being
visible, we had little to say, but sat absorbed in
thought, or in silence listened to the monotonous
sound of our oars, a sort of rudimental music,
suitable for the ear of Night and the acoustics of
her dimly lighted halls;

> "Pulsæ referunt ad sidera valles,"

and the valleys echoed the sound to the stars.

As we looked up in silence to those distant
lights, we were reminded that it was a rare
imagination which first taught that the stars
are worlds, and had conferred a great benefit
on mankind. It is recorded in the Chronicle of

Bernaldez, that in Columbus's first voyage the natives "pointed towards the heavens, making signs that they believed that there was all power and holiness." We have reason to be grateful for celestial phenomena, for they chiefly answer to the ideal in man. The stars are distant and unobtrusive, but bright and enduring as our fairest and most memorable experiences. "Let the immortal depth of your soul lead you, but earnestly extend your eyes upwards."

As the truest society approaches always nearer to solitude, so the most excellent speech finally falls into Silence. Silence is audible to all men, at all times, and in all places. She is when we hear inwardly, sound when we hear outwardly. Creation has not displaced her, but is her visible framework and foil. All sounds are her servants and purveyors, proclaiming not only that their mistress is, but is a rare mistress, and earnestly to be sought after. They are so far akin to Silence, that they are but bubbles on her surface, which straightway burst, an evidence of the strength and prolificness of the under-current; a faint utterance of silence, and then only agreeable to our auditory nerves when they contrast themselves with and relieve the former. In proportion as they do this, and are heighteners and intensifiers of the Silence, they are harmony and purest melody.

Silence is the universal refuge, the sequel to all dull discourses and all foolish acts, a balm to our every chagrin, as welcome after satiety as after disappointment; that background which the painter may not daub, be he master or bungler, and which, however awkward a figure we may have made in the foreground, remains ever our inviolable asylum, where no indignity can assail, no personality disturb us.

The orator puts off his individuality, and is then most eloquent when most silent. He listens while he speaks, and is a hearer along with his audience. Who has not hearkened to Her infinite din? She is Truth's speaking trumpet, the sole oracle, the true Delphi and Dodona, which kings and courtiers would do well to consult, nor will they be balked by an ambiguous answer. For through Her all revelations have been made, and just in proportion as men have consulted her oracle within, they have obtained a clear insight, and their age has been marked as an enlightened one. But as often as they have gone gadding abroad to a strange Delphi and her mad priestess, their age has been dark and leaden. Such were garrulous and noisy eras, which no longer yield any sound, but the Grecian or silent and melodious era is ever sounding and resounding in the ears of men.

A good book is the plectrum with which our else silent lyres are struck. We not unfrequently

refer the interest which belongs to our own unwritten sequel, to the written and comparatively
lifeless body of the work. Of all books this
sequel is the most indispensable part. It should
be the author's aim to say once and emphatically,
"He said," "ἔφη," ἔ. This is the most the book
maker can attain to. If he make his volume a
mole whereon the waves of Silence may break, it
is well.

It were vain for me to endeavor to interpret
the Silence. She cannot be done into English.
For six thousand years men have translated
her with what fidelity belonged to each, and still
she is little better than a sealed book. A man
may run on confidently for a time, thinking he
has her under his thumb, and shall one day ex-
haust her, but he too must at last be silent, and
men remark only how brave a beginning he
made; for when he at length dives into her, so
vast is the disproportion of the told to the un-
told, that the former will seem but the bubble
on the surface where he disappeared. Nevertheless, we will go on, like those Chinese cliff
swallows, feathering our nests with the froth
which may one day be bread of life to such as
dwell by the seashore.

We had made about fifty miles this day with
sail and oar, and now, far in the evening, our
boat was grating against the bulrushes of its

native port, and its keel recognized the Concord
mud, where some semblance of its outline was
still preserved in the flattened flags which had
scarce yet erected themselves since our departure; and we leaped gladly on shore, drawing it
up, and fastening it to the wild apple tree,
whose stem still bore the mark which its chain
had worn in the chafing of the spring freshets.